R06068 00048

ND
2639.3
.A35
P75
2000

LEGLER

W9-DBC-275

Chicago, IL 60624

Chicago Public Library

REFERENCE

Form 178 rev. 11-00

CHICAGO PUBLIC LIBRARY
LEGLER BRANCH
115 S. PULASKI RD. 60624

WALLS OF HERITAGE
WALLS OF PRIDE

African American Murals

JAMES PRIGOFF
ROBIN J. DUNITZ

Pomegranate

San Francisco

Published by
Pomegranate Communications, Inc.
Box 6099, Rohnert Park, CA 94927
www.pomegranate.com

Pomegranate Europe Ltd.
Fullbridge House, Fullbridge
Maldon, Essex CM9 4LE, England

Catalog Number A567
ISBN 0-7649-1339-5

All images © the individual artists
Foreword © Edmund Barry Gaither
"Keeping Hope Alive: the Story of African American Murals" © Floyd Coleman, Ph.D.
"Urban Totems: the Communal Spirit of Black Murals" © Michael D. Harris, Ph.D.
Other text and photographs © James Prigoff and Robin J. Dunitz, unless otherwise indicated.
No part of this publication may be reproduced or transmitted in any form or by any means, electronic
or mechanical including photocopy, recording, or any information storage or retrieval system, without
permission in writing from the copyright holders.

Library of Congress Cataloging-in-Publication Data
Prigoff, James and Dunitz, Robin J.
      Walls of Heritage, Walls of Pride: African American Murals / by James Prigoff, Robin J. Dunitz
          p. cm.
      Includes bibliographical references.
      ISBN 0-7649-1339-5
      1. Afro-American mural painting and decoration. 2. Mural painting and decoration—20th
      century—United States. I. Prigoff, James. II. Title.

      ND2639.3.A35 D86 2000
      751.7'3'08996073—dc21   00-029133

Cover and interior design by Laura Lind Design
PRINTED IN CHINA

09 08 07 06 05 04 03 02 01 00   10 9 8 7 6 5 4 3 2 1

CONTENTS

CHICAGO PUBLIC LIBRARY
LEGLER BRANCH
115 S. PULASKI RD. 60624

Foreword

No quality defines black Americans' experiences more saliently than struggle— the struggle to gain simple human recognition, to claim the rights of citizenship, and to be secure in exploring the infinite potential of creative autonomy. This struggle is rooted in fundamental inequalities that marked the encounter between Africans and Europeans when America was first formed. Racism, dehumanization, undervaluation, color prejudices, paternalism—all of these demons attended the transformation of newly arrived Africans in America into African Americans, yet these demons did not succeed in choking the extraordinary personal and collective reinvention of black people in what has become these United States. Instead, they challenged and inflected African American experience in ways that have simultaneously spawned black nationalist and assimilationist sentiments. Permutations of these sentiments have expressed themselves in the formation of a complex, fluid identity that combines many cultural strains with a heightened consciousness of African remembrance. One fruit of this complicated, painful, and often internally contradictory layering of collective and personal experiences has been the birth of expressive traditions in the arts. Horrific distortion and misrepresentation have been transmuted into a counternarrative celebrating the triumph of the imagination and the power of the spirit. These dynamic forces are the engine of African American mural making.

Aaron Douglas introduced and established two central themes that remained dominant throughout the twentieth century. First, Douglas related his visual language to the murals of ancient Egypt and Nubia. By doing so, he connected African American experience to the black symbolic legacy represented by Africa, and reclaimed Africa as a black legacy. Second, Douglas used the mural to express a comprehensive vision of black history. In this way he established the scope of the mural as a device capable of advancing a unified narrative of singular historical power, a narrative which suggested a different and noble history of black Americans, a narrative which reached farther back than slavery, farther even than colonialism. Indeed, he asserted for black people the existence of roots stretching to the dawn of human civilization along the Nile six thousand years ago. What was missing from his approach, however, was an engagement with specific historical events of the recent American past.

United States history has been dominated by issues related to race. Racial conflicts have called forth some of the most heroic black figures and have posed many of the most dramatic events of our national story. No true telling of the nineteenth-century record, for example, could exclude the insurrections of Nat Turner, Denmark Vesey, and John Brown; the declarations of David Walker, Frederick Douglass, and Sojourner Truth; the bravery of Harriet Tubman and the Massachusetts Fifty-fourth Regiment in the Civil War; or the coming of emancipation. Yet these stories are strangely rare in the history painting of the period. With the exception of Edmonia Lewis and her sculpture *Forever Free* (1867), African Americans, for whom these personalities and events were particularly relevant, did not turn to such historical themes until the twentieth century.

Part of the problem arose from the fact that murals using historical themes were generally commissioned for great public spaces, and African Americans controlled few such public spaces. Nor was their story—at least as they might tell it—a high priority in the larger national saga as it was being developed in Work Projects Administration–sponsored murals across the country in the thirties and early forties. It remained for black institutions to take on the combined role of commissioner and venue for history paintings from an African American perspective.

Hale Woodruff *(Amistad Mural)* and Charles White *(The Contribution of the Negro to Democracy in America)* soundly anchored the tradition in African American murals of presenting historical personalities in heroic action. Inspired by the great Mexican muralists, they, and later John Biggers, celebrated the strength and righteous character of ordinary black people whose faith and conviction buttressed the race and advanced it against heavy odds.

By mid-century, black muralists had brought together: 1) a profound awareness of Africa as part of the African American symbolic legacy; 2) an appreciation of the need to tell a comprehensive story that contained and defined the intervening experience of slavery; and 3) a focus on black history painting, referencing actual historical episodes and personalities as viewed from an African American perspective.

The sixties were volatile, moving from the terrifying threats and vicious attacks on peaceful southern civil rights protestors to full-blown riots in urban centers all across the country. The new militancy that underpinned this shift also manifested itself in the visual arts, where two bold directions emerged: 1) black art, a self-consciously political tradition aimed at offering an analysis of the black condition and a prescription for changing it, appeared and in time dominated critical discussion, and 2) a neo-African perspective gained currency in which African inspirations—historical, political, and cultural—were synthesized and adapted to address African American needs. Both of these forms quickly found expression in murals.

When the Organization of Black American Culture (OBAC) brought about the creation of the *Wall of Respect* in Chicago in 1967, it precipitated a seminal event. The *Wall of Respect,* in creating an art form immediately accessible on the streets of black communities, spoke in a barrier-free language that integrated text and generated instant impact. It pushed viewers to take sides, to be for or against "the black revolution." Its boldness and daring inspired scores of similar walls across the United States. These new murals became increasingly political, their iconography often integrating contemporary figures such as H. Rap Brown, Stokely Carmichael, and Malcolm X, and making frequent use of red, black, and green, the colors of black nationalism associated with Marcus Garvey.

As the number of urban murals grew, their visual language widened and became richer. Regional differences appeared, and the range of subject matter again broadened, reaching well beyond political and nationalist polemics. Several black museums embraced these fresh works and in time the visual arts canon

began to shift, finally admitting to the existence of a distinct tradition of black murals. Historically black colleges and universities retained their place as leading sites for the commission of narrative murals, as demonstrated by comparatively recent unveilings at Winston-Salem State University, Texas Southern University, and Hampton University.

The narrative mural, in contradistinction to decorative murals, has been a predominantly minority form in the second half of the twentieth century. It has been important to Latino and Chicano artists, and to programs introducing minority youths to the visual arts in inner cities, but nowhere has it been so vital and creatively alive as among black muralists. The story of American art in the twentieth century cannot be told without accounting for the magnificent contribution of African American muralists who, acting upon their need to visualize and represent a counternarrative, expanded and enriched both the form and content of American painting, forever stretching it toward a greater truth.

EDMUND BARRY GAITHER
Director, Museum of the National Center of Afro-American Artists

Acknowledgments

The contributions of many generous people made this book possible. First and foremost we would like to thank the muralists for creating their beautiful and meaningful work in communities all over the country, for showing us the importance of public art in our lives, and for inspiring us to put together this book in order to showcase their work. Our deepest thanks to those artists who spoke with us at length, sharing their personal perspectives and insights. Their contributions have added greatly to the substance and value of this book.

Dozens of individuals at educational institutions, community arts centers, public and private agencies, museums, and libraries have given us assistance along the way. We would especially like to single out a few key people: John Pitman Weber, author, scholar, muralist, and a friend of Jim's for more than twenty years, has followed this project since day one and made many valuable suggestions; Paul Von Blum—lecturer in African American studies at UCLA—and Alan Barnett—mural historian, author of *Community Murals,* and a very close friend—both gave us considerable help and encouragement; and Richard Powell, who, although too involved with other projects to personally contribute to the book, directed us to our two outstanding essayists, Floyd Coleman, Ph.D., and Michael Harris, Ph.D.

A special acknowledgment must go to the late Eva Cockcroft, a muralist and author with a lifelong commitment to social justice, for suggesting that the two of us collaborate on this book.

Jim also thanks his wife, Arline, a professor of social work at California State University, Sacramento—who produced a book on issues of globalization during this same time—for her comments, feedback, and encouragement. He also extends thanks to his longtime friend Mark Rogovin, founder of the Public Art Workshop in Chicago, for stimulating his early interest in and knowledge of murals.

Robin would like to acknowledge the contribution of Cecil Fergerson, a Los Angeles–based art historian and community arts activist, for educating her about African American murals and history when she first began her research seven years ago. She also extends thanks to the nonprofit Mural Conservancy of Los Angeles for providing a vehicle for her involvement in the mural movement. Finally, she is grateful to her parents and her son Ricky for their support and patience while she ate, breathed, and talked almost nothing but murals for these many years.

Preface

CHICAGO PUBLIC LIBRARY
LEGLER BRANCH
115 S. PULASKI RD. 60624

"How did you become interested in documenting murals?" is the most commonly asked question at the conclusion of my slide lectures. Obviously, it is not a very common vocation, avocation, or hobby. For me, however, it seemed very natural. In the mid-70s, I attended a lecture by Victor Sorrel given at the University of Illinois Circle Campus. Professor Sorrel taught at Chicago State, had published a guide to Chicago murals, and was a very knowledgeable authority on public art. His talk was very stimulating and although I had seen some of the Chicago murals he discussed, I had paid little attention to them. During the show I remembered all the murals I had seen and photographed in Mexico in the '60s, and the frescoes I had admired in churches throughout Europe. I quickly found that documenting murals satisfied three interests that strongly motivated me: I enjoyed photography, I respected the community aspect of public art, and I had a strong concern for social and political justice—often the subject matter of street art. As a Jewish person, the history of my own people plus my involvement with the civil rights struggles of the '60s taught me to care about the quality of life for all people. In sharing the images I documented over a twenty-five-year period, I could speak to the politics of social change as well as the aesthetics of the art itself.

Tracking down murals in Chicago in those early years was like a treasure hunt. It was exciting to discover the works of the many African American artists who were painting at that time. I came to know such great artists as Calvin Jones, Mitchell Caton, and my personal "Diego Rivera," Bill Walker. Over the years I was fortunate enough to meet John Biggers, Richard Wyatt, Dewey Crumpler, Marcus Akinlana, and many of the other muralists, as well as to establish close communications with the newest generation of artists, like Brett Cook (Dizney).

The Chicano Mural Movement, spanning the last thirty years, has been reasonably well documented in books such as *Signs From the Heart* from SPARC in Los Angeles and the Durphy Foundation Project, which archived twelve hundred slides of California Chicano Art. Likewise, the eighteen-thousand-slide collection at the University of California, Santa Barbara, library pulled together Chicano imagery from a number of California institutions.

In the many fine books on African American art, attention was given to the great murals of a brilliant group of artists, including Aaron Douglas, Charles White, Hale Woodruff, Charles Alston, and even the works of John Biggers. But the public art of the last thirty years received little more than a paragraph, which usually noted the Chicago *Wall of Respect*. Alan Barnett's *Community Murals* is an outstanding resource, but unfortunately only covers the early years of the mural movement.

In many respects, African American murals, with their very public personae, help to establish a visual rebuttal to the racist, derogatory, and insulting imagery so often used by upper-class groups that want to maintain power and position at the expense of the African American community. There is pride and a sense of dignity in much of the art portrayed in this book, as well as the strength that comes from resistance to tyranny and injustice. Hopes and aspirations are also part of the legacy of shared imagery. Unfortunately, racist stereotyping can easily become embedded in a culture. People of color, immigrants, and many minority groups have all been victims of such tactics. Given limited access to the more formal art venues, African American artists chose the streets and other public places to create images that challenged negative messages. The very large format of the mural images tended to foster a sense of pride not only for those who lived in the local area but also for many others who passed through and saw the energy, vitality, and compassion of these works.

Feeling the need to supply some of the missing information, I met with Eva Cockcroft, a fine muralist, author, and artist, to discuss my thoughts. Eva quickly shared with me the fact that Robin Dunitz, a Los Angeles mural documentor and author, had talked to her about the same project idea. "You two should do it together," was Eva's pronouncement, and so it came to be. Our history of African American murals starts one hundred fifty years ago, covers the great artists from the '30s through the '50s, and then adds what I think is the missing piece of the tapestry: the wonderful African American public art of the last thirty years. Many of these murals no longer exist, some are faded, some have been repainted to glow with all their former vibrancy, and many just look great, waiting for the public to pass their way.

This book is a work-in-progress. No two people could hope to identify all the images and works of art that have been created over so many years. The authors hope that this investigation will stimulate sufficient interest to ensure that the documentation becomes even more complete.

—JAMES PRIGOFF

As a college student during the height of the anti–Vietnam War movement in the late 1960s, I received a street-level education in the politics of power in America and developed a lasting disdain for elitism. During this formative period of my life, I marched on Washington, D.C., did an independent study on the blues, and majored in "People's History."

My first important exposure to murals was the Olympics Murals Project in 1984: the organization bringing the summer games to Los Angeles commissioned ten murals along the freeways around downtown L.A. Although there were hundreds of murals in the city by then, I lived in murally challenged Westwood and hadn't seen many. I spent weeks photographing these works-in-progress. I loved that they were beautiful—obviously created by talented artists—and that they were out in the public realm where everyone could see and enjoy them.

Two years later my interest in murals was further expanded by a visit to the National Palace in Mexico City where Diego Rivera's dramatic depiction of the pageantry and struggles of history—politically engaging and speaking for the disenfranchised—thrilled me. In 1989 I stumbled across a brochure for the Mural Conservancy of Los Angeles, a group then unknown to me. I immediately joined, and shortly thereafter volunteered to help organize a mural tour for teachers. When I discovered that there was no resource book of local murals, I decided to write one.

In the course of putting together my first book, *Street Gallery: Guide to 1,000 Los Angeles Murals,* I learned that African Americans had painted many significant but little-known murals around town. Like too many others, I had associated mural making primarily with Latino artists. Few of the people who purported to be knowledgeable about L.A.'s murals knew about Charles White's tribute to Mary McLeod Bethune at the public library branch in Exposition Park, about Golden State Mutual Life Insurance Company's then forty-year-old gem by Charles Alston and Hale Woodruff, or about Charles Freeman's powerful collage about American justice inside a small storefront law office. These and countless others were a revelation to me.

The stories behind the artists drew me in deeper. The resource that first educated me about the history of black murals was Samella Lewis's *African American Art and Artists.* I was amazed and angry to learn that as a teen Charles White had won two scholarships to art school and then had been denied entrance when the administrators saw the color of his skin. I was excited to read about Hale Woodruff's *Amistad Mural* at Talladega, which depicted an important episode in American history seldom taught in school. And I was surprised to learn that many consider the *Wall of Respect* the first street mural, the one that started a whole movement eventually taken up by artists of many ethnicities.

Before I'd even finished *Street Gallery,* I knew that my next project would be to learn more about African American murals and to share more broadly those I'd become aware of. To start, I decided to self-publish a book of postcards showcasing twenty-five African American murals in Los Angeles. I also received the Mural Conservancy Board's blessing to organize a public mural bus tour of African American murals in South L.A. I invited Cecil Fergerson, a highly regarded community arts activist, to guide the tour. I was disappointed when only fifteen people signed up. I came to realize that, along with ignorance of the fact that black people have created beautiful and important art, fear keeps most people from venturing into the poorer parts of town.

The last piece of the puzzle that became this book was connecting with Jim Prigoff. I knew Jim, but we had never worked together. His expertise on spraycan art was well known to me. Artist and mural historian Eva Cockcroft brought us together upon hearing that we both were embarking on the same project separately. Jim's vast twenty-five-year-old archive of community mural imagery nationwide became the core of the book. I contributed my skills as a researcher and journalist, conducting interviews and uncovering background information on the murals and their creators. If it hadn't been for Jim's perseverance during a frustrating two-year search, we still might not have had a publisher. Also, his unrelenting networking with experts in the field of African American art over many months happily brought Floyd Coleman, Michael Harris, and Edmund Barry Gaither into the project.

—Robin J. Dunitz

Keeping Hope Alive: The Story of African American Murals

Floyd Coleman, Ph.D.

The black American struggle for survival and equality has been sustained by word (religion and literature), song (spirituals, gospel, blues, jazz, and hip-hop) and image (graphic arts, painting, photography, film, and other forms of visual culture). Much has been written about African American religion, music, and literature, but only in the last thirty years have the visual arts received the serious scholarly attention they deserve. The visual arts provide a face—a concrete manifestation of the hopes and aspirations of black Americans. Thus, murals—the largest and, by extension, the most compelling genre of the visual arts—are celebrations of skill, intelligence, ingenuity, imagination, and spirit that form an important thread in black America, inspiring and shaping a culture of hope.[1]

From unknown enslaved craftspeople to sophisticated fine artists, writers, and intellectuals, many have explored and affirmed the changing identities of black Americans. In mid-seventeenth-century communities throughout the South, newly arrived Africans utilized their pre-American experiences and skills to produce pottery, ironwork, carpentry, carvings, and quilts that not only met the functional needs of the plantations but also reflected self-affirming intentions and cultural values. Black productions then and since Emancipation reflected these African Americans' will to survive, creating metaphors that expressed hope and celebrated culture through form and design.

In African American culture there has been a distinct leitmotif of hope. This can be heard in spirituals and traditional lore and observed in the earliest creations of Africans in America. In the twentieth century, one need only think of James Weldon Johnson's and John Rosamond Johnson's "Lift Every Voice and Sing" (1900, often referred to as the "Negro National Anthem"), Martin Luther King's "I Have a Dream" speech at the 1963 March on Washington, Jesse Jackson's exhortation to "Keep Hope Alive," or the jeremiad of recent hip-hop.

The mural, an interior or exterior wall painting, connects art and history in powerful and compelling ways. It engages the viewer in a dialogue that is determined by the architectural space, the illusion of pictorial space, and images that may be drawn from historical, religious, or literary sources or from the artist's imagination. Formal values are expressed through scale, proportion, composition, pattern, color, and line. Painted and incised images on cave walls and cliff faces date as far back as 30,000 B.C.E.; the mural, with its strong narrative or symbolic abstract format, has been seen throughout Africa, Asia, Europe, and the Americas. Western expectations of the painted wall as mural were set by the work of fifteenth- and sixteenth-century artists of the Italian Renaissance. Twentieth-century American conceptions of murals have been shaped by the works of Mexican muralists of the 1920s and 1930s. The mural serves as a means of publicly communicating ideas, ideals, values, hopes, and aspirations of a people. For blacks in particular, the mural has been a symbol of pride, dignity, endurance, and hope. It has served as an alternative vision of history as well as a major medium of social criticism and protest.

The public mural came to the immediate attention of hundreds of thousands of African Americans when the December 1967 issue of *Ebony* magazine featured modified panels of the *Wall of Respect,* the originals of which were painted earlier that year in Chicago by the artists of OBAC. The *Wall,* as it was most frequently called, was a direct, raw, expressive work that communicated through formal and symbolic means that a new attitude was abroad in black America.

Expressing solidarity and unity through visual and formal means, the artists were creating community. They explored culture and history, affirming ties to Africa and the Caribbean. By claiming space, the artists demonstrated self-worth and demanded respect, calling for resistance to oppression and recognition of the redemptive nature of struggle and resistance.[2]

The story of African American murals, however, did not begin with the *Wall of Respect* in 1967. It began in a much less public way in Cincinnati, Ohio, more than a century earlier.

Cincinnati, one of the thriving art centers of nineteenth-century America, was where African American skill and perseverance and white abolitionist interests and wealth intersected, setting in motion a tradition of fine arts patronage that involved race and the use of the arts to promote social change. In 1850 Nicholas Longworth (1782–1863) commissioned Robert Scott Duncanson (1821–72) to paint landscape murals for his Belmont mansion, now the Taft Museum. Duncanson, a skillful house painter and interior decorator, taught himself to be a fine arts painter by copying European engravings, sketching, and painting portraits.

In 1852 Duncanson completed the Belmont murals: eight wall panels, three over-door floral vignettes, and two patriotic eagles over arched entrances. Although the artist had no previous experience in this medium, his work reflected the accomplished landscape style of the Hudson River School of Thomas Cole (1801–1848), Thomas Doughty (1793–1850), and Asher B. Durand (1796–1886).

For any artist to get a commission to paint a mural is rare. That Longworth chose Duncanson over better-known Cincinnati artists to paint the murals at Belmont raises issues that go beyond talent and notoriety. This achievement is all the more significant considering that at the time Duncanson was being recognized as "the finest landscape painter in the West," chattel slavery was the status of most blacks in the United States. The Longworth-Duncanson relationship[3] should be seen in light of the saga that was still unfolding across the nation. Antislavery groups, organized as early as 1775, had in 1825 intensified their efforts to eliminate slavery through both moral persuasion and political activism. Nicholas Longworth and abolitionists throughout the country and abroad supported black achievement, which they believed would advance their efforts to eliminate slavery in America.

Abolitionist support of Duncanson and other artists helped to establish the idea that achievement in the fine arts was sufficient proof of black humanity.

Sunset Mural, Robert Scott Duncanson, 1850–52. The Taft Museum, 316 Pike Street, Cincinnati, Ohio. Oil on plaster, one of eight panels, 109⅞" x 86¼". Originally sponsored by Nicholas Longworth (the museum was originally his home). Bequest of Charles Phelps and Anna Sinton Taft. Photograph © The Taft Museum.

This perspective on the importance of achievement in the fine arts to the social status of a people influenced how late-nineteenth- and early-twentieth-century African Americans and their European and European American allies viewed and promoted black creativity.[4]

Since the eighteenth century, blacks had been forming political and spiritual organizations such as the African Union Society in Rhode Island (1780), the Philadelphia African Society (1787), and the network of African Free Schools and societies. From the 1890s on, black Americans began to build an infrastructure to promote achievement and to express their cultural heritage. In 1896, Mary Church Terrell (1863–1954) helped organize the National Association of Colored Women, which promoted educational programs and social reform.

In 1900, W. E. B. Du Bois and others, with the blessing of Booker T. Washington (1856–1915), attended the First Pan-African Congress held in London. In that same year, Booker T. Washington organized the National Negro Business League, which sought to promote black businesses and entrepreneurship. In 1905, W. E. B. Du Bois, William Monroe Trotter (1874–1934), and others organized the Niagara Movement at a meeting in Canada. The Movement provided impetus for white and black leaders to establish the National Association for the Advancement of Colored People (NAACP) in 1909.[5] In 1914, with the financial support of Joel A. Spingarn, the NAACP established the Spingarn Medal for the "highest or noblest achievement by an American Negro during the preceding year" in any area of endeavor. Du Bois saw the awards as "an important step to advance the race."

In 1924, with support from Amy Spingarn, the NAACP launched the Amy Spingarn Prizes for literature and the arts. The Harmon Foundation started its awards program in 1926 and expanded it to the visual arts, offering annual exhibitions and awards available to artists across the United States. NAACP-published magazines *Crisis* and *Opportunity*, edited by W. E. B. Du Bois and Charles S. Johnson (1893–1956), respectively, frequently featured cover and interior art by black artists. These magazines engaged in a systematic effort to develop a modern black society by reinterpreting and reevaluating black history in light of black creativity in the arts.

The last decade of the nineteenth century ushered in the era of the "New Negro." Throughout this decade, educated blacks sought to define themselves in opposition to the "Old Negro" postbellum stereotypes of blacks as lazy, ignorant, cunning, and oversexed. Alain Locke (1885–1954), W. E. B. Du Bois, James Weldon Johnson (1871–1938), Charles S. Johnson, and other leaders of the cultural phalanx of the movement believed that artists should provide the visual images of the New Negro.[6] They wanted images that would serve to uplift the race and would help to actualize an American model democracy in which blacks would be viewed and treated with the respect and dignity accorded others.

Unprecedented cultural and intellectual activity, increased support, and publicity helped to fuel the productivity of black artists from the 1890s to the 1930s, giving them confidence in their own ability to produce works of exceptional quality.

AFRICAN AMERICAN MURALS: THE TWENTIETH CENTURY—BEGINNINGS

A full appreciation of the long tradition of African American murals must acknowledge the underrecognized predecessors of middle- and late-twentieth-century works.

William Edouard Scott (1884–1964) grew up during the first phase of the New Negro movement. Scott studied at the School of the Art Institute of Chicago and continued his education in Paris, where he was befriended by Henry Ossawa Tanner, an important role model to generations of black artists. Tanner's life and art served as refutation of the belief that blacks did not have the aesthetic sensibility or skill needed to produce works of art worthy of serious intellectual contemplation. Scott followed in the footsteps of Tanner, who became his idol and mentor.

In 1915, Scott traveled to the South to study and paint black people. Booker T. Washington, founder of Tuskegee Institute in Alabama, hosted Scott's visit to the South. Scott was to have painted Washington's portrait, but the educator died before the artist could do so. In 1931, Scott received a Julius Rosenwald

Fellowship to paint in Haiti, where he immersed himself in the life of the people. Following his determination to focus on the subjects immediately available, he concentrated on the common people, not the cultural elite. Scott spent a successful period in Haiti and is often given credit for getting the artists involved in painting local landscapes and people, paving the way for the development of Centre d'Art by DeWitt Peters in 1944.

In 1909, Scott painted his first mural—for Lane Technical High School in Chicago—while still enrolled at the School of the Art Institute of Chicago. Called *Commerce,* it is a large panoramic view focused at eye level, the middle ground bathed in light—a visually engaging composition held together by a strong sense of design. Scott painted murals for churches, recreation halls, organizations, and governments. He became the most prolific African American muralist of the first half of the twentieth century, completing more than seventy-five murals in Illinois, Indiana, New York, and Washington, D.C. He depicted black subject matter in twenty-five murals, making him an important part of the cadre of artists fashioning the image of the New Negro. Throughout the 1940s Scott worked within late-nineteenth-century and early-twentieth-century realms of realism, completing *Frederick Douglass Appeals to President Lincoln* (1943), one of his most important and mature public murals, for the Recorder of Deeds Building in Washington, D.C.[7]

While William Edouard Scott exemplifies the first phase of the New Negro movement, Aaron Douglas (1899–1979) embodies the Harlem Renaissance, the movement's "cultural peak." As a student and later an art teacher in Kansas City, Douglas was an avid reader of *Crisis* and *Opportunity,* two of the most influential magazines in the New Negro movement.

Recruited by the Urban League to come to Harlem, Aaron Douglas was encouraged by Locke, Johnson, and Du Bois. Shortly after his arrival in Harlem, Douglas was introduced to the Austrian artist Weinold Reiss (1887–1953) and began to study with him. Reiss had gained a reputation for his sympathetic depictions of blacks and Native Americans. Reiss had a strong influence on Douglas, encouraging him to capture the physical features of black folk and to study African sculpture. Working closely with Reiss, Douglas developed his skills and gained confidence in his artistic abilities. His work frequently appeared in *Opportunity* and *Crisis,* and both black and white authors used his illustrations and designs in their books and magazine articles on black subjects.

Less than two years after arriving in New York, Douglas was commissioned to paint his first mural, *Jungle and Jazz,* for Club Ebony in Harlem. In 1930, Fisk University commissioned him to paint a series of murals for the university's library. These murals gave Douglas an opportunity to explore a wide range of themes within his carefully constructed style, inspired by Egyptian art, Orphism, Art Deco, and Synthetic Cubism.

Also in 1930, Douglas was commissioned by the Sherman Hotel in Chicago to paint a mural for its College Inn. *Dance Magic,* like *Jungle and Jazz,* suggests a primitivistic intentionality, no doubt inspired by popular perceptions of jazz and of exotic blackness. The heroic, larger-than-life image is explored in his Bennett College mural of 1931, which portrays Harriet Tubman (1821–1913), the legendary nineteenth-century abolitionist who brought more than three hundred enslaved Africans out of the South through the Underground Railroad.

In 1934, Douglas completed a mural for the 135th Street Branch of the New York Public Library, which has become his best-known work. Called *Aspects of Negro Life,* the mural consists of four panels, each representing a phase of African American history. Focusing on the African background, the first panel, *The Negro in an African Setting,* shows two dancing figures surrounded by drummers and other stylized figures. Concentric bands of high-key colors connect the sections of the panel. From the top of the panel a ray of light cuts across the images, breaking up the space and creating a more abstract composition. At the topmost center of the panel an African sculpture from the western Sudan region combines Bamana and West Coast Mende forms. The panel symbolizes Africa, the ancestral homeland of black people in America.

Panel two, *An Idyll of the Deep South,* depicts several figures in a field, carrying hoes and surrounded by stylized plants. The center of the panel portrays

An Idyll of the Deep South, from **Aspects of Negro Life,** Aaron Douglas, 1934. Schomburg Center for Research in Black Culture, New York Public Library, 515 Lenox Avenue, Harlem. One of four panels, oil on canvas, 60' x 139'. Sponsored by the New York Public Library, Countee Cullen branch. © Schomburg Center for Research in Black Culture, Art & Artifacts Division, The New York Public Library, Astor, Lenox and Tilden Foundations.

several musicians and dancers flanked by images of working and praying. This references the period after Emancipation, when blacks were still tied to the land. Images of music and dance occur in each panel of the mural.

Panel three, *Slavery Through Reconstruction,* depicts several groups of figures: hooded Klansmen appear to be entering the space while a contingent of Union soldiers are receding into the distance; a large orator and a top-hatted figure suggest the Emancipation Proclamation and the president who signed it; cotton plants span the bottom of the panel and tree leaves run across the top. The composition is framed by silhouetted figures: a drummer on the left side and a trumpet-blower on the right. The balance contributes to the formal stability of the composition and conveys the centrality of music to black culture.

The fourth panel, *Song of the Towers,* depicts two black men on a large wheel amid towering smoke stacks. At the center, a standing figure holds a saxophone. Tall buildings in the background suggest that the African American has moved from a rural to an urban environment. The panel is animated by an unbalanced figure in the lower-left section of the panel; a black figure on the lower right runs from hovering Klan-like vegetal forms below. Light concentric circles contrast with the dark silhouette of the central figure, drawing the eye. The mural is replete with ideological references that are attributed to the artist's association with socialist and communist groups.[8]

Aspects of Negro Life summarizes Douglas's efforts to firmly connect black Americans to their African roots through subject matter, color, and line. The costumes, the spirited dancers and drummers, and the Sudanic statue are thematic ties to Africa. The silhouettes and sharp angles throughout the mural are Douglas's way of translating the feel of African sculpture into a two-dimensional format. This mural is an icon in the history of African American modernist art and is unquestionably one of the most inventive murals in the history of the Work Projects Administration (WPA) art projects.

Douglas, perhaps more than any of the other early muralists, was the first to create works that were expressions of an African American sensibility and

Song of the Towers, from **Aspects of Negro Life,** Aaron Douglas, 1934. Schomburg Center for Research in Black Culture, New York Public Library, 515 Lenox Avenue, Harlem. One of four panels, oil on canvas, 94" x 88". Sponsored by the New York Public Library, Countee Cullen branch. © Schomburg Center for Research in Black Culture, Art & Artifacts Division, The New York Public Library, Astor, Lenox, and Tilden Foundations.

ethos. *Aspects of Negro Life* is a radical departure from the genre paintings of Henry Ossawa Tanner and William Edouard Scott; it is stylistically experimental and reflects a decidedly black consciousness in subject matter.

Aaron Douglas is important to the history of African American murals because he took the image of the lived experience of blacks and created powerful works that combined the "felt" and the "imagined" experiences of black people. Douglas expanded the art language of black modernist artists with his high-key colors, abstract forms, and overlaying of flat planes of color and shapes, creating authoritative and imaginatively conceived works that were superbly and skillfully executed.

MEXICAN INFLUENCES

More often than not, African American murals painted after 1930 reflected influences of the Mexican muralists: Diego Rivera (1886–1957), José Clemente Orozco (1883–1949), and David Alfaro Siqueiros (1896–1974). However, African American contact with Mexican artists occurred even earlier. Miguel Covarubbias (1904–1957) lived in Harlem as early as 1917 and was a participant-observer throughout the Harlem Renaissance. Orozco first visited Harlem in 1917; he later returned to the United States to paint the murals at Pomona College (1930) and Dartmouth College (1932–34). While exiled from Mexico, Siqueiros spent time in the United States in 1932 and from 1934 to 1936. His workshop in New York City attracted artists such as Jackson Pollock and others who would become important figures in the 1940s and 1950s. The murals of Rivera, Orozco, and Siqueiros were well known to African American artists, particularity Hale Woodruff and Charles Alston.

While Hale Woodruff did not complete a large number of murals, his venture into the genre is significant. Woodruff was invited by Atlanta University's president John Hope to launch an art program in 1931. The WPA artists' programs were started in 1933 and Woodruff joined the program in 1933–34, when, with the assistance of Wilmer Jennings, he painted *The Negro in Modern American Life: Literature, Music and Art* for David T. Howard High School in Atlanta. Other murals from Woodruff's early phase included *Shantytown* and *Mudville,* both destroyed by fire. These two works were strongly praised by Ralph McGill, a reporter (and, later, editor) of the *Atlanta Constitution,* who wrote that the murals came from "the hands of a master artist."[9] More praise came from art historian James A. Porter: "Woodruff has always demonstrated his ability to render the broad essentials of a scene and to make the most of a story; none of his expressionist experiments has diminished this ability."[10]

Although his early murals received considerable critical acclaim, Woodruff felt that he did not know very much about murals. In 1936 he applied for and received a grant to study with Diego Rivera. Rivera accepted Woodruff as an apprentice. While working with Rivera, Woodruff learned fresco painting techniques and later traveled to Cuernavaca and other locations to view murals.

In his travels Woodruff saw how the Mexican mural movement focused on the resistive spirit. Rivera, Orozco, and Siqueiros all sought to use public mural art to mobilize critical consciousness about neglected features of Mexican history. Woodruff applied this lesson to an African American historical episode in his Talladega College murals, commissioned by President Buell Gallagher to commemorate the *Amistad* mutiny of 1839 and the founding of Talladega College by the American Missionary Society in 1867.

The *Amistad* mutiny is presented in three panels: *Mutiny Aboard the Amistad; The Amistad Slaves on Trial at New Haven, Connecticut, 1840;* and *The Return to Africa, 1842.* In the first panel Woodruff shows the moment the captured Africans, led by Cinque, fought to overpower the captain and crew and take control of the *Amistad.* The second panel shows the trial after the successful *Amistad* mutineers were captured by the USS *Washington* and taken to New London, Connecticut. The third panel shows Cinque and his group, along with black and white missionaries, returning to West Africa after litigation by abolitionist-funded lawyers to prohibit the captured Africans from being returned to Spain, and after former president John Quincy Adams's successful defense of their case before the United States Supreme Court. Woodruff's storytelling and his ability to use the

formal elements of scale, pattern, color, and line to communicate in compelling ways are clearly demonstrated in the *Amistad Mural.*

Woodruff utilizes stylistic devices of Diego Rivera and other Mexican muralists; neo-Baroque paintings of French artist Theodore Gericault (1791–1824), particularly his *Raft to the Medusa* (1819); and Italian Renaissance paintings with marine subject matter, such as *The Birth of Venus* (1482) by Sandro Botticelli (1445–1510), to produce one of the most powerful murals in the history of American art. The orientation of the figures, the repetition of colors, the recurrence of objects (particularly machetes) are carefully orchestrated within the relatively shallow space of the mural panel. In all three panels, Woodruff has heightened the illusionist effects and patterns to make the viewer engage in dialogue with the work, responding to rhythmical lines, carefully modulated colors and shapes, and the expressive faces of the principal players in this dramatic event in American history.

Art historian M. Akua McDaniel is one of the few scholars to have called attention to the companion murals to the *Amistad* mutiny that focus on the founding of Talladega College.[11] Here, as in the *Amistad* panels, Woodruff presents an epic narrative. The first panel depicts scenes associated with the Underground Railroad. The second panel is called *Opening Day* and shows students enrolling at the college. The third panel, *Building the Library,* shows students and white workers constructing the library. These murals show stronger stylistic affinity to the American Scene murals of Thomas Hart Benton than does the *Amistad Mural.* Both works, however, represent Woodruff's mature style and underscore his mastery of color and composition.

A decade after completing the *Amistad Mural,* Woodruff, in collaboration with Charles Alston, completed *The Negro in California History.* His panel *Settlement and Development,* which focused on the years 1850 to 1949, demonstrates his technical proficiency and his ability to create compelling visual narratives. Woodruff and his colleague told the relatively unknown story of black participation in the development of California, the nation's largest state.

The call to use African sources was answered in Woodruff's *Art of the Negro,* a six-panel mural commissioned for the rotunda of the Trevor Arnett Library by Atlanta University President Rufus Clement and unveiled in 1952, five years after Woodruff left Atlanta to accept a professorship in the Art Education Department at New York University. Alain Locke in *The New Negro* (1925) and *Negro Art: Past and Present* (1936) had maintained that the path to recognition and respect for black artists was through utilizing their unique heritage. Artists immersed in their culture can make a significant contribution to what art historian Edmund Barry Gaither called "an evolving cultural democracy." The iconographical program of the mural reflects a concern for establishing African art at the center of the world "cultural democracy."[12]

Native Forms is the first panel. At the top center of the panel, a composite Yoruba (Nigerian) figure featuring generic West African sculptural forms rests upon a base on which is painted an image of a Dogon (Mali) granary door. Left of this sculpture, the artist has painted images of Melanesian figures with strong Sepik River area features. To the right of the central figure, the artist places animated and colorful post-Columbian Mexican masked figures. In bottom sections of the panel, the artist presents a medley of forms: discretely defined shapes that show prehistoric wall paintings; two figures working cooperatively; a lone left-handed artist with black physiognomic features engaged in painting a wall.

Throughout the murals Woodruff juxtaposes images that collapse time and geography. In the second panel, *Interchange,* Woodruff places figures representing African and Mediterranean cultures in an inverted triangular format, spatially separated by painted shields, relief sculptures, and architectural forms. In the third panel, *Dissipation,* the artist shows European invasion and destruction of Africa; however, he painted outlines of African sculptures in the lower part of the panel, some transformed into abstract sculptures—perhaps a reminder that the vocabulary of modernist abstraction was long ago forecasted by traditional African art. The fourth panel, *Parallels,* features three totemic sculptures—composite African flanked by composite U.S. Northwest Coast (left) and composite Melanesian (right)—that

dominate the top center of the panel. Painted panels of pre-Columbian Mexican sculpture and codices, as well as painted panels of composite African and Melanesian forms, fill the space. The fifth panel, *Influences,* shows Baule (Ivory Coast) figures, and a myriad of flat shapes that show Haitian *veve* drawings. An abstract Henry Moore (British) sculpture and abstract surrealist forms are distributed throughout the mural.

It is the sixth panel, *Artists,* that reveals Woodruff's ideological position. The panel depicts black artists from prehistory to the 1950s, among them Sebastian Gomez (seventeenth-century Spain), Joshua Johnston (late-eighteenth- and early-nineteenth-century America), Richmond Barthé, Charles Alston, and the young Jacob Lawrence (twentieth-century America). Examples of the artists' work are also shown; Richmond Barthé's *Blackberry Woman* is an easily recognizable piece. Placed above this august gathering of black artists, Woodruff depicts African and Greek muses, reflecting a cultural democracy in which African art is not on the margins but is a vital part of the core cultural traditions that greatly influenced twentieth-century aesthetic production. Woodruff's *Art of the Negro* signals the new directions taking place in American art at mid-century. Here figurative and modernist biomorphic abstraction are combined with Abstract Expressionism.

Woodruff sums up his long and fruitful interest in African art when he intones: "I have tried to study African art in order to assimilate it into my being, not to copy but to seek the essences of it, its spirit and quality as art."[13] He succeeded in *Art of the Negro,* one of the most important murals in American art.

Of the black artists working in New York City at the start of the WPA art programs, few were more prepared to participate than Charles Alston. Like Aaron Douglas, Alston (1907–1977) was a university graduate (Columbia), hence more broadly educated than many of his artist friends and associates. Alston was one of the few black artists in the country awarded a supervisory position within the WPA art program; Sargent Johnson of California and Archibald Motley of Illinois were the only others. Alston was very much aware and appreciative of the work of the Mexican muralists, particularly Diego Rivera and José Clemente

Mystery and Magic and **Modern Medicine**
Charles Alston, 1935–36.
Harlem Hospital, Women's
Pavilion Lobby, 506 Malcolm X
Boulevard, Harlem, New York.
Oil on canvas, 17' x 9' (each).
Sponsored by the Federal Art
Project of the Works Progress
Administration. Photograph
courtesy of the National
Archives.

Orozco, both of whom he met when they visited and painted murals in New York City. In 1936, Alston and his twenty assistants, including artists such as Beauford Delaney (1901–1979), Georgette Seabrooke (b.1916, now Georgette Powell), and Vertis Hayes (b.1911), were assigned to paint murals in the Harlem Hospital. Their selection of black subject matter for the murals was initially rejected by the hospital's white administrators; however, after subsequent delay and negotiations, the murals were painted in the pediatric and nursing units. Alston himself painted two murals, *Mystery and Magic* and *Modern Medicine,* for the lobby of the building. Alston's murals deal with the development of medicine from traditional African to modern surgical practices. Alston presents an engaging visual story of the evolution of modern medicine. Bearden and Henderson maintain in *A History of African American Artists from 1792 to the Present* that Alston's Harlem

Hospital murals are the finest produced in New York City in the 1930s.

Having visited Hale Woodruff in Atlanta when he was painting the *Amistad Mural* for Talladega College, Alston was asked to join Woodruff on a commissioned mural project for Golden State Mutual Life Insurance Company, a black-owned firm founded in Los Angeles in 1925. *The Negro in California History* shows Alston and Woodruff at their best in reconciling American scene and Mexican muralist painting styles. Alston's panel *Exploration and Colonization* depicts the years from 1527 to 1850. Using the horizon line as a strong compositional element, Alston's larger-than-life figures cut across the prominent skyline, giving explorer-scout James Beckwourth a powerful presence in the top center portion of the panel. The mural tells the story of black involvement in the exploration, settlement, and development of California, and, by extension, the United States. As a tribute to his talents, Alston was invited to return to Harlem Hospital in 1969 to create a mosaic mural for its newly remodeled structure.

Mexican muralist influence cannot be more appropriately illustrated than in the work of Charles White (1918–1979). White, deeply immersed in the history and culture of black Americans, devoted his life to analyzing and interpreting that culture visually. White's commitment to telling the African American's story was total. Greatly influenced by Locke's *The New Negro,* Marxist ideas, Taller de Grafica Popular (TGP), and the muralists of Mexico, White saw himself as a cultural warrior, one who made images that would reveal the beauty of black people and give them the confidence and pride to move beyond victimization. After studying at the School of the Art Institute of Chicago, White was accepted for the WPA arts program, which enabled him to devote more time to his work. The Federal Art Project and his knowledge of Mexican art helped him to understand how art could be used to promote social change. Although White produced murals such as *Five Great American Negroes* (1939) for the Chicago Public Library, *History of the Negro Press* (1940) for the Negro Exposition at the Chicago Coliseum, and *Mary McLeod Bethune* (1978) for the Los Angeles Public Library in Exposition Park, he is best known for *The Contribution of the Negro to Democracy in America* (1943), a virtual visual history of black America from the colonial era of Crispus Attucks to the mid-twentieth-century era of Paul Robeson. In this mural, White used a limited palette to achieve a powerful tableau of human forms, depicting ordinary black folk in bold, monumental ways.

White's influence on African American artists has been profound. Perhaps more than any other black artist of his generation, he has produced images that reveal the pride and dignity of black Americans. His devotion to portraying black people in positive ways was not lost on the Hampton Institute student who was his volunteer assistant when painting *The Contribution of the Negro to Democracy in America:* John Biggers.

Over the past half-century, John Biggers (b. 1924) has thoroughly promoted mural painting as an artist, teacher, and advocate. He produced murals as an undergraduate art student at Hampton Institute, and mural production was the focus of his doctoral dissertation at Pennsylvania State University under the directorship of Viktor Lowenfeld (1903–1960), his mentor at Hampton.

When John Biggers moved to Texas in 1949 to head the art department at Texas State University for Negroes (now Texas Southern University), he incorporated murals in common educational experience by establishing mural painting as a part of the art curriculum. As an artist and teacher, Biggers used murals to produce affirming and educational images for black Americans. In 1996 he wrote: "My murals have been the central focus of my life as an artist. From my earliest artistic beginnings at Hampton Institute, I have told stories about life through my paintings on the wall."[14]

Enrolling at Hampton Institute in 1941 brought Biggers in contact with the people who would shape his life. When Biggers changed his major from plumbing to art, he came under the tutelage of Viktor Lowenfeld, an Austrian Jew, a teacher and scholar who understood what it was like to be a despised minority. Biggers would also meet and interact with Charles White, Elizabeth Catlett, and fellow student Samella Sanders (now Lewis), and would receive the encouragement of Alain Locke. At Hampton he learned from Lowenfeld, White, and Catlett that to be an artist was a serious undertaking, and that one had a responsibility not only to oneself but also to one's people. The Hampton experience was pivotal to Biggers's development as an artist.

Like others working after 1930, John Biggers was greatly influenced by the Mexican muralists—and by Diego Rivera's *Detroit Industry* cycle murals of 1932 and 1933 in particular—but his direct experience with murals and a broader understanding of the Mexican muralists came from Charles White. In 1943, White was awarded a Rosenwald Fellowship to paint *The Contribution of the Negro to Democracy in America* at Hampton Institute. The visual language and compositional conventions of White's mural influenced how Biggers would design his murals for more than a decade. All these influences can be seen in *Sharecroppers* (1946–47), a benchmark work in Biggers's early development as a mural painter. Further maturation is seen in Biggers's *The Contribution of Negro Women to American Life and*

Education (1953), a monumental work for the Blue Triangle Branch YWCA in Houston, and *Web of Life* (1957–62). The latter work marks the beginnings of the artist's deeper understanding of African culture and its people, and his effort to develop a new visual vocabulary.

Working with his nephew James since 1989, Biggers has completed murals that will assure his place in the history of American art. *Origins* and *Ascension* at Winston-Salem State University Library and *House of the Turtle* and *Tree House* at Hampton University Library, all completed from 1990 to 1992, create a tapestry of black American and African history and culture unlike any monumental works of African American art to date. Biggers created these murals for the "edification and enjoyment" of all who see them, particularly the students, whom he wanted to inspire. The interplay of ground plane and imagery create a structure that is both emphatic and elusive, and multiple perspectives add to the complexity of the composition of each mural. For forty years, Biggers has combined an incipient surrealism and the design authority of African art with the color intricacies of geometric abstraction, informed by the structure and rhythm of African American quilts.

Fully aware of the educative power of the mural, Biggers felt that his work could instill pride and promote social equality. But perhaps most of all he realized that the mural could visualize and memorialize the connections between African Americans and Africans.

Biggers engages his art in the black struggle for freedom, dignity, and equality in America. His murals are a virtual lexicon of the influences, styles, and ideologies that have shaped twentieth-century African American art. Fulfilling the call of the New Negro in the 1920s, he connects the traditions of the 1930s and 1940s with the efflorescence of mural activity of the 1960s and beyond.

Stagecoach and Mail (also known as **U.S. Mail**), Archibald Motley, 1937. Wood River Post Office, Wood River, Illinois. Oil on canvas, approximately 6' x 5'. Sponsored by the U.S. Treasury Department's Section of Fine Arts. Collection of the U. S. Postal Service.

OTHER MURALISTS

Archibald Motley and Sargent Johnson, twentieth-century African American artists, both explored black subject matter in their work. Motley's paintings of the black church after his visit to the Deep South make a contribution to the black image in American art.[15] However, his works with the WPA Federal Arts Project, including several murals, are in keeping with the thrust of the federal program; his figures are generic. Motley painted *Stagecoach and Mail* (1937) for the post office in Wood

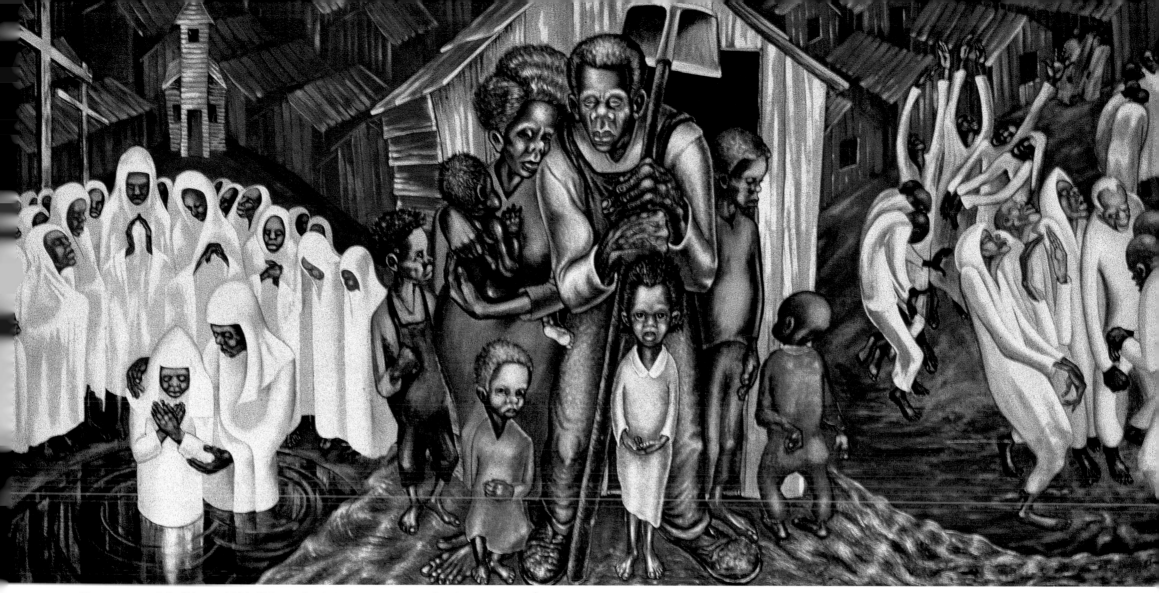

Sharecroppers, John Biggers, 1946–47. Pennsylvania State University, Paul Robeson Cultural Center, State College, Pennsylvania. Egg tempera on muslin, 46" x 93".

River, Illinois, across the Mississippi River and not far from St. Louis, Missouri.

Sculptor Sargent Johnson, unlike Archibald Motley, was greatly influenced by Alain Locke. He was a frequent participant in Harmon Foundation exhibitions, and was the virtual West Coast point man for the visual arts of the Harlem Renaissance.[16] In many of his public works, which were mural-like sculptural friezes, he included Asian and pre-Columbian imagery. His smaller pieces were noted for their exploration of African and black American themes. His work, like that of Hale Woodruff, is a manifestation of African American artists making art by drawing upon sources and images from around the world.

Georgette Seabrooke Powell painted in the American Scene style of her instructors at Cooper Union and her mentor Charles Alston. In *Recreation in Harlem* (1936) at Harlem Hospital, Powell depicts blacks and whites engaged in dancing and other activities. Within the shallow space, an overall tonality unifies the composition.

No artist of the earlier generation produced work that reflected the mood, the perspectives, and the metaphysical reality of the urban black experience of the 1960s more than Romare Bearden (1912–1988). Bearden, employing collagelike techniques and improvisational patterns, created murals of great variety. In *Baltimore Uproar* (1982) and *Communications* (1982) Bearden returns to figuration seen in earlier works, but with more highly saturated color. In *Before Dawn* (1989) and *Cityscape* (1976), Bearden uses the space and figuration seen in his collages, a synthesis of the abstract and the representational. His conceptualized images have great presence and power.

Murals constitute a relatively small part of the oeuvre of Jacob Lawrence (b.1917), yet his work has the clarity of form, implicitly narrative image, historical reference, and serialization of themes most appropriate to mural painting. Lawrence's murals in Howard University's Blackburn Center are typical of his style, as established by his famous *Migration Series* (1940–41). *Explorations* (1980) and *Origins* (1984) each consist of twelve fabricated baked enamel panels. They are dedicated to educator Mary McLeod Bethune and actress Ruby Dee, respectively. The red, brown, blue, and yellow chromatic colors, along with neutral black and gray areas and lines, create the visual structure for the artist to tell the story of African American struggles and triumphs.[17]

Three of Lawrence's murals—*Community* (1989) in the Addabbo Federal Building in Queens, New York, *Theater* (1978) at the University of Washington, and *Games* (1978) originally at the Kingdome (both in Seattle)—demonstrate his uncanny ability to monumentalize scenes and create a tapestry of darks and lights, large and small forms that result in powerful visual narratives.

AFRICAN AMERICAN MURALS IN CONTEXT

Beginning with Aaron Douglas, African American murals moved past wall decorations to become African-centered modernist works of art. Douglas was very much aware of the work of leading artists and of current issues in criticism, but followed the admonitions of Locke to uplift the race by producing works of great skill that had meaning and significance to the black community. Woodruff, Alston, White, and Biggers continued in that tradition.

The African American muralists have connected with the black community through formal elements of color, line, pattern, space, and subject matter. Through their interpretations of the history of peoples of African ancestry in the diaspora, they instilled meaning and purpose in the lives of black Americans. They have made centuries-old events relevant and new. Their life-affirming works have reflected both a social and spiritual consciousness—essentially, art for life's sake.

NOTES

1. I wish to thank art historian Raymond G. Dobard and cultural critic/choreographer Carolyn Shuttlesworth for their helpful suggestions in the preparation of this essay.

2. For a participating artist/scholar's perspective of the *Wall* and of this era, see Jeff R. Donaldson and Geneva Smitherman Donaldson, "Upside the Wall: An Artist's Retrospective Look at the 'Original' 'Wall of Respect,'" in *The People's Art: Black Murals, 1967–1978* (Philadelphia: African American Historical and Cultural Museum, 1986). Donaldson discusses the making of the "original" *Wall of Respect,* pointing out that the mural's overall design and images were changed by the time the mural was featured in popular media.

3. Longworth thought very highly of Duncanson. In 1853 he wrote a letter of introduction to the eminent American sculptor Hiram Powers for Duncanson when he and fellow artist William Sonntag traveled to Europe. Duncanson also received a portrait commission from Longworth, which he completed in 1858. See Joseph D. Ketner, *The Emergence of the African-American Artist: Robert S. Duncanson, 1821–1872* (Columbia: University of Missouri Press, 1993), 72, 108, 110.

4. For a discussion of abolitionist patronage of African American artists see Sharon F. Patton, *African-American Art* (New York: Oxford University Press, 1998), 74–77.

5. For a most informative overview of postbellum black American history and culture, see Arnold Taylor, *Travail and Triumph: Black Life and Culture in the South Since the Civil War* (Westport, Connecticut: Greenwood Press, 1977), and John Hope Franklin, *Racial Equality in America* (Columbia: University of Missouri Press, 1993).

6. For an insightful discussion of the concept of the New Negro, see Lizzetta LeFalle-Collins, "Re-Defining the African-American Self," in Lizzetta LeFalle-Collins and Shifra Goldman, *In the Spirit of Resistance: African American Modernists and the Mexican Muralist School* (New York: The American Federation of Arts, 1996), 19–26.

7. Little has been written about Scott's murals. The most important discussion of his murals appears in Edmund Barry Gaither, "The Mural Tradition," and William E. Taylor, "Echoes of the Past: Artists' Biographies," in William E. Taylor and Harriet G. Warkel, *A Shared Heritage: Art by Four African Americans* (Indianapolis: Indianapolis Museum of Art, distributed by Indiana University Press, 1996), 123–146, 160–166.

8. Amy Helene Kirschke, "The Depression Murals of Aaron Douglas: Radical Politics and African American Art," *International Review of African American Art* 12, no. 4 (1995): 19–29.

9. See Romare Bearden and Harry Henderson, *A History of African American Artists from 1792 to the Present* (New York: Pantheon Books, 1993), 208.

10. James A. Porter, *Modern Negro Art* (Washington, D.C.: Howard University Press, 1992), 109. First published in 1943.

11. See M. Akua McDaniel, "Reexamining Hale Woodruff's Talladega College and Atlanta University Murals," *International Review of African American Art* 12, no. 4 (1995): 4–17.

12. For a discussion of Alain Locke's philosophy of art, see Edmund Barry Gaither, "John Biggers: A Perspective," in Alvia J. Wardlaw, *The Art of John Biggers: View from the Upper Room* (New York: Harry N. Abrams, Inc., in association with the Museum of Fine Arts, Houston, 1995), 76–79, and Tommy L. Lott, *The Invention of Race: Black Culture and the Politics of Representation* (Malden, Massachusetts: Blackwell Publishers, Inc., 1999), 69–70.

13. Bearden and Henderson, *A History of African-American Artists,* 213.

14. Olive Jensen Theisen, *The Murals of John Biggers: American Muralist, African American Artist* (Hampton, Virginia: Hampton University Museum, 1996), viii.

15. See Jontyle Theresa Robinson and Wendy Greenhouse, *The Art of Archibald J. Motley Jr.* (Chicago: Chicago Historical Society, 1991), 16–17.

16. See Porter, *Modern Negro Art,* 108, and Lott, *The Invention of Race,* 69–70.

17. See Michelle-Lee White, "Common Directions, Epic Dimensions: Jacob Lawrence's Murals at Howard University," *International Review of African American Art* 12, no. 4 (1995): 30–37.

Urban Totems: The Communal Spirit of Black Murals

Michael D. Harris, Ph.D.

Murals are public-access stained-glass windows. They sanctify the community like the Stations of the Cross sanctify the church.
—NELSON STEVENS

A black creation
Black art, of the people,
For the people,
Art for people's sake
Black people
The mighty black wall
—DON L. LEE

(read at the dedication of the *Wall of Respect,* Chicago, 1967)

1967–1975: ART FOR THE PEOPLE

Floyd Coleman remembers his first glimpse of Hale Woodruff's *Amistad Mural* at Talladega College, completed in 1939 to commemorate the centennial anniversary of the revolt led by Cinque aboard the slaver *Amistad*. Coleman was stunned. Not only were the murals visually captivating, but here for the first time was an image of a black man *winning*. In the first panel of the mural, African captives physically subdued whites in a violent repudiation of enslavement. The middle panel presented a well-dressed, gentlemanly Cinque participating in his own legal defense, seeking to legitimate his refutation of enslavement. The final panel showed the Africans of the *Amistad* preparing to return to their West African homes after securing their freedom in 1841. This mural, completed during the midst of the horrific period of apartheid (Jim Crow) in the southern United States, provided a visual catalogue of hope and inspiration for young African Americans in Alabama.

Abolitionists worked to make the 1839 *Amistad* incident symbolic of larger issues of slavery. The American Missionary Association got involved, and in the second half of the nineteenth century made possible the opening of more than one thousand schools and colleges for blacks. One of those schools was Talladega College and, according to Woodruff, the mural was a gesture of the school's appreciation.

If we jump to 1967 Chicago we find the famed *Wall of Respect* mural going up on the city's South Side with the participation of Jeff Donaldson, Wadsworth Jarrell, Barbara Jones, and Carolyn Lawrence—four of the founding members of the artist group AfriCobra—as well as Norman Parish, Eliot Hunter, William Walker, and others[1] who were members of the newly formed Organization of Black American Culture (OBAC, pronounced "Obasi"). Nearly thirty years after the *Amistad Mural,* it remained difficult to find images of blacks winning. It was difficult to find images of blacks on television, in print media, or in film. It also was difficult to find images *by* blacks in museums, galleries, or art texts. Echoing the earlier effort of Woodruff, and building upon the social activism of the work of contemporaneous Mexican muralists, the *Wall of Respect* was intended to present images of significant, heroic, recognizable African Americans. It was meant to inspire the South Side black community with the faces of black success, creative genius, and resistance: Muhammad Ali, John Coltrane, Nina Simone, Marcus Garvey, and Malcolm X appear in the original mural. The *Wall of Respect* represented a rallying point for the community and a visualization of some of their collective values and successes. It lifted them from collective invisibility. The list of heroes to be included on the wall, chosen because their lives and works exemplified the ideals of the OBAC Visual Art Workshop, was approved by the community. The mural was painted outdoors without official sanction or sponsorship. The *Wall of Respect* truly was a community project.

The Wall of Respect
(REVISED VERSION), Sylvia
Abernathy, Jeff Donaldson,
Eliot Hunter, Wadsworth
Jarrell, Barbara Jones,
Carolyn Lawrence,
Norman Parish, William
Walker, and Myrna
Weaver; photographers
Billy Abernathy, Darrell
Cowherd, Roy Lewis, and
Robert A. Sengstacke;
Edward Christmas, mixed
media commercial artist,
1967 (destroyed in 1971).
43rd and Langley,
Chicago, Illinois.
Self-sponsored.
Photograph © 1967
Public Art Workshop.

Jeff Donaldson has written that the mural was conceived as "an adoption and an aesthetic extension of the turf-identifying graffiti scrawled on neighborhood buildings by Chicago street gangs for more than a decade before the creation of the *Wall of Respect*."[2] Donaldson points out that while the mural was being painted, the powerful Blackstone Rangers gang sanctioned the effort and protected the wall. People from the community gathered to watch the artists work, often bringing them food and drink. Sometimes a call-and-response developed as people offered critiques and commentary to the artists. According to Donaldson, the mural sparked a community murals movement that led to "more than 1,500 murals in virtually every urban black community in the nation," with two hundred produced by 1975 in Chicago alone.[3] By the mid-1970s, however, the official support of arts organizations and government agencies generated murals that became more graphic and abstract in nature. Still, the *Wall of Respect* revitalized the murals movement in this country and inspired other ethnic groups to erect murals for social criticism and protest, or to celebrate their cultures.

Most of the murals prior to the *Wall of Respect* had been executed on interior walls. They were created in black institutional spaces and many were designed by iconic artists such as Aaron Douglas, Charles White, Charles Alston, Hale Woodruff, and John Biggers. An interior mural theoretically is not openly available to everyone. With the *Wall of Respect,* murals began to be staged outdoors in community, rather than institutional, settings. When a mural is painted in and for a community, it has moved into vernacular space and popular culture. Black British cultural theorist

Stuart Hall notes that, "in one sense, popular culture always has its base in the experiences, the pleasures, the memories, the traditions of the people. It has connections with local hopes and local aspirations . . . the everyday practices and the everyday experiences of ordinary folks."[4] As a part of popular culture, outdoor murals directly engaged the community: "[Popular culture] is an arena that is *profoundly* mythic. It is a theater of popular desires, a theater of popular fantasies. It is where we discover and play with the identifications of ourselves, where we are imagined, where we are represented. . . ."[5] The early murals were urban totems operating as emblematic, idealistic, often mythic signs (in the semiotic sense) for black folk.

The *Wall of Respect* engaged issues of black cultural accomplishment, radical protest against oppression, and contemporary heroism, rather than historical narratives. The content of most of the murals that preceded it "reflected a vision of Black progress through hard work and individual achievement" rather than

making direct challenges to the oppressive American political system. Historian Reginald Butler suggests that this indicated the "gradualist approach of the Roosevelt/Truman era of Black activism" and was consistent with the nonviolent, rural-based civil rights movement of the late 1950s.[6] By moving outdoors, murals were to directly engage the community, invite their responses and criticism, and serve as catalysts for community action. Because the *Wall of Respect* was to belong to the community, the OBAC artists agreed that there would be no signatures to draw attention to individuals, which would also protect the artists from media exploitation and police harassment, which did become a problem. Individualism was subordinated to group effort and communal benefit.

The content of the Chicago *Wall of Respect,* the 1968 *Wall of Dignity* in Detroit, and Atlanta's *Wall of Respect* (c. 1974) sought to counteract the stigmatization that blacks experienced. Social psychologist Claude Steele writes that stigma,

Wall of Dignity
Eugene Wade (Eda),
William Walker,
Edward Christmas, and
Eliot Hunter, 1968.
Mack and Lillibridge
(across the street from
St. Bernard's Church),
Detroit.

Wall of Respect, Amos Johnson, Vera Parks and Nathan Hoskins, 1976.
Downtown Atlanta.

"the endemic devaluation many blacks face in our society and schools," is "its own condition of life, different from class, money, culture."[7] He argues that:

> devaluation grows out of our images of society and the way
> those images catalogue people. The catalogue need never be
> taught. It is implied by all we see around us: the kinds of people
> revered in advertising (consider the unrelenting racial advocacy
> of Ralph Lauren ads) and movies (black women are rarely seen
> as romantic partners, for example); media discussions of whether
> a black can be President; invitation lists to junior high school
> birthday parties; school curricula; literacy and musical canons.[8]

These early murals appeared in an era when blacks seldom appeared on television or in advertisements other than as Aunt Jemima, Uncle Ben, or Cream of

Wheat's Rastus. Oppression had a visual component that had operated effectively since the 1830s in art, minstrelsy, and eventually in popular media. It was only in the streets that blacks found visibility and a means to vent frustration and anger about their stigmatization and oppression in American society. There had been at least fifty-eight major uprisings and police-citizen confrontations from 1964 to 1967. This was an era when the Black Panther Party slogan, "Power to the People," became widely known and outdoor communal murals took inspirational images and lessons in political action directly to masses of people.

The outdoor murals brought into play the vernacular tradition of call-and-response because the images needed community approval to survive without being defaced. Los Angeles muralist Elliott Pinkney says that people would come and ply him with questions while he was up on the scaffolding. Sometimes he stopped and spent a few hours talking to people in the neighborhood about what he was doing and why.

Outdoor murals sought to place images of success, positive images, in front of people for their everyday consumption. Heroic or accomplished individuals such as Muhammad Ali, John Coltrane, W. E. B. DuBois, Angela Davis, Bobby Seale, and Malcolm X appeared. Integrationists like Martin Luther King Jr. and Roy Wilkins did not appear in most of the early murals because many of the artists preferred a more aggressive response to racial oppression. African symbols and imagery in the murals linked African Americans to a cultural legacy preceding the Atlantic slave trade and the stigmatization that followed. Many of these early murals were created by artists collaborating in the communal spirit of their messages.

If one thinks about black folks' identification with Joe Louis before World War II, how neighbors crowded around a radio to hear each fight and shared so much joy in each victory, it then becomes easy to imagine the symbolic potential of murals. Joe Louis's glory was our glory. He represented the race, and, like Woodruff's *Amistad* image, here was a black man winning against whites. He was not prevailing as a trickster of folklore like Br'er Rabbit, the Signifying Monkey, or the older African tricksters Ananse the spider from Ghana and Eshu Elegbara from Nigeria and the Caribbean. Louis stood and fought and prevailed. And it was in that tradition that Muhammad Ali and Malcolm X were celebrated. The Cream of Wheat chef was a white fantasy of a black person and we had seen enough of him.

More decorative, stylized, symbolic, and colorful mural imagery developed in the early- to mid-1970s as can be seen in Don McIlvaine's *Black Man's Dilemma* (1970) in Chicago, and Dana Chandler's *Knowledge Is Power, Stay in School* (1972) in Boston. McIlvaine worked with a local gang, the Conservative Vicelords, on the creation of his mural of street-scene images. Chandler concocted simplified figures in a symbolic array: Two fists emerge as flames from the mouth of Martin Luther King Jr., who is helping to crack open an egg of oppression. On the opposite side of the mural, another figure aids in the opening of the egg, pointing his finger in a gesture approximating Adam's in Michelangelo's Sistine Chapel fresco. The black nationalist colors of red, black, and green color Malcolm X's glasses. Chandler says that he was indicating that blacks have the power to free themselves and rise to their fullest potential individually and collectively. He says that the work was an effort to visually encourage people to stay in school to acquire the transformative power of knowledge.

On occasion, heroic figures and community messages were joined by calls for unity. Nelson Stevens, an AfriCobra artist who had joined the faculty at the University of Massachusetts, Amherst, completed the mural *Work to Unify African People* (1973) in Boston in collaboration with Dana Chandler, whose mural *The Black Worker* was adjacent to his. Like Charles White in the 1950s, Stevens presented everyday people from the black community as iconic figures in his work. Sculptor Howard McCaleb formulated text at the bottom to stabilize the composition and Stevens incorporated it into the image.

Part of the power of this image comes from its composition. Two monumental heads anchor the image. They rest atop the word "African," which is part of a horizontal register across the bottom of the work. To the viewer's right, a small image supports the theme, but the remainder of the mural is organized around the heads and the textual message. The work is colorful and symbolic, but its simple organization of forms and space is as cohesive as a painting might be. This differs from many murals that surge with complicated activity and imagery, or that patch a series of images together. Stevens's figures combined the naturalism of the Atlanta *Wall of Respect* with the color and stylization seen in Chandler's murals. The Pan-African message is in line with Stevens's sense that murals form an "outdoor gallery glorifying, warning, and restoring."[9]

One of the more memorable indoor murals of the 1970s was Leroy Foster's *Life and Times of Frederick Douglass* (1972, installed in 1973) in the Frederick Douglass branch of the Detroit Public Library. It was conceived around

Life and Times of Frederick Douglass, Leroy Foster, 1973. Detroit Public Library, 3666 Grand River, Detroit. Oil on canvas, 10' x 12'. Photograph courtesy of Detroit Public Library.

a Detroit meeting between Douglass and John Brown on March 12, 1859, seven months before Brown's attack on Harper's Ferry. This work also incorporates characteristics of Michelangelo's Sistine Chapel fresco, particularly the heroic, muscular form of an angry young Douglass breaking the shackles of slavery. Douglass's face was configured to suggest the qualities of many nationalities to enable many people to see themselves in the image, and as a way of saying that freedom will be possible for all only when racism, brutality, and ignorance are ended. Scenes from the life of Douglass surround this figure, including his meeting with a determined-looking Brown. In the upper-right-hand corner is a large portrait of an older, white-haired Douglass with a wizened intensity in his eyes.

A number of murals improvised upon the original *Wall of Respect* both in name and in the use of imagery celebrating black achievers and leaders. In addition to Detroit's *Wall of Dignity* and Atlanta's *Wall of Respect,* there was a *Wall of Respect* in St. Louis, the 1972 *Wall of Consciousness* by Bernard Young in Philadelphia, and Arnold Hurley's *Frederick Douglass* mural in Boston. Around 1969 the *Wall of Truth* was completed in Chicago across the street from the original *Wall of Respect.* However, by the mid-1970s the exuberant nationalism and communal narratives began to give way to new content, and the work exhibited a new style and eclecticism.

Stevens points out that the early murals began as an "oasis of color and form and message" in the urban desert.[10] Their presence was a testimony to the many exposed walls and buildings in need of attention in black communities. These were harsh environments, often overcrowded yet filled with vacant lots, abandoned cars, and drab buildings in need of paint and repair. Their vibrant color brought excitement and visual stimulation to otherwise bleak, often depressed urban landscapes. The walls were oases of spirit as well, providing a place to come for hope and inspiration. They nourished the community spiritually, and in gratitude the community often brought food, iced tea, Kool-Aid, and bean pies to the artists as they worked. Stevens, for one, felt that most of the art that blacks came in contact with at that time was detrimental to their mental health. Murals offered ocular therapy.

Wall of Consciousness, designed by Bernard Young and painted by Haddington Leadership Association and West Philadelphia artists (project coordinated by Clarence Wood), 1972. 57th Street and Haverford Avenue, Haddington, Pennsylvania. Sponsored by the Philadelphia Museum of Art's Department of Urban Outreach.

Aesthetically, the early murals brought a new style to mural painting, allowing many artists to confront the issue of distance relative to the reading of an image. Imagery that might seem abstract at a close distance might "assemble" into a readable image as the viewer moved further from it. Donaldson wrote that black artists brought their "penchant for high energy color, bold, uncompromising design techniques, and non-Western patterns and symbols" to mural painting. These stylistic elements influenced other groups such as the Mujeres Muralistas, the Chicago Mural Group, the Haight-Ashbury Muralists of San Francisco, and foreign muralists such as the Atelier d'Art Public in Paris, the Dusseldorfer Wandmal-Gruppe of West Germany, and the Canberra City Mural Art Group of Australia.[11] However, the political and communal consciousness of the early black murals was not present in the content of many subsequent murals, even those by black artists.

The dictionary defines a totem as the emblem of a clan, family, or group, and as anything serving as a distinctive, often venerated, emblem or symbol. Murals by African American artists, especially during the period from 1967 to 1975, functioned in this way. They attempted to embody a collective realization of identity, a communal awareness of being. They were, in many ways, urban totems symbolizing the creativity, accomplishment, and worth of people of African descent. Many other ethnic communities were inspired by this functionality and the potential of murals to visually represent some perceived communal essence.

Interestingly, the *Wall of Respect* and other works like it reflected a political and philosophical consciousness that increasingly acknowledged the problem articulated by W. E. B. Du Bois in his 1903 volume *The Souls of Black Folk*. In theorizing the idea of double consciousness among African Americans, Du Bois suggested that Negroes struggled with the binary opposition of being Negro and American, particularly since the realities of power and oppression enforced that dialectical opposition with dire physical and psychic consequences. Du Bois wrote, "One ever feels his two-ness,—an American, a Negro; two souls, two thoughts, two unreconciled strivings; two warring ideals in one dark body, whose dogged strength alone keeps it from being torn asunder."[12]

Du Bois suggested that black people desired a shift in the conjunction from *or* to *and,* asserting that the Negro "simply wishes to make it possible for a man to be both a Negro and an American, without being cursed and spit upon by his fellows, without having the doors of Opportunity closed roughly in his face."[13] During the late 1960s and early 1970s, a number of artists instead began to accept the imposed binary opposition and began to turn their consciousness inward for strength and resistance. The *or* became the site of "constant contestation" in aggressive, urban, radical black thought.

1975–1990: FROM REVOLUTIONARY EFFORT TO CREATIVE DECORATION

The Yoruba of Nigeria have a term, *nà,* that refers to art or design. It is the transformation of materials into art. However, Nigerian artist and scholar Moyo Okediji says that *nà* is more than this: "Any transformation of the material into advanced levels is the *nà*. It is making *nà* out of that material. So, in a way, we are not talking merely of a transformation of artistic materials. That is merely a symbol of the transformation of the society itself, of Man, into a more advanced, a more human, into a more useful, a more creative person."[14] *Nà* is the creative, transformative means of elevating the ordinary to the extraordinary, the mundane to an expression of the spiritual—the communicative link between humankind and the divine. To adorn a vessel for *Shango,* the Yoruba deity of adjudication, is to enhance the potency of that vessel through *nà*. In the same way, black artists elevated the walls of their urban landscape by putting up murals. They transformed their environment and often tried to transform members of their community by encouraging more proactive, self-celebratory, or politically assertive attitudes and behaviors.

In the mid-1970s, especially, due to the support of various educational and governmental institutions and publicly sponsored arts agencies, murals began to showcase individual creativity and reflect more individual initiative. The use of black imagery and the style of high-affect colors continued, but the call-and-response dialogue with the community faded. Government initiatives brought new highways and interstates slashing through old black communities and urban renewal projects razed large areas and relocated communities. Still, the artists persisted in asserting black visibility and creativity. African American artists were still underrepresented in museums, galleries, and major collections; black expression rooted in African or African diaspora sensibilities seldom drew interest from the mainstream art world. The Boston Museum of Fine Arts, New York's Guggenheim Museum, and the Los Angeles County Museum of Art catered to their traditional audiences of wealthy patrons, but the street galleries catered to folk who had difficulty finding their own lives and images in museums. Many artists capitalized upon the notion of murals composing an outdoor urban gallery offering exhibition opportunities unavailable to them in downtown museums and galleries.

Pontella Mason (black) and James Voshell (white) collaborated in 1975 in Baltimore to put up a mural of a young boy watching two men play checkers, the kind of subtle moment that might have happened frequently in local neighborhoods. This image articulates an intergenerational passing of tradition: the young men learn how to play checkers or dominoes while listening to the conversations of older men.

Untitled (men playing checkers), James Voshell and Pontella Mason, 1975. C & P Parking Lot, Edmondson and Franklin Streets, Baltimore, Maryland. 28' x 40'. Funded by CETA through Beautiful Walls for Baltimore.

Malcolm X and Martin Luther King Jr. were common icons on many walls, including Menelek's *Malcolm X* at Brooklyn's Public School 262. In 1977 William Walker painted *St. Martin Luther King* in Chicago celebrating King as a Christlike figured martyred on the cross. Both figures appeared in Nelson Stevens's extraordinary interior mural *Centennial Vision* (1980) at Tuskegee Institute, now Tuskegee University.

Centennial Vision, commissioned to commemorate the centennial anniversary of the founding of Tuskegee Institute, features an image of four of the college's presidents, most prominently Booker T. Washington. Agricultural and scientific images accompany George Washington Carver, and a section to the left celebrates Gen. Chappie James and the Tuskegee Airmen of World War II who trained there. The bottom register features a number of figures who contributed to black resistance, uplift, and success before and during the tenure of the college. Stevens states that Cinque begins the row on the left and Malcolm X completes it on the right, though his image is twinned with Martin Luther King Jr. Also represented are Frederick Douglass, Ida B. Wells, Mary McLeod Bethune, W. E. B. DuBois, and Marcus Garvey. "I Am Because We Are," a phrase attributed to African scholar John S. Mbiti, is inscribed just below Washington's head to iterate the artist's collective outlook. Although the mural was painted on an interior wall on the campus of Tuskegee Institute, Stevens's experience as an outdoor muralist and his membership in AfriCobra added the character of the earlier outdoor murals to the work. *Centennial Vision* is more intricate than Stevens's earlier mural, but remains true to its spirit visually and philosophically.

During that same year, Mitchell Caton and Calvin Jones completed *Ceremonies for Heritage Now* at Chicago's Westside Association for Community Action building. The mural's image began in a rectangular space to the left and continued along the block to impose itself on an area of the building with pilasters and windows with bars. Decorative elements take up the small area above the windows, and below them parts of the image bleed over the pilasters to segue into the next section. Though colorful, the mural was not just the decoration of architectural space such as one might find on houses in Haiti; its effect transformed the architectural structures rather than accenting them. The complexity of the image belies the simplicity of the vertical pilasters and the rectangular spaces between them.

A mural Caton and Jones completed together in 1979, *Another Time's Voice Remembers My Passion's Humanity,* uses large images to anchor the composition and points up the adjustments the artists made in the *Ceremonies* mural to accommodate the wall's broken space. Both murals reveal wonderful draftsmanship and use of high-octane color, and both appeal to the community through cultural celebration and inspirational themes. Jones commonly designed his walls with human forms and African patterns to express the continuity of the past and the present.

Builders of the Cultural Present
Calvin Jones and Mitchell Caton, 1981. 71st and Jeffery Boulevard, Chicago.
22' x 45'. Funded by the Illinois Arts Council, National Endowment for the Arts, Chicago
Council on Fine Arts, and the South Shore Cultural Council.

In 1981 Caton and Jones collaborated again on *Builders of the Cultural Present,* a masterpiece in which African symbols and icons are integrated with images of contemporary public figures. For instance, a Ghanaian Adinkra symbol known as *gye nyame* ("fear none but God") appears in the lower part of the left panel. The work is made up of three panels: the left addresses science and health, the second deals with the arts, and the third references literature. The mural was completed in a rejuvenated part of Chicago's South Shore, and Jones wanted the work to have a contemporary feel. As a result, each panel is rendered with a diagonal slant to the right, creating a sense of motion that adds dynamism to the standard rectangular format of murals.

Boston artist Paul Goodnight painted *Jazz History/Tribute to Black Classical Music* in 1982 on the side of Walter Jo's jazz club in South Boston. The club was on Tremont Street, a section of town Goodnight says was active with nightlife like New Orleans' Bourbon Street and was often visited by many jazz greats. The work picked up a thread from early murals, a thread woven through a good deal of African American visual art: the celebration of black music. Blues and jazz musicians of the twentieth century have been seen almost as custodians of culture, and their creative verve was made heroic in a number of murals. Goodnight's economical composition depicts saxophonist Johnny Hodges, a Dorchester, Massachusetts, resident who went on to fame with the Duke Ellington and Count Basie big bands. John Coltrane, Cannonball Adderly, Miles Davis, and Sarah Vaughan are also pictured in the work.

A variety of official sources began to offer support for murals in the 1970s and 1980s. Through VISTA and ACTION, federal programs supported the creation of thirty-five murals in the Springfield, Massachusetts, area from 1973 to

1978. Students were paid to work summers and often received college credit at the University of Massachusetts in nearby Amherst. The mayor's office in Baltimore launched a program funded with federal CETA money. The Cleveland Area Arts Council funded a neighborhood murals program, and the Bureau of Cultural Affairs for the City of Atlanta sponsored several public art projects. Government-funded "1 percent for the arts" programs led to many commissions for federal and local government buildings. These funds encouraged a proliferation of murals—a good number by African American artists—but the political and communal nature of the images had changed from the black nationalist fervor of earlier walls. Notably, in this period spraycan art began to appear in New York as an aggressive quest for visibility by urban youths—and almost the antithesis of the

officially sponsored murals. Jean Michel Basquiat, whose tag was SAMO, emerged from this group to become one of the most celebrated black artists of the decade.

Chicago muralist William Walker painted two optimistic murals with childhood themes, *Childhood Is Without Prejudice* and *You Are as Good as Anyone,* a mural that echoed Jesse Jackson's chant of self-affirmation, "I Am Somebody." Both murals used simple imagery. *Childhood* was painted as a tribute to a nearby school's promotion of racial harmony. The image was formed of a series of large, simply drawn heads of children from different ethnic groups. The second mural was composed of three vignettes showing children in different settings. *History of the Packinghouse Worker,* another mural by Walker from that same period, was a more complex composition, full of figures in the left half. The right side was

Jazz History/Tribute to Black Classical Music
Paul Goodnight, 1982
(destroyed in 1985).
Walter Jo's, 981 Tremont
Street, South Boston.
23' x 14'.
Sponsored by the owner
of Walter Jo's.

broken into three sections, each portraying a worker performing a specific job within a distinct industry. This work had more of the visual character of the old WPA murals, which featured voluminous figures and general-interest labor themes.

Official sponsors helped spawn a great many murals, but these works had the effect of muting the nationalist or Pan-Africanist sentiments found in the *Wall of Respect* and its immediate successors. Integrationist and multicultural themes appeared more frequently, and Dr. King gained more visibility than Malcolm X. Individual artists worked with fewer collaborators on mural projects and a sense of individual creativity prevailed over a communal vision. In many ways, mural compositions had become so complex and refined by the early- to mid-1980s that the *Wall of Respect* seemed a bit naïve by comparison. Images and themes had become more diverse. Perhaps the high volume and visibility of murals combined with the experiences of prolific muralists like Nelson Stevens, Calvin Jones, William Walker,

Elliott Pinkney, and Dewey Crumpler in San Francisco contributed to the aesthetic refinement of the genre.

In 1982 Walker turned back to political content with *Reaganomics*. Richard Nixon had attempted to subvert African American protest by taking an approach of "benign neglect" toward civil rights issues and the black community. Ronald Reagan took a more conservative, more hostile approach toward blacks after his 1980 election, and his policies attempted to roll back many of the legal and social gains the nation had made toward racial justice in the preceding two decades. His economic policies were especially harmful to those below the poverty line and his administration instigated a redistribution of the nation's wealth upward toward the wealthy, shifting a balance that had remained stable since the Great Depression and initiating the sharp rise in homelessness that still lingers as a problem today. Walker's mural caricatured Reagan as a jack-in-the-box figure and articulated a social critique of his policies.

Untitled
Alvin Carter, 1982.
People's Choice,
920 Selby Avenue,
St. Paul, Minnesota.

Walker, who conceived of and worked on the *Wall of Respect,* has been one of the more prolific muralists of the past thirty years. Many of his works were self-sponsored. In 1984 he completed an interesting wall entitled *Peace, Peace* in Chicago on the façade of Norwood's liquor and grocery store. Among the portraits featured in the composition is a somber memorial with Martin Luther King Jr., The Honorable Elijah Muhammad, and El Hajj Malik Malcolm X seated together on a bench, dressed in black. The artist intended their appearance together to suggest the importance of a harmony inclusive of all points of view. Perhaps the jarring juxtaposition of these three religious leaders and social activists and the sign "Liquors & Groceries" directly overhead unintentionally reflects the unsettling conflicts revealed posthumously about the private lives of King and Muhammad, and the sordid early years of street hustling by Malcolm Little before his conversion to Islam and his transformation into Malcolm X. Somehow those contradictions speak to the potential for transformation in even the most degraded among us while also reminding us of the human frailty of heroes and saints.

Alvin Carter painted a mural on a storefront in St. Paul, Minnesota, foregrounding the fabulous golden mask of the eighteenth-dynasty Egyptian pharaoh Tutankhamen against an interpretation of the pyramids of Giza. Subtle transformations of the golden mask give it features more obviously identified with blacks, accentuating the Afrocentric focus upon ancient Egypt as a civilization that is a part of the heritage of African Americans.

Alonzo Davis produced an abstract mural along a freeway in Los Angeles for the 1984 Olympics. This work was one of ten murals done along freeways in the downtown area for a project that was an amended version of a Davis idea. The mural was colorful and decorative, and its spare design was appropriate for its location because viewers would be traveling at great speed and would not be able to comprehend the sort of complex, roiling imagery of some of the Chicago murals. These two works point up the diversity of imagery and types of murals that emerged during this period.

One of the masterworks produced in the 1980s was John Biggers's 1982 mural in Adair Park in Houston. Biggers, who in 1957 became one of the first African American artists to visit West Africa, developed a patterned aesthetic in his work while maintaining perspectival depth and chiaroscuro to articulate forms. The patterns create a sense of rhythm and their varying sizes form symbiotic musical time signatures. This mural reads as a holistic composition rather than as a series of images blended together. The detail is overwhelming, but larger compositional elements stabilize the visual space and move the eye from one passage to the next. The images are symbolic more than narrative, yet the mural's various passages narrate messages so the whole seems like a series of scenes in a long visual tale.

Just to the right of center a section of triangular forms brilliantly reenvisions the shotgun house so common in southern black neighborhoods—particularly in the Gastonia, North Carolina, community of Biggers's youth—as a pattern and an icon. Shotgun houses, which are small, narrow structures with three or four rooms sequentially aligned, testify to the poverty of their residents. The arrangement of the rooms forces occupants to interact with each other as they move through the house, and, like the small two-room West African structures they resemble, shotgun houses encourage people to move outside into communal space. Front porches, unlike the decks, back porches, and patios of many modern suburban dwellings, are places for interaction with one's neighbors and passers-by. In Biggers's mural, railroad tracks run in front of the houses, making tangible the idea of southern blacks living "across the tracks" in a poorer section of town. The tracks also contain implications about the movement and migrations that are so much a part of twentieth-century African American history.

Several women stand on the porches of Biggers's shotgun houses as caryatids metaphorically supporting the black household. The gables of the houses suggest the pattern of a patchwork quilt, an expressive form associated with women. These themes celebrating black women continued in Biggers's painting during the 1980s, particularly his *Shotguns* series.

The colors in the mural are mostly muted earth tones and their effect is one of warmth, but the color scheme—perhaps inadvertently—in part replicates the way color is used to paint much West African sculpture. Yoruba women use

Crossroads (detail), Carole Byard and Marilyn Lindstrom with local youth, 1997. The Cultural Center of Minnesota, 3013 Lyndale Avenue South, Minneapolis, Minnesota. Latex on concrete block, 12' x 112'. Sponsored by Neighborhood Safe Art, the Cultural Center of Minnesota (owned and directed by African Americans) and the Lyndale Neighborhood Association. Photograph courtesy of Marilyn Lindstrom.

this scheme to paint shrine walls because the colors are drawn from pigments found in the natural environment. Rather than name each tone, the Yoruba suggest polytonal ranges of value with the terms *fúnfún* (whites and light tones), *púpà* (warm reds and yellows), and *dùdù* (blues, blacks, and dark tones). Whites might be made from chalk or eggshells, and charcoal is used for a range of blacks. Camwood powder is a source for a rust red. This color scheme generates a sense of continuity in Biggers's work, and an intensity that is digestible, not overwhelming. The wall is warm, complex, full of meaning, and visually arresting.

During the '80s a number of powerful indoor murals were painted, and several notable artists designed walls. Jacob Lawrence designed a lovely horizontal mural at the University of Washington, Seattle, for a theater named after him. A number of black artists were involved in projects at the Boys and Girls High School in Brooklyn and the Addabbo Federal Building in Queens. The work of Norman Lewis, Vincent Smith, and Eldzior Cortor was installed at the high school. Partly in response to black protests against a lack of commissions, the Addabbo project included murals by Lawrence, Howardena Pindell, Romare Bearden, Frank Smith, Ed Sorrells-Adewale, and Richard Yarde.

A Romare Bearden composition, *Before Dawn,* was executed in mosaic at the Charlotte Public Library in North Carolina. The work appears to have been drawn from Bearden's earlier *Mecklenberg* series, which dealt with his experiences growing up in the Charlotte area. Michigan artist Jon Lockard, who had painted several murals in the Detroit/Ann Arbor area in the 1970s, completed indoor murals at Wayne State University (*Continuum,* 1980) and at Central State University (1982) in Wilberforce, Ohio. Lockard's powerful figures and black nationalist sentiments were continuations of the spirit found in the early walls.

FIN DE SIÈCLE: THE 1990s

When the *Wall of Respect* was dedicated on August 27, 1967, "the street was . . . filled with people" and the atmosphere was "festive, and vibrant with music. Gwendolyn Brooks and Don L. Lee [Haki Madhubuti] read poems dedicated to the wall and Val Ward, founder of the Kuumba Theatre Workshop, recited."[15] The mural became a source of pride in the neighborhood and, for a quarter, children would explain the wall to visitors, naming each portrait and symbol. William Walker, who made the original proposal and obtained permission from the owner of the building to paint the mural, remembers a young man who studied the *Wall* for a long time before saying, "I'm gaining my strength."[16] Rival gangs the Almighty P. Stone Nation and the Disciples declared the site a neutral ground and leaders of the Stones met with the artists and offered to help secure materials. The *Wall of Respect* became a landmark of the old Black Belt on Chicago's South Side. It was Art for the People sanctioned by the people.

Murals were necessarily topical because buildings are torn down or renovated, and sunlight and weathering age painted walls. By 1971 a fire and demolition had destroyed both the *Wall of Respect* and the *Wall of Truth* across the street. Some murals have been restored in recent years, but the urgency of the condition inspiring a mural may have abated a decade after its creation. Muhammad Ali was a vital, defiant hero in 1967 because of his refusal to be inducted into the armed services on the grounds of religion, his affiliation with the Nation of Islam and its challenge to the American Judeo-Christian orthodoxy, and his standing as the Heavyweight Champion of boxing, a symbol of masculine power. Ali had appeared on the cover of *Esquire* in 1968 riddled with arrows in "mock anguish, in the manner of Mantegna's *St. Sebastian*,"[17] a third-century Roman Christian martyr persecuted for his faith. By the mid-1970s Ali had become an icon and a beloved figure in many parts of the world, and in 1996 his appearance at the Atlanta Olympics was nostalgic and touching. He was honored and embraced by many whites and no longer was a symbol of black masculine defiance.

By the 1990s many murals by black artists had become more personal than communal and their subject matter was often more socially critical than inspirational, more decorative than political. Integration, urban renewal, and the upward mobility of the growing black middle class changed the character of many black communities across the nation, and the flood of drugs in America in the 1980s devastated impoverished areas. The beating of Rodney King by the Los Angeles police and the 1992 acquittal of the four officers who were captured on videotape violently beating him led to a new uprising in Los Angeles. Racism was, and still is, a problem.

The Reagan-Bush years and the conservative climate they instilled combined with a loosening of regulatory and tax restraints upon big corporations intensified the business atmosphere in the nation. Corporate takeovers and "downsizing" layoffs became a way of life, and monied interests bought influence in Congress and in presidential politics. Professional sports and significant sports events were taken over by corporations, and games began to seem more like advertising events or television programs. Marketing, advertising, and mural painting often overlapped. Large advertisements in New York's Times Square, or on well-traveled streets in West Hollywood, California, became like murals and some murals became more like advertisements.

The art market had become volatile in the 1980s and major works began to command exorbitant prices. Black artists largely were excluded from these developments and the conservative ethos led to political assaults on those public agencies such as the National Endowment of the Arts that had begun to fund black, Hispanic, Asian, female, and gay artists. Jean-Michel Basquiat, a former graffiti writer, became the most celebrated black artist in the country, but he was more closely associated in the public mind with Andy Warhol and Julian Schnabel than with any particular community base. Perhaps the raw, painful power of his work was more appealing than the sophisticated virtuosity of Romare Bearden—who did receive a level of respect and notoriety—or the patterned mastery of John Biggers, both of whom rooted their work in the black experience. Black artists continued to find their museums in the streets.

Richard Wyatt's *Hollywood Jazz 1945–1972* (1990) at Capitol Records depicted a number of musical legends including Duke Ellington, Nat King Cole, and Billie Holiday. The mural was lovely and eye-catching, but it was aimed at the general public, not a particular black community. Similarly, Dewey Crumpler's *Black and Tan Jam* (1984) was a visual feast for the entire community to share. Spencer Taylor and Solomon Thurman produced *Black Americans in Flight* (1990) for the St. Louis airport, and Alice Patrick's colorful *Women Do Get Weary But They Don't Give Up* (1991) for the National Council of Negro Women in south Los Angeles, like *Hollywood Jazz,* presented a series of well-known personalities. These murals were concerned with creative commemoration.

Increasingly, murals served aesthetic or commemorative purposes, or represented organizations, government agencies, or corporations. How was a viewer to differentiate between a Michael Jordan Nike ad and the 1988 three-story portrait of Julius Erving in a suit done by non-black artist Kent Twitchell in Philadelphia, or the 1999 mural ad of Michael Jordan and Dennis Rodman along a Chicago expressway? What seems most important is that African American personalities and personae were visible on a superhuman scale as signifiers of something other than racial representation. The dilemma of being Negro *or* American was evolving toward the possibility of being black *and* American. The personalities put forth as heroic or notable had evolved so that a student at San Francisco's Balboa High School produced a mural of bad-boy rapper and actor Tupac Shakur in 1997. Jordan and Rodman were great basketball players but their involvement in black communities or the issues affecting them was negligible. They were not defiant, nor were they producers of black culture: they were black and famous. Shakur was talented and defiant, but his anger was not politically directed toward transformative strategies or ideologies.

Genocidal Tendencies
Ian White, 1990.
2526 West Jefferson
Boulevard, South
Los Angeles.
Acrylic.
Sponsored by the Social
and Public Art Resource
Center.
© Social and Public Art
Resource Center.

Still, black style deeply infiltrated American culture and stars such as Michael Jordan created a new aesthetic and a new industry with the force of their talents and personalities. Just as black community murals changed the landscape of American cities by establishing the aesthetic of wall decoration, black style and presence changed sports and affected corporate images and advertising. Baggy shorts, inventive athletic shoes, and shaved heads became accepted athletic display and marketing icons, and Michael Jordan led a sports-corporate link that sent Nike's revenues skyrocketing from $270 million in 1980 to $9 billion by 1997. By the end of 1999, Kentucky Fried Chicken plantation icon Colonel Sanders was a rapping cartoon in television commercials. Many city centers and public buildings were colorized and invigorated by various murals just as decaying neighborhoods had been vitalized a generation earlier. But the content of murals had changed; by the 1990s references to the black community were more often symbolic and metaphorical than geographic.

Social activism did not vanish in mural painting. Ian White, the son of Charles White, painted a wall in Los Angeles called *Genocidal Tendencies* (1990) that critiqued nuclear reactors and their potential to harm children. The child's face depicted in the work could have come from a number of backgrounds, indicating that the work was for the community-at-large. Elliott Pinkney completed a wall at the Watts Towers Arts Center, Los Angeles, *Community Anti-Tobacco Mural* (1991), linking cigarettes with death and suggesting to young people that they "Say No to Smoking." Bernard Williams painted *Feed Your Child the Truth* (1994) in Chicago using a colorful style that drew upon that used by Caton and Jones a decade or so earlier. African imagery, patterns, and symbols formed the ground for representational images from black history and culture. Perhaps Williams understood the power a public wall has to inform and inspire, to be a source of strength like the *Wall of Respect*.

Noni Olabisi painted *Freedom Won't Wait* (1992) in Los Angeles with stark black-and-white images on a deep red background and a message panel to the right with the headline "No justice, no peace." The artist put out another call for social awareness with *Wake Up!*, created in downtown Los Angeles in 1996. Perhaps her most notorious work was the 1995 mural *To Protect and Serve,* titled after the idealis-

tic credo of the police. Ironically, the wall was dedicated to the Black Panther Party, the group founded in Oakland in 1966 that fought against the police and equated them with racist "pigs" in its literature and rhetoric. The Panthers, in opposition to Martin Luther King Jr., preached a doctrine of armed self-defense and viewed white police in black communities as an occupation army. Huey P. Newton in his signature black beret is very prominent in the mural. The work is bracketed on the left by a black man with a rifle, and on the right by a crouching black panther. Like Olabisi's other murals, the images are in black and white on a bright red ground. At the center, on Newton's beret, there is a circular yellow medallion. The limited palette creates an intensity and focus that adds to the power of the work.

Olabisi's use of the police slogan transfers its values to the Panthers. She says that the group was there to *protect* the community when lynching seemed to be the order of the day. They armed themselves with guns and law books to combat societal oppression on their own terms. They were there to *serve* the community through programs such as free breakfast for schoolchildren (created with the understanding that hungry children do not learn well), free clinics, and free clothing. Statements from the Black Panther Party's ten-point manifesto make *To Protect and Serve* an in-your-face black nationalist statement:

> *We want an immediate end to POLICE BRUTALITY and*
> *MURDER OF BLACK people!*
> *We want land, bread, housing, education, clothing, justice and peace.*
> *ALL POWER TO THE PEOPLE!*

The brutal assault of Haitian immigrant Abner Louima, who was beaten and sodomized with wooden objects by two New York policemen, and the shooting of unarmed African immigrant Amadou Diallo more than forty times by New York police officers, both in the mid- to late-1990s, indicate that the relationship of white police and black communities has not completely become peaceful and just.

There were several new tributes to Dr. King, including C. Siddha Sila Webber's *Have a Dream* (1995) in Chicago and Alexander Austin's *Go For Your*

Dream (1994) in Kansas City, Missouri. Austin's self-sponsored wall was an effort to counteract inner-city violence with a tribute to a champion of nonviolence. The artist began with only several gallons of paint and set up a sign saying "Accepting Donations" to solicit community support. He says that this type of work lifted him from homelessness: he was asking for donations but giving back at the same time. The mural was up for only a short time before the city began to tear it down for a highway extension that had been under discussion for ten years but never acted upon. In addition to showing a range of expressions from King's "I Have a Dream" speech, it told the story of the artist's homelessness and his commitment to finally acting on his potential as an artist. Austin had channeled the communal spirit of early murals into autobiography and a message of personal transformation. His concept was to tell people not to be afraid to pursue their dreams.

John Biggers painted several amazing murals at historically black colleges: *Ascension* and *Origins* (1991–92) at Winston-Salem State University in North Carolina, and *House of the Turtle* and *Tree House* (1992) at Hampton University in Virginia. These murals combined symbols, images, and complex patterns to provide inspirational messages and historical references to African and African American cultures.

The impact of murals diminished as they proliferated in cities around the nation, and decorative murals and large-scale advertisements adorned an increasing number of urban buildings. The invisibility that was a partial inspiration for the early murals changed as blacks began to be more visible in professional sports, on television, in advertisements, and as popular musical entertainers. In the 1980s MTV had been pressured to show more videos by black entertainers, and by the 1990s rap music was regularly featured and black youth style was widely emulated by young whites. Afrocentric efforts to revise public school curricula, the development of African and African American studies programs at white universities, and a growing body of African American scholarship had begun to change what could be taught in American schools and colleges. More accurate information became available, challenging many of the racist or erroneous assumptions of Eurocentric

scholarship. These efforts were so successful that there was a conservative backlash against multicultural curriculum efforts and affirmative action admissions to integrate university student populations, and many called for a return to a Western canon of great books and culture. However, the reactionary forces have been unable to stop the force of black cultural presence and influence. Perhaps the urban totems revived ancestral deities and invited them to work in places they had never been.

INSURGENCY: URBAN SPRAYCAN CALLIGRAPHY

One of the most fascinating twists in the story of African American murals is the growth of spraycan art. The form revived the renegade spirit of the *Wall of Respect* but for totally different purposes. Often young people tagged subway trains and a variety of urban spaces devising unique styles and signatures as if shouting to be recognized against the dehumanizing forces of modern city life. The "writers," as they called themselves, had styles and tags, and many worked in crews. In some ways, their work paralleled the gang graffiti that inspired the *Wall of Respect*. They developed a particular language and engaged in an underground dialogue. The City of New York mounted an effort to stop the graffiti, which forced artists to maintain a code shielding their actual identities. Perhaps this was hip-hop calligraphy, but the spread of the form among poor and working class youths in major cities around the Western world inevitably affected mural painting. They were too much of a force to be ignored.

Spraycan art became so ubiquitous that it was soon an acceptable aesthetic in communities. Its transgressive origins, its function as a voice for the voiceless and a vocabulary for people too often left out of mainstream dialogues, made the work seem like the protest of outsiders. It was the language of youth. It had congruencies with the braggadocio of early rap music: artists devised pseudonyms and competed stylistically through verbal assaults. Often the rhetoric had the exaggeration and humor found in the old game of playing the dozens, or snapping. Ultimately spraycan art is about language the same way the dozens might be. One must be inventive, stylish, and strong. Spraycan art has calligraphic characteristics and often the style supercedes the message. Because our society reads written language from left to right, our visual compositions often are read that way. This fact may have helped spraycan calligraphy evolve more easily into murals.

Blade, an early "king" of the New York City subway system, claimed to have sprayed his stylized name on more than five thousand subway cars over a period of years. Remarkably, each Blade "piece" was carefully crafted to differ from the previous ones. To this day his "Blade" canvasses are purchased by collectors in the European market.

One example of spraycan art, *L.A.-Berlin Exchange* (south Los Angeles, 1992)—by Toons, DruOne, A-One, Mith, and Hex—in collaboration with young artists from Berlin, squeezed in a woman's face and several images among a cacophony of stylized words. Unlike earlier work that suddenly imposed itself upon flat surfaces, subway cars, and buses in cities, this mural was tailored to the space it occupied. There is a logic to the composition that is similar to the teeming style of the mid- to late-1970s murals. The image has a density that speaks of layers that must be excavated slowly by viewers.

Spon and Vulcan, two New York writers, created *Roughneck Reality* in the Graffiti Hall of Fame in 1993 with the same density of words and images, but the figures in the lower portion of the work seem to be cartoon characters. Spraycan work is often done quickly and many of the forms and figures are outlined, much like in graphic work. The hypernaturalism or voluminous, muscular figures of classic black murals are seldom used. Vulcan was able to produce another colorful density on the side of Detroit's "art train."

E-Z One sprayed a wall on 110th Street paying tribute to Malcolm X. The name "Malcolm" is the central element in the work and it seems to be undulating and crackling with lightning and energy. The color intensity of the mural is focused here as well. There is a portrait of Malcolm to the left of his name, and

WANE, Wane and COD, 1993. Bronx. Self-sponsored.

from the right of his name bursts his fist. The message's content is written conventionally above the right-hand section of the name. The work is a simple one, but it points up the adoption of a spraycan aesthetic in the approach some young artists took to mural painting.

"Wane" of the COD crew subordinated imagery in his Bronx wall, which is completely devoted to stylizing his name. Non-black San Francisco artist Booker did a wonderful section of a wall featuring a partial portrait of rapper/actor Ice Cube in 1992. The word "Cube" covers his mouth and contains the only color in the portrait beyond the sepia tone used to paint it. This is one of the few spraycan works in which the image supercedes the language.

One particularly remarkable spraycan artist is Brett Cook (Dizney). His 1989 San Francisco wall *Why Fight for A Crayon That's Not Our Color?* shows two crayon-headed blacks struggling over a "flesh"-colored crayon. A long message runs above their heads, and typical calligraphic marks and doodles appear to the left. The communal, social message and the large figures are unusual for spraycan walls. The image seems to be a hybrid of urban mural genre and spraycan style.

Cook moved to the New York area in 1994 and has since exhibited at the Studio Museum in Harlem. He has evolved as an artist and the growing complexity of his work has challenged his commitment to the tradition in which he works. Spraycan artists usually produce work that does not have sanction or permission. A great deal of it is done late at night in three- or four-hour sessions. At a certain point, Cook no longer wished to sacrifice technical complexity to that kind of speed. Interestingly, he found that when he worked in daylight, passersby usually assumed that the work was sanctioned and he could take the time he needed.

Interaction with the people of a community is critical to his work and his motivation. Spraycan art, in its essence, has been concerned with giving a voice to the unheard folk. It has been an expression of presence and the establishment of a type of identity. The irony of the genre is that pseudonyms and nicknames prevail. We find writers such as Blade, Phase 2, Dondi, Quik, Vulcan, Noc, and Kase 2. These become similar to stage names for rappers (i.e. Snoop Dogg, Ice-T, Mase, Puff Daddy, and L. L. Cool J.) and suggest invented personae. Their names become a layer of protection codifying their true personalities.

Cook uses his work to give voice to the people in the communities where he paints. Often he paints their images and quotes their words, removing their anonymity. As a part of his Harlem project, he did seventeen paintings without permission or support. In 1999 he indicated that fifteen of them were still standing. His work has recaptured some of the communal spirit of those early murals.

> As a young black writer, I was expected to act the victim. But to do
> so would be to corroborate all the things that had oppressed me in the
> first place.
>
> —JAMES BALDWIN from a radio interview, National Public Radio

The sheer number and variety of African American murals since 1967 makes it impossible to mention them all. Many more than have been touched upon here warrant careful discussion. Their colorful, powerful presence in our cities enhances the potency of our urban environments in the sense of the Yoruba concept of *nà*. They provide a barometer for gauging the social climate in the United States, and point out the various social functions of art in this society. Murals are not without precedent in the history of people of African descent. Rock paintings in the Sahara date back to 10,000 B.C.E.; French researcher Henri Lhote described their magnificence:

> Some of the figures stood alone, others formed complex group-
> ings. Sometimes the scenes were clear enough and related to
> everyday life or to the spiritual and religious existence of the
> different peoples which followed on, one after another. . . . We
> were astounded by the diversity of styles and subjects and by the
> great number of overpaintings. . . .
>
> In a word, we were confronted with the greatest
> museum of prehistoric art in the whole world.[18]

All those millennia ago African people expressed their existence in paint on walls. Their museum was their environment, not a hermetic space.

Urban murals were, and continue to be, vehicles of empowerment for African Americans. They signify a resistance to victimization and a refusal to act the part. They articulate hope, celebrate history and achievement, and show off the creativity of artists. They teach, inspire, affirm, critique, document, and sometimes just plain strut their colorful stuff. Many of them emblematize the conditions and potential of African Americans. They visually insist that people on the margins of society have a presence and a say in the central dialogues.

Perhaps the communal flavor of black murals offers an antidote to the introspective, often esoteric expression of late modern and postmodern art and its hermeneutical specialists. The audience was and is a primary concern of the artists, and, like an expressive preacher giving a sermon, the response is immediate and instructive. Can I get an "Amen?"

NOTES

1. Each artist was given a section of the mural and a category of people to represent. For example, Wadsworth Jarrell painted rhythm & blues personalities, Jeff Donaldson focused upon jazz, and Norman Parish painted statesmen.

2. Jeff R. Donaldson and Geneva Smitherman Donaldson, "Upside the Wall: An Artist's Retrospective Look at the Original 'Wall of Respect,'" in *The People's Art: Black Murals, 1967–1978* (Philadelphia: African American Historical and Cultural Museum, 1986).

3. Donaldson and Donaldson, "Upside the Wall."

4. Stuart Hall, "What is This 'Black' in Black Popular Culture?," in *Black Popular Culture* (Seattle: Bay Press), 25.

5. Ibid., 32.

6. Reginald Butler, "Black Murals: Introductory Essay," in *The People's Art: Black Murals, 1967–1978* (Philadelphia: African American Historical and Cultural Museum, 1986).

7. Claude M. Steele, "Race and Schooling of Black Americans," *Atlantic Monthly* (April 1992): 69.

8. Ibid., 72.

9. Nelson Stevens, interview by the author, 7 December 1999.

10. Nelson Stevens, interview by the author, 9 December 1999.

11. Donaldson and Donaldson, "Upside the Wall."

12. W. E. B. Du Bois, "Of Our Spiritual Strivings," in *The Souls of Black Folk* (1903; reprint, New York: New American Library, 1969), 29.

13. Ibid.

14. Moyo Okediji, interviewed by the author, Ile-Ife, Nigeria, August 1991.

15. Eva Cockcroft, John Pitman Weber, and James Cockcroft, "Beginnings," in *Toward a People's Art: The Contemporary Mural Movement* (New York: E. P. Dutton & Co., 1977).

16. Ibid.

17. Richard J. Powell, *Black Art and Culture in the 20th Century* (London: Thames and Hudson, 1997), 97.

18. Henri Lhote, *The Search for the Tassili Frescoes: The Story of the Prehistoric Rock-Paintings of the Sahara,* trans. Alan Houghton Brodrick (New York: E. P. Dutton & Co., 1959), 12.

Mural Time Line of Key Historical Events

1850   Robert Scott Duncanson is commissioned to paint a series of murals in the Cincinnati home of Nicholas Longworth. This is the first known African American mural.

1909   William Edouard Scott paints his first mural, *Commerce,* for Lane Technical High School in Chicago, while still a student at the Art Institute of Chicago. He goes on to paint approximately seventy-five murals in Illinois, Indiana, New York, and Washington, D.C., making him the first African American muralist of the twentieth century.

1925   Aaron Douglas moves to Harlem from Kansas and soon becomes the leading visual artist of the Harlem Renaissance.

1930–34   Three of Mexico's most famous muralists, Diego Rivera, David Alfaro Siqueiros, and José Clemente Orozco, spend time painting murals at sites in the United States, inspiring many American artists.

1934   Aaron Douglas paints his four-panel mural *Aspects of Negro Life* for the Countee Cullen branch of the New York Public Library.

1936   Under the auspices of the New Deal's Federal Art Project, Charles Alston directs a group of African American artists in the creation of murals for Harlem Hospital. The project generates controversy when the hospital's white administrators express opposition to the murals' black themes.

1938   Hale Woodruff paints the *Amistad Mural* for Talladega College in Alabama.

Early 1940s   Samella Lewis and John Biggers study mural painting at Hampton Institute with Viktor Lowenfeld, an inspirational art teacher who came to the United States to escape the Nazis' rise to power in Germany.

1943   Charles White completes *The Contribution of the Negro to Democracy in America* at Hampton University and *History of the Negro Press* for the American Negro Exposition at Chicago Coliseum. The current whereabouts of the latter work is unknown.

1943   In a national competition sponsored by the Treasury Department, William Edouard Scott is the only African American selected to paint a mural depicting an episode from black history for the Recorder of Deeds Building in Washington, D.C. He is one of seven winners chosen from three hundred entries.

1947–48   Samella Lewis and William Walker paint murals while at the Columbus Gallery School of Arts in Ohio.

1949   John Biggers becomes chair of the art department at Texas State University (later Texas Southern University) and begins teaching mural painting as part of the curriculum.

1952   William Walker travels to the South and paints murals in Memphis.

1966   African American students at Washington High School in San Francisco, protesting school-site WPA murals that depict George Washington and his slaves, demand that Dewey Crumpler be commissioned to paint a contemporary mural portraying the strengths and positive contributions of peoples of color. The mural is finally completed in 1977.

1967   The *Wall of Respect,* probably the first outdoor community mural, is painted in Chicago's South Side. Created through OBAC Visual Art Workshop with leading artist participants Jeff Donaldson, Eliot Hunter, Barbara Jones, Norman Parish, Wadsworth Jarrell, William Walker, Edward Christmas, Myrna Weaver, Sylvia Abernathy, and Carolyn Lawrence, plus a number of other artists and photographers. Coverage in *Ebony* magazine inspires artists in other cities.

1968   Dana Chandler and Gary Rickson begin painting militant murals in Boston, funded by Summerthing, a project of the Mayor's Office of Cultural Affairs.

1968   Cityarts Workshop starts in New York City. Its first mural, for the entrance hallway of the Alfred E. Smith housing project's recreation center, involves hundreds of local African Americans.

1968   William Walker and Eugene Wade (Eda) paint murals in Detroit.

1968   Cornbread and Topcat 126, two notorious taggers in Philadelphia, bring their "style" to New York City to start a long evolution that becomes the worldwide hip-hop youth culture of spraycan art.

1969   Muralists Rozzell and Roderick Sykes bring together a group of artists to create St. Elmo Village in Los Angeles, an ever-expanding collection of houses and garages (and later apartments) that becomes a creative arts neighborhood. Mural making has always been an integral part of the village's creative process.

1968–70 Smokehouse artists William T. Williams, Melvin Edwards, Guy Ciarcia, and Billy Rose are active in Harlem.

1971 Mitchell Caton, William Walker, and John Pitman Weber launch an artists' collective, which they call the Chicago Mural Group (later renamed the Chicago Public Art Group), currently one of the major mural-producing organizations in the United States. They are later joined by other artists, including Calvin Jones.

1971 *Murals for the People* exhibit at the Museum of Contemporary Art in Chicago features William Walker, Eugene Wade (Eda), Mitchell Caton with John Pitman Weber, and Mark Rogovin. The "Artists' Statement" from that exhibit is the first real mural manifesto.

1971 The Philadelphia Museum of Art's Department of Urban Outreach hires Clarence Wood (black) and Don Kaiser (white) to assist with neighborhood-based public art, including murals.

1970s Spraycan art takes off on the New York subway trains and on neighborhood walls. Among the early writers are young African Americans Blade and Phase 2.

1975 Beautiful Walls for Baltimore gets started, funded with federal CETA money and supported by the Mayor's Office of Manpower Resources and the Mayor's Advisory Committee on Art and Culture.

1977 A group of eight artists in Portland, Oregon, seven of them black, begin a multipanel mural on the contributions of African Americans to Portland and the Northwest.

1978 Franklin "Franco the Great" Gaskin begins painting the security gates along 125th Street in Harlem.

1978 Jacob Lawrence is commissioned by the King County Percent for Art Collection to create his first public mural, *Games,* for the Kingdome Stadium in Seattle.

1983–84 Ten murals are painted on downtown Los Angeles freeways in celebration of the coming Olympics. The project is the brainchild (in a somewhat amended form) of community artist Alonzo Davis. Davis, Roderick Sykes, and Richard Wyatt are among those muralists contributing.

1986 Philadelphia's African American Historical and Cultural Museum mounts an exhibition called *The People's Art: Black Murals, 1967–1978.*

1986 Paul Goodnight's *Jazz History* in Boston is destroyed. He sues the landlord and later wins an out-of-court settlement.

1991 The African Burial Ground, the largest and only known urban pre-Revolutionary African cemetery in America, is uncovered in New York City at the site of construction of a new federal building. Amidst ongoing controversy, several public art works, including a mural, are commissioned for the new Foley Square Federal Building memorializing the African Burial Ground.

1992 Noni Olabisi paints her first mural, *Freedom Won't Wait,* in south-central Los Angeles after a violent, citywide upheaval in the aftermath of the acquittals of four white police officers whose beating of black motorist Rodney King was videotaped and broadcast around the world. Three years later she completes a mural of the Black Panther Party, *To Protect and Serve,* after unsuccessful attempts by the local Arts Commission, the Los Angeles Police Department, and others to stop it.

1993 The Birmingham Museum of Art in Alabama starts a community mural program and hires Toby Richards as muralist. The next year she becomes outreach coordinator of the mural program, a position she still holds.

1995 *The Art of John Biggers: View From the Upper Room,* the first major retrospective of John Biggers's work, opens at the Museum of Fine Arts, Houston, and later travels to museums in North Carolina, Connecticut, Virginia, Massachusetts, and California.

1995 *In the Spirit of Resistance: African American Modernists and the Mexican Muralist School* is organized by the Studio Museum in Harlem, the Mexican Museum in San Francisco, and the American Federation of Arts. Among the black muralists whose work is featured are Charles Alston, John Biggers, Dewey Crumpler, Jacob Lawrence, William Walker, Charles White, and Hale Woodruff. A detail of Charles White's mural *The Contribution of the Negro to Democracy in America* is featured on the cover of the exhibition's catalog. After opening at the Studio Museum in Harlem, the show travels to Michigan, North Carolina, Texas, Ohio, and California.

1996 *A Shared Heritage: Art by Four African Americans* opens at the Indianapolis Museum of Art. Two of the featured artists are muralists: William Edouard Scott and Hale Woodruff.

1997 Spraycan artist Brett Cook (Dizney) takes to the streets of Harlem to create and install his series of portraits honoring local residents. His street work started ten years earlier in the San Francisco Bay Area with major public, nonpermission spraycan renderings of a wide variety of political and socially conscious subjects.

THE MURALS

Pre–1967 Murals

Aspects of Negro Life: The Negro in an African Setting

The library murals attempt to give a symbolic representation of certain aspects of Negro life. The first of the four panels (The Negro in an African Setting, 72' x 72') reveals the Negro in an African setting and emphasizes the strongly rhythmic arts of music, the dance, and sculpture which have influenced the modern world possibly more profoundly than any other phase of African life. The fetish, the drummer, the dancers in the formal language of space and color recreate the exhilaration, the ecstasy, the rhythmic pulsation of life in ancient Africa.

The third panel (Slavery Through Reconstruction, 60' x 139') is composed of three sections covering the periods from slavery through the Reconstruction. From left to right, the first section depicts the slaves' doubt and uncertainty transformed into exultation at the reading of the Emancipation Proclamation. The third section shows the departure of the Union soldiers from the South and the onslaught of the Klan that followed.

AARON DOUGLAS
From a rededication statement after the mural was restored by the artist
Aaron Douglas papers, Smithsonian Archives of American Art, 1949

Aspects of Negro Life, Aaron Douglas, 1934. Schomburg Center for Research in Black Culture, New York Public Library, 515 Lenox Avenue, Harlem, New York. Oil on canvas, four panels. Sponsored by the New York Public Library, Countee Cullen Branch. © Schomburg Center for Research in Black Culture, Art and Artifacts Division, The New York Public Library, Astor, Lenox, and Tilden Foundations.

Aspects of Negro Life: Slavery Through Reconstruction

Aspects of Negro Life: An Idyll of the Deep South

Recreation in Harlem, Georgette Seabrooke (Powell), assisted by Beauford Delaney and Louis Vaughn, 1936. Harlem Hospital, Nurses' Recreation Room, 506 Malcolm X Boulevard, Harlem, New York. Oil, 5' x 19'5". Sponsored by the Federal Art Project. Photograph courtesy of the National Archives.

We were supposed to give twenty hours a week to the project, but there was a two-year holdup in getting the project started. The Superintendent of Hospitals decided that it was not going to be a colored hospital, and he did not feel that we should have those kinds of paintings within the building. Sara Murrell and I were the only women affected by it. Selma Day and Elba Lightfoot were not affected because they had chosen subjects from fairy tales, nothing to do with black anything. I told them that I had black and white in the picture, but it was directed at blacks.

GEORGETTE SEABROOKE
From *Artist and Influence,* 1993, pp. 87–88

The mural depicts a series of events that began in 1839 when fifty-three African captives who, en route to slavery in Cuba on the Spanish ship *La Amistad,* mutinied under the leadership of Cinque. Upon arrival at the tip of Long Island, New York, the ship was seized by a U.S. naval vessel. The Americans claimed salvage rights to the ship and "cargo," while the Spanish claimed that their property rights had been violated. The mutineers were jailed in Connecticut and accused of piracy and murder. A committee of abolitionists was formed to defend the captive Africans. The case was eventually argued by John Quincy Adams before the U.S. Supreme Court, which ruled that the Africans should be freed and allowed to return to Africa.

Amistad Mural: Mutiny Aboard the Amistad, Hale Woodruff, assisted by Robert Neal, 1939. Talladega College, Savery Library, Talladega, Alabama. Oil on canvas, three panels, 6' x 20'. Sponsored by Talladega College. © Talladega College.

The mutiny took place in 1839. My mural was painted in 1939, the one hundredth anniversary of the event. Out of this mutiny people like Josiah Willard Gibbs, the Baldwins, Tappan and so forth, formed what was called the American Missionary Association (AMA). That was about 1840. It was out of the efforts of this organization that many of the Negro schools in the South were founded—LeMoyne, Talladega, and so forth. So this mural was a gesture of appreciation on the part of Talladega for the AMA. The mural was also painted in honor of the slaves and their mutiny and their final freedom.

HALE WOODRUFF
Interview with Al Murray
From the Smithsonian Archives of American Art, 1968

**Frederick Douglass
Appeals to President Lincoln**
William Edouard Scott, 1943.
Recorder of Deeds Building,
Washington, D.C.
Oil on canvas.
Sponsored by the U.S. Treasury
Department Section of Fine Arts.
Photograph © Steven Cummings
Photography.

This mural depicts a historical meeting during which Frederick Douglass attempted to convince President Lincoln and his cabinet to enlist black soldiers in the Union Army.

A national competition was held for the mural commissions in the Recorder of Deeds Building, all of which were to depict episodes from African American history. Seven winning artists were chosen from three hundred entries; Scott was the only African American selected. The subjects of the other panels are Crispus Attucks (the first American killed in the Revolutionary War); Benjamin Banneker (who assisted in the surveying of federal territory that later became the District of Columbia) displaying a map of the city of Washington to Thomas Jefferson; the death of Colonel Shaw at Fort Wagner; slaves building bulwarks out of cotton bales at the Battle of New Orleans; Cyrus Tiffany saving the life of Commodore Perry during the Battle of Lake Erie; and Matthew Henson planting the American flag at the North Pole.

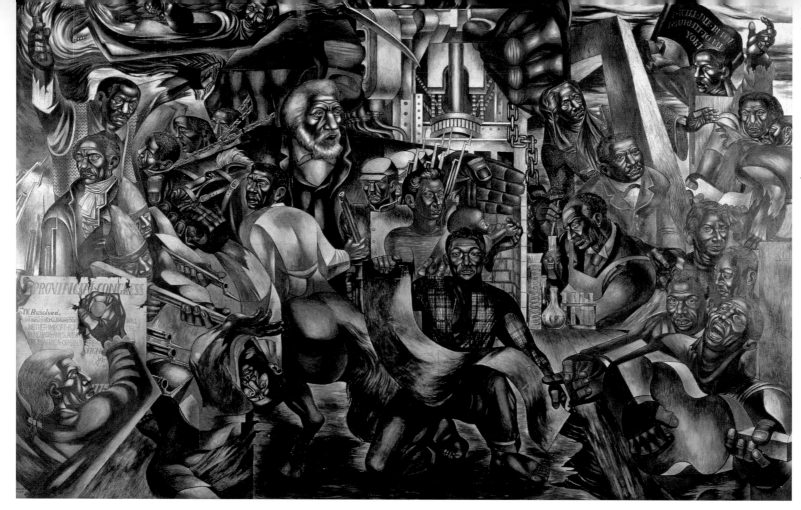

**The Contribution
of the Negro to
Democracy in America**
Charles White with
students (including
John Biggers), 1943.
Hampton University,
Hampton, Virginia.
Egg tempera, 12' x 18'.
Sponsored by the Art
Students League.
© Hampton University
Museum, Hampton,
Virginia.

P*art of the project under the [Rosenwald] Fellowship was to do three months of studying at the Art Students League [in New York City] and the rest of the time was to be devoted to doing a mural at some Negro college in the South. The school for the mural was to be my choice for which I took a trip to a number of Negro universities and finally picked Hampton Institute, where I spent the final nine months of my fellowship executing the mural at the school.*

I started with the American Revolution, depicting Crispus Attucks as the first man to die in the Revolution, came on through using individuals like Frederick Douglass, Booker T. Washington, George Carver, Harriet Tubman and Sojourner Truth, and Marian Anderson. The object was to take the contributions through physical revolt of fighting for the abolition of slavery and also the contributions that had been made in the sciences, the arts, as well as politics.

CHARLES WHITE
Interview with Betty Hoag
From the Smithsonian Archives of American Art, 1965

I take the title from "The Chambered Nautilus" by Oliver Wendell Holmes. The central idea in this design is the progression of cultures and civilizations from the dawn of recorded history to the present. Each new generation can and must look back on, face up to, and learn from the greatness, the weaknesses and failures of our past with the firm assurance that the strength and courage certain to arise from such an honest and dutiful approach to our problems will continue to carry us on to new and higher levels of achievement.

AARON DOUGLAS
From *Mural Decoration—Build Thee More Stately Mansions*, Aaron Douglas papers, Smithsonian Archives of American Art, 1945.

Building More Stately Mansions
Aaron Douglas, 1944.
Fisk University
International Student
Center, Nashville,
Tennessee.
Oil on canvas, 4' x 3'.
Sponsored by Fisk
University.
Photograph © Fisk
University Galleries,
Nashville, Tennessee.

The Negro in California History: Exploration and Colonization (Panel 1), Charles Alston.

The mural was commissioned for the Golden State Mutual Life Insurance Company's new home office. The artists worked closely with architect Paul R. Williams, and extensive research was done by local librarian Miriam Mathews and historian Titus Alexander. Alston and Woodruff traveled around California for three weeks in August 1948 visiting historical sites, examining original records in state libraries and museums, and sketching native flora and landscapes as well as costumes, art, and equipment of earlier periods.

The first panel covers 1527 to the mid-nineteenth century. The following individuals are pictured: Estevanico, guide with Cabeza de Vaca; Biddy Mason, one-time slave and later philanthropist who won her freedom in a Los Angeles court; James Beckwourth, discoverer of the lowest pass through the northern Sierra mountains; the grave of Ignacio Ramirez, the first Christian buried in California; William Leidesdorff, a San Francisco city official; U.S. Consul Thomas O. Larkin; and Jacob Dodson, who accompanied explorer Captain John C. Fremont.

The second panel encompasses California's achievement of statehood in 1850 until 1949. Pictured is African American participation in the building of Golden Gate Bridge and Boulder Dam, Pony Express riders, the *Elevator* (a militant newspaper of the 1860s), William Shorey (captain of a whaling ship), and Mammy Pleasant (a civil rights crusader).

The Negro in California History: Settlement and Development (Panel 2), Hale Woodruff.

The Negro in California History
Charles Alston (Panel 1) and Hale Woodruff (Panel 2), 1949.
Golden State Mutual Life Insurance Company, 1999 West Adams Boulevard, Los Angeles, California.
Oil on canvas, two panels, 16'5" x 9'3¼".
Sponsored by Golden State Mutual Life Insurance Company.

Art of the Negro (panels from left to right): **Influences, Artists, Native Forms**

Art of the Negro: Interchange

Art of the Negro: Native Forms

There are many artists and other people today who believe that we have no part of Africa's history. I look at the African artist certainly as one of my ancestors regardless of how we feel about each other today. I've always had a high regard and respect for the African artist and his art. So this mural is for me a kind of token of my esteem for African art. Also, I wanted it to be something of an inspiration to the students who go to the library, to see something about the art of their ancestors.

HALE WOODRUFF
Interview with Al Murray
From the Smithsonian Archives of American Art, 1968

Art of the Negro
Hale Woodruff, 1950–51.
Clark-Atlanta University, Trevor Arnett Library, Atlanta, Georgia.
Oil on canvas, six panels, 11' x 11' each.
Commissioned by Rufus Clement, then president of Atlanta University.

Masculine society has been inclined to place woman in a minority role; yet in the history of our country no more heroic work has been done than that performed by woman. She has not only organized the family but has had to lead in struggles to build a society in which the family could grow. She has been the leader in public, rural, and informal education. In depicting the contributions of Negro women, it was but natural that those should first be known who were interested in the struggle for freedom. Notable were Sojourner Truth and Harriet Tubman. . . .

No attempt has been made to include every character in the mural, but to symbolize through two main characters the sociological, historical, and educational contributions of Negro women to American life and education. The right side represents slavery, out of which Harriet Tubman leads people. . . . the Tree of Life embraces the balance of the mural, depicting progress in education, science, music, and healthful living, with Sojourner Truth as the pioneer teacher. The search for knowledge in a free society becomes available to the old and young, men and women, as symbolized by the old man reading by [lamplight]. The contribution of a third woman, Phyllis Wheatley, appears in the [depiction of] the book being read by the mother [to her child]. All of that embraced by the Tree of Life is in contrast to the hopelessness expressed in the figures at the far right.

The church on each side symbolizes the spiritual background of those women who have maintained leadership roles in our society.

JOHN BIGGERS
From *Black Art in Houston*, 1953, p. 63

The Contribution of Negro Women to American Life and Education
John Biggers, 1953
YWCA (Blue Triangle Branch), 3005 McGowen, Houston, Texas.
Oil on canvas, 8' x 24'.
Sponsored by Reverend Fred T. Lee in memory of his wife, Della.

Murals 1967–Present: Midwest

The fleshed-out idea of a collective mural project was exceedingly compelling to the [Visual Art] Workshop for many reasons, not the least of which was that black artists like William E. Scott, Aaron Douglas, Archibald Motley, Hale Woodruff, Charles Alston, Charles White, and John Biggers had been producing (since the 1920s) outstanding interior murals portraying black heroes and epochs in black history. Some Workshop members were aware of this glorious legacy. But the exciting part about this project was that it was an exterior mural with high visibility in a well-traveled section of the city. In a way, it was in the time-honored tradition of the great Mexican muralists such as Diego Rivera and José Clemente Orozco whose works had inspired earlier black muralists. The fact that the Mexican muralists were revolutionaries made the group's public mural project even more compelling. But what proved to be the single most important factor in convincing the group to adopt the project was the fact that it would be a "guerrilla mural." While Mr. Baker, occupant of the grocery and liquor store at 43rd and Langley, welcomed the idea, the absentee white owner of the building was never consulted. The unauthorized painting of the wall was to be a revolutionary act in and of itself even beyond the astounding effects the project would itself engender. Before the Wall was finished on August 24, 1967 it had become an instantaneous shrine to black creativity, a rallying point for revolutionary rhetoric and calls to action, and a national symbol of the heroic black struggle for liberation in America.

JEFF DONALDSON
From *The People's Art: Black Murals, 1967–1978*, 1986

People had a great attachment to that wall. I suppose maybe it was because they didn't have anything. We came in the spirit of love and respect and giving. We didn't ask anything other than their cooperation, and once we got into it, we could even (safely) leave our paint on the scaffold in a community that was dominated by drugs, drug dealers, drug users, thieves, rapists, robbers, murderers.

That wall meant many things to many people. I saw a young man sitting in front of the wall. His back was just resting on the wall. So I said, 'How are you doing, brother?' He said, 'I'm gaining my strength.' I saw people cry. I suppose the people in that community realized they had something that other people wanted to share and deal with. I don't think we, the artists, fully realized what we had created in relation to how people would attach themselves to it. As far as doing anything to the wall, that was unheard of. When the wall was first executed, the people would come all hours of the night. It was a truly wonderful thing.

WILLIAM WALKER
Interview with Victor Sorell
From the Smithsonian Archives of American Art, 1991

Wall of Respect (ORIGINAL VERSION), Painters and printmakers, Sylvia Abernathy, Jeff Donaldson, Eliot Hunter, Wadsworth Jarrell, Barbara Jones, Carolyn Lawrence, Norman Parish, William Walker, and Myrna Weaver; photographers Billy Abernathy, Darrell Cowherd, Roy Lewis, and Robert A. Sengstacke; and Edward Christmas, mixed-media commercial artist, 1967 (destroyed in 1971). 43rd and Langley, Chicago, Illinois. Self-sponsored. Photograph © 1967 Robert A. Sengstacke.

This mural is widely believed to be the first grassroots community mural. In one corner of the mural it was written: "The wall was divided into sections, covering political leaders, athletes, musicians, poets, and religious leaders."

Wall of Respect, Leroy White and six others, 1968. St. Louis, Missouri. Self-sponsored.

Most of the artists were sign painters. They saw an article in *Ebony* about the Chicago *Wall of Respect* and decided to paint their own. This photo was taken many years after the wall was painted.

The reason we named it the Wall of Truth was because we dealt with subject matter relating to what was happening in that community. In other words, we'd gotten away from the hero-type thing. I painted a scene of some starving children. We started painting about things that the people were actually experiencing, such as hunger, the reality of the Klan, the reality of hatred, the reality of things that we felt the community should deal with.

WILLIAM WALKER
Interview with Victor Sorell
From the Smithsonian Archives of American Art, 1991

Wall of Truth
Eugene Wade (Eda) and
William Walker, 1969.
Across the street from the
Wall of Respect,
Chicago, Illinois.

The mural compares the suffering of African Americans to the struggles of the Israelites in the Old Testament book of *Exodus*. The idea for the mural came from a history class in the church's Community School.

In the center panel, Eugene Wade painted a black Moses confronting a black Pharaoh. In one corner the generation gap is portrayed by a youth standing in a pose of rebellion while an older man is bent in a posture of despair and submission. Another panel pictures such black leaders as Martin Luther King Jr., Malcolm X, and Elijah Muhammad, with their followers in the background.

A*s our world shrinks rapidly into a small community, the need for respect and understanding between nations and races becomes more and more essential. Unless we unite all men, we will be drowned in ignorance and unleash the forces of hate.*

I have tried to show that the good people of our time cannot sit on the sidelines. They have to become involved. Someone recently said that we are living in the darkness of the lies that have been taught about black people. I hope these paintings will help to deliver the message of respect and understanding, for that was the intent.

WILLIAM WALKER
Comments at the mural's unveiling, quoted in the
Michigan Chronicle, January 25, 1969

Harriet Tubman Memorial Wall (also known as **Let My People Go**), Eugene Wade (Eda) and William Walker, 1968. Five panels, St. Bernard's Church, 11031 Mack Avenue (at Lillibridge), Detroit, Michigan. Sponsored by St. Bernard's Community School and the Inter-Parish Sharing Program of the archdiocese of Detroit.

Black Man's Dilemma, Don McIlvaine, 1970. West Side of Chicago, Illinois.
Sponsored by the Art and Soul Workshop.

Between 1969 and 1970, I did about six murals, three on the West Side and three in tunnels leading to Lake Michigan. At that time there were only three of us in Chicago actively doing murals. Bill Walker, Eugene Wade (Eda) and me. Walker and I worked on a couple together around Cabrini Green. After that, everybody started to do them.

    I was running an art workshop on the West Side for youngsters interested in art. It was sponsored by private donations and the University of Illinois. We got money from Playboy, the Contemporary Art Institute, and others. We were given a lot of materials by local art suppliers.

    Black Man's Dilemma was my second mural. I was working with a gang, the Conservative Vicelords. They had a vacant wall. I got a theme together, street scenes—the kinds of things that went on in the community—and put a mural up to decorate the wall.

DON MCILVAINE
Markham, Illinois
June 1999

Thoughts of the past and present: Egyptian figures on the left, involved in cultural pursuits, are balanced on the right by a militant Black Panther and others breaking out of their chains.

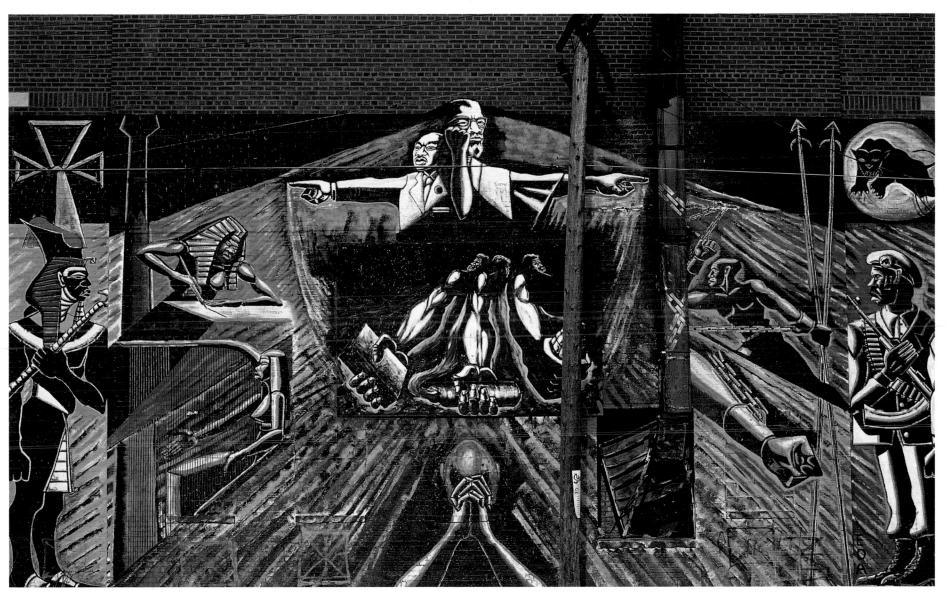

Wall of Meditation, Eugene Wade (Eda), 1970.
Olivet Community Center, 1441 North Cleveland Avenue, Chicago, Illinois.

Universal Alley/Rip-Off, Mitchell Caton, assisted by C. Siddha Sila Webber, 1968–1973. 50th Street between Champlain and St. Lawrence Avenues, Chicago, Illinois. Self-sponsored plus community donations.

I had a good friend, Mitchell Caton. He was a canvas painter. Bill Walker talked him into getting involved in the mural thing. At that time, it was about giving the art to the people, making art relevant to the people, raising the level of consciousness, community participation through art.

In 1968 we did a mural called Universal Alley. Mostly it was just the two of us with people in the community. He did most of the painting. My job was to create poetry for the mural and act as social liaison. It was a very dangerous area with a lot of heavy gangs at that time. I would work with the kids and grown-ups that would pass by, so they could take ownership through involvement.

As an artist, Caton had extremely high expectations, was extremely gifted, and totally committed to art, art, art. He was very passionate about what he was doing. He looked on much of the system as a rip-off. When we painted this mural, he called it Rip-Off, but I called it Universal Alley. I wrote the poem called "Universal Alley" [on the mural], so more people stuck with that. Over the years, I don't know which name won out.

I had a vision that if we did the mural in a prayerful manner to uplift the community, it would create a safe-zone and people would come from all over the world to see the mural. It worked. It went from fifty people celebrating on a Sunday to five thousand. The mural created a vibration. For about five years, every Sunday during the summer, between two thousand and five thousand people would dance in the alley and read poetry. The jazz was in the garage that the mural was painted on.

Then different activities started to happen that scared people away. Drug people, gamblers, street people, homosexuals, vendors. It went from a high spiritual thing to more or less a free-for-all.

Caton and I did seven or eight murals together. My thing was to deal with the spiritual aspect and his approach was to deal with everyday stuff, harshness and realities of life. We complemented each other, but we also battled a lot of times. I guess that's part of the art process.

C. SIDDHA SILA WEBBER
Chicago
July 1999

A powerful visual remembrance of those who gave their lives in the struggle for social justice.

I think Father Kendricks might have had a little problem because I didn't have the traditional symbolism that Catholic churches often have.

WILLIAM WALKER
Interview with Victor Sorell
From the Smithsonian Archives of American Art, 1991

All of Mankind (Why Were They Martyred?), William Walker, 1971–73. Strangers Home Missionary Baptist Church (originally San Marcellus Catholic Church), 617 West Evergreen Avenue (at Clybourn), Chicago, Illinois. Funded by the Chicago Mural Group (now the Chicago Public Art Group) and others.

I *read* The Jungle *by Upton Sinclair, and it dealt with the subject of the Lithuanian family. The man Jurgis was one of the major characters in the book. I was able to see the deplorable working conditions of the packinghouse workers through his eyes, and how they were just ground down and exploited. So I tried to deal with that history in relation to seeing it visually as best I could.*

I used the chessboard to relate how the supervisors at the stockyards would exploit the women, some of those Lithuanian and Slavic women. I used it to make a statement about the chessboard of life, and how people are oftentimes manipulated when they are in certain positions, not fully understanding how they are being manipulated. Sometimes we are controlled by things that are much bigger than ourselves because of circumstances.

WILLIAM WALKER
Interview with Victor Sorell
From the Smithsonian Archives of American Art, 1991

**History of the
Packinghouse Worker**
William Walker (restored in
1998 by Bernard Williams
with Derrick Holley), 1974.
Amalgamated Meat Cutters
Union Hall (now the
Charles Hayes Family
Investment Center),
4859 South Wabash, South
Side of Chicago, Illinois.
Sponsored by the Illinois
Labor History Society.

This was an important mural because of the location. What was and is still happening in the community is primarily a drug scene, a scene of all sorts of ills that exist within that community. There seemed to have been some concern during the time that we painted the wall that some people would rebel against what Mitchell was doing because Mitchell dealt with the subject of drugs. But we didn't have any real problems in the community.

WILLIAM WALKER
Interview with Victor Sorell
From the Smithsonian Archives of American Art, 1991

Wall of Daydreaming/Man's Inhumanity to Man
William Walker, Mitchell Caton, and Santi Isrowuthukal, 1975.
47th Street and Calumet Avenue, Chicago, Illinois.

A Time to Unite, Mitchell Caton, Calvin Jones, Justine DeVan, Tony Campbell, Grant York, and community supporters, 1976. 41st Street and Drexel Boulevard, Chicago, Illinois. 16' x 50'. Sponsored by the Chicago Mural Group (now the Chicago Public Art Group).

This was my very first mural. I asked Caton if I could just hang out with him, clean his brushes, and watch him paint a mural, to find out what it's all about. At that time in my life, I had very few challenges in my work. I could do anything I wanted. Justine would tease me about my being the master artist, because I had the previous celebrity of being a painter and illustrator whose work had been around the world in various publications.

I asked Caton to let me just check out working on a mural. I had planned on being an apprentice and just watching Caton. Caton had an altogether different agenda, which I did not know at the time. His agenda was to study and learn from me. He knew my reputation. We knew each other since I was eighteen, but not by our art.

When we first got there, I had some frustration. Justine had a prepared sketch of something she wanted to illustrate up on the wall. I stood back and watched. Caton was waiting for me to do what I do. I was waiting for everyone else to do what they were going to do. Caton then expressed those well-received words, "Do it, Jones, do it, even if it's wrong. Do it!"

From that point on I went directly to the wall. My approach to painting a mural was no different from how I would attack an easel. The first image I put up there was the blues player on the far right end, the opposite end from where Justine was working. After that Caton just fed off what I was doing. He saw the direction I was going and started doing the magic he does to reflect off of the images I was putting down. When I did the blues singer, Caton did the blue African mask.

Our skills overlapped and it appeared as if the images were all done by one person. That was when I realized the final imagery of any mural project should have continuity, not be separated or divided. Caton and I would bounce off each other. Nobody knows who did what and that is important in any public art collaboration.

CALVIN JONES
Chicago
1994 and 1999

Three dimensions of an African American woman's life: on the left, her historical ties to Africa; in the center, her professional aspirations; and on the right, the home and her role as mother.

Black Women Emerging, Justine DeVan and Mitchell Caton, 1977. 4120 South Cottage Grove Avenue, Chicago, Illinois.

St. Martin Luther King
William Walker, 1977.
40th Street and Martin Luther King Drive,
Chicago, Illinois.

This is the first mural in which I used one fig-
ure to make a statement, standing in a cross. Of course, that was viewed in many ways by different people. I guess they had different attitudes about that. But they didn't particularly like
my having him standing in the cross. They saw him as hanging on the cross, but actually he
was standing in the cross.

Then [Martin Luther King Jr.'s] father was kind enough to dedicate the wall.

WILLIAM WALKER
Interview with Victor Sorell
From the Smithsonian Archives of American Art, 1991

Children Are the Future (also known as **Childhood Is Without Prejudice**), William Walker (restored in 1993 by Bernard Williams and Olivia Gude), 1977. 56th and Lake Park, Chicago, Illinois.

Originally painted as a tribute to nearby Bret Harte School's promotion of racial harmony in the classroom. Walker's children had attended the school.

I love children. I love all children. I think they are just wonderful. Their innocence, their attitudes toward the rest of humankind. I just can't express and do justice to my feeling that I have for little children.

WILLIAM WALKER
Interview with Victor Sorell
From the Smithsonian Archives of American Art, 1991

I *wanted to start out with a statement of strength within family and community. The ram's horns symbolize strength in Yoruba African cultures. In keeping with our theme, Caton suggested we use one of the ancient traditions of family—the Kente. The tradition of the Kente is design in five-inch strips. It's only worn on very special first-time occasions—baptisms, deaths, births, weddings, etc. That is where Kente comes from in all of my public art pieces, because each mural is a first-time occasion.*

To me doing drawings and grids are a waste of time and energy. The amount of time it takes to do, I could be up doing it live.

CALVIN JONES
Chicago
1994

Another Time's Voice Remembers My Passion's Humanity Calvin Jones and Mitchell Caton (Restored in 1993 by Bernard Williams and Paige Hinson), 1979. Acrylic, 22' x 48'. Elliott Donnelley Youth Center, 3947 South Michigan Avenue, Chicago, Illinois.

Continuum (detail)
Jon Onye Lockard, 1980.
Wayne State University,
Manoogian Hall, Detroit,
Michigan.

In this mural cycle there are five parts. It is a history of African and African American people. We start in Africa with the figure of Shaka Zulu, who was central in the history of the African continent. This is a very Pan-African mural. Shaka Zulu holds bolts of lightning in his hand—he has the grasp and ability to hold that kind of energy. He represents the power of the past and the possibilities of the future.

JON ONYE LOCKARD
Detroit
1994

This work is especially addressed to the children. My first painting projects were in Memphis and Nashville, Tennessee (1954). When I visited West Memphis and found out about the plantations and how people chopped cotton and the very low wages they were receiving and the conditions in general, that was the experience that changed my entire life about trying to get fame and fortune. It was as though the curtain of history of 200 years had just appeared before me and someone had pulled the curtain back. . . . It was in Memphis that I first became aware of the fact that black people had no appreciation for art or artists—they were too busy just struggling to survive. I then decided that a black artist must dedicate his work to his people.

In questioning myself as to how I could best give my art to black people, I came to the realization that art must belong to all people. That is when I first began to think of public art.

WILLIAM WALKER
From "The Artists' Statement," Museum of Contemporary Art, Chicago, 1971
and an interview with Victor Sorell
From the Smithsonian Archives of American Art, 1991

You Are as Good as Anyone
William Walker, 1980.
47th Street, Chicago, Illinois.

Ceremonies for Heritage Now
Calvin Jones and Mitchell Caton, 1980.
Westside Association for Community
Action, Chicago. Acrylic, 22' x 75'.
Sponsored by the Chicago Mural Group
(now the Chicago Public Art Group).

The building was a neighborhood facility for health care and youth programs. Young people would meet here before going out on their field assignments.

This was my first time doing a mural on the West Side. When blacks migrated to Chicago from the South, those from Mississippi, Alabama, and Tennessee went to the West Side while those from Georgia, Arkansas, Louisiana, and Florida went to the South Side. Blues singers Muddy Waters, Howlin' Wolf, and John Lee Hooker were all from Mississippi and they all migrated to the West Side. Martin Luther King Jr. lived two blocks away when he lived in Chicago. When Louis Armstrong came up from New Orleans, he lived on the South Side.

The first image we put up was the plantation couple in the Mississippi cotton field looking down at the continent of Africa. To the left is a mask of spiritual health and rituals. Moving right from Africa it's the still dances of Senegal, then the blues player just left of the door. The mural continues on down the wall. There's the head of a local woman who was a community organizer and activist. She initiated programs for young people and had an annual awards ceremony.

If you look at any of my murals, where you see the human form, you will also see the patterns and designs of Africa in order to represent the continuity between the past and present.

CALVIN JONES
Chicago
August 1999

The text within the mural reads:

EARTH IS NOT OUR HOME

EARTH IS A PREPARER PLACE WHERE KING, MALCOLM, JESUS, JOHN BROWN, LINCOLN, GHANDI, MOHAMMAD, BUDDA, & THEM DIED — 4 LOVE WE MUST DIE 4 LOVE ALONE WE R. EARTH IS NOT OUR HOME

(OUR FATHER WHICH ART IN HEAVN) PREPARETH A PLACE) 4 US — HERE NOW! WE MUST BE FRUITFUL & MULTIPLY, HAVE DOMINION OVER THE EARTH &

IN GOD

The Lord is my shepherd; I shall not want. He maketh me to lie down in green pastures: he leadeth me beside the still waters. He restoreth my soul: he leadeth me in the paths of righteousness for his name's sake. Yea, though I walk through the valley of the shadow of death, I will fear no evil: for thou art with me, thy rod and thy staff they comfort me. Thou preparest a table before me in the presence of mine enemies: thou anointest my head with oil; my cup runneth over. Surely goodness and mercy shall follow me all the days of my life: and I will dwell in the house of the Lord for ever.

Earth Is Not Our Home, C. Siddha Sila Webber, 1981. Martin Luther King Jr. Boulevard, Chicago, Illinois. Self-sponsored.

This was the second mural I did by myself. Bill Walker had painted on this wall, but it never took off. It had ugly colors and somebody wrote graffiti on it. Walker and I talked and he gave me the wall.

When you don't get paid, you can fall in love deeply. I was in love with this wall all summer. Mostly I wanted to say something to the community to give people hope and pride and beauty.

My grandmother was an American Indian and she taught me a lot. My mother was consciously very spiritual. My father was an extremely religious, positive person. They all had profound spirituality about them, and I inherited that type of a personality.

My thinking is that we're here on earth getting ready. The people in the mural are mostly cosmic people. We don't come from Earth. We came from heliocentric space, or you might call it heaven. Malcolm, Martin, John Brown, Gandhi, and Buddha died, having come to Earth to prepare us to be better people. Inside the sun is an Indian. He has a sign under him, like on a coin, that reads, "In God," instead of "In God We Trust."

The whole thing was to get people thinking how we're not limited to this hell that we're getting here. I put in the Twenty-third Psalm [The Lord is my shepherd…], and it was amazing how many people stopped by and read it.

C. SIDDHA SILA WEBBER
Chicago
July 1999

Reaganomics
William Walker, 1982
Chicago, Illinois
Self-sponsored

A jack-in-a-box-like Reagan grins under a list of itemized statistics on budget cuts in community social services. Directly to Reagan's right is a woman holding an empty plate. At the mural's other end a confrontation is taking place between Klansmen and Nazis, and members of local neighborhood organizations. A caption reads, "How Come We People Can't Be More Together?"

The Tallest Tree in the Forest, Jon Onye Lockard, 1982. Central State University, Robeson Center for the Performing Arts, Wilberforce, Ohio.

The mural is a montage, touching on all major events of Paul Robeson's life. From his childhood to his college experience to his involvement in music and drama, his legal experience, the effect and influence of his wife and children, his involvement in politics, the world at that time, and his impact in the movies.

JON ONYE LOCKARD
Detroit
1994

A master painter with a keen eye for color, shape, and form, Mitchell Caton painted this small abstract wall as part of a world-wide support network during the height of the antiapartheid struggles in South Africa. The mural is not very visible from the street, so the viewer needs to come close to the wall to feel its power and interpret its imagery. Early markings of the Dutch East India Trading Company in the center are flanked by newspaper headlines describing the riots of Soweto and Capetown, while painted African masks stare out in juxtaposition to a face covered by a gas mask.

South Africa Exposed
Mitchell Caton, 1985.
Chicago Defender Building,
2400 South Michigan,
Chicago, Illinois.

Peace, Peace, William Walker, 1980. Chicago, Illinois. Self-sponsored.

Wall of Community Respect, William Walker, 1985. Chicago, Illinois. Self-sponsored.

In the vicinity of 47th and Calumet, William Walker painted some of his most important murals, supplying his own paint, time, energy, and remarkable talent. One of the key walls he received permission to paint was the side of Norwood Liquors, thanks to owner Tom Norwood. Often referred to as the *Wall of Community Respect,* this wall was repainted by Walker on at least three different occasions, the last honoring Harold Washington, the first African American mayor of Chicago.

During a visit to the *Peace, Peace* wall with Walker, he talked about his interest in contrasting light and shadows. Also, note the trompe l'oeil columns. His trademark children of all colors, interlocked in close embrace, underscore his hatred of racism in any form. The hooded Klan figures create artistic as well as real tension with figures of community people. While painting, locals would often come up to him and ask if they could have some of their poetry included on the wall, and, more often than not, he would oblige. Although the political views of Martin Luther King Jr., Malcolm X, and Elijah Mohammad appealed to very different elements in the community, Walker painted them together to suggest the importance of harmony inclusive of all points of view.

I had a friend who was an alderman. He wanted me to do something in his area and helped me get a few dollars. He wanted something that would just be about the community, so that's what I did. It took practically all summer. I used a lot of color and a lot of imagination.

This mural got a great response from the community. There was a bus stop near the wall. When the high school and college students got off the bus, they would tell me how much they liked it.

C. SIDDHA SILA WEBBER
Chicago
July 1999

Untitled
C. Siddha Sila Webber, 1985.
1031 Cottage Grove,
Chicago, Illinois.
Funded by the Chicago
Cultural Affairs Department.

Art Train (Aerosol Ecstasy), Vulcan, 1986. Detroit, Michigan.

Henry Chalfant was asked to bring ten premier spraycan artists to Detroit to paint the sides of five railroad cars called the *Art Train*. The train would roll through the Michigan countryside from town to town. Students were brought to the stations for an art lesson inside the cars, which were fitted out as a moving museum. *Pop Art* was the subject matter for this particular show. Vulcan was one of the team of nine spraycan artists and one traditional brush-using artist who helped create the final images.

The owner of this movie theater, Ed Gardner, was restoring the building, built in 1926. On the South Side, at 47th and South Park, there had once been a theater called the Regal—the mecca of the black community during the Depression years and World War II, but it was torn down in the '60s. Gardner's vision was to recreate the old Regal Theater that we'd all grown up with.

All the personalities on the wall performed at the original Regal, and I saw many of them during my childhood. On the left side, closest to the street, I wanted to do a retrospective of those persons that appeared there from the '20s to the '50s. However, I wanted it to be in the spirit of the theater, not just a who's-who of favorite people.

I selected for the comedy area Redd Foxx, who was from the neighborhood where I was born, and Moms Mabley. For musicians—Duke Ellington, Nat King Cole, Billie Holiday, Sarah Vaughan, Ella Fitzgerald, Dinah Washington, who was a local, Miles Davis, Joe Williams, Dizzy Gillespie, Count Basie, and Louis Armstrong. Throughout the portraits I wanted to have the rhythm of continuity so I wove various African patterns in and through the figures.

Local composer Evod Magek wrote a musical composition for Bright Moments called Blues for Five Beat. The first two bars for piano run through the area where piano players Count Basie and Duke Ellington are. The music for the saxophone is in the silhouette of the jitterbug dancers, and around Louis Armstrong are the bars written for trumpet.

The Regal used to have lavish production numbers. It was famous for its dancers and big bands. I felt no one would be more fitting for the central position than Josephine Baker. I didn't want it to be a portrait, but rather an image in the spirit of all those beautiful women who performed there. On the right side I wanted to put the youngsters who'd appeared on stage. The most famous and recognizable that I recall is "Little Stevie Wonder." I saw him when he first performed there at twelve years old, so he's in there at that age down by the synthesizer. I also did the large adult Stevie Wonder. The last image, at the far right, is Aretha Franklin. The African symbols near her have the double entendre of the gold and platinum records performers receive as awards. The large musical score is "Stompin' at the Savoy" of the '30s.

The idea for the title of the mural came from the song I sang every morning when Caton would pick me up—Bright Moments by Rasan Roland Kirk.

CALVIN JONES
Chicago
August 1999

**Bright Moments,
Memories of the Future**
Calvin Jones and
Mitchell Caton, 1987.
New Regal Theater,
79th and Stony Island,
Avalon, Chicago, Illinois,
Keim paint, 24' x 125'.
Sponsored by Ed Gardner
(building owner).

The Blue Nile
Charles McGee, 1987.
Detroit People Mover
Broadway station,
Detroit, Michigan.
Outdoor enamel paints.
Funded by The Hudson
Webber Foundation, City of
Detroit, and Detroit People
Mover Art Commission.
Photograph courtesy of
Irene Walt.

I believe all things are equal under nature. Most people think that people are the greatest thing that walked the earth, but I feel our role is as humble as the ant or the fly or whatever. All of us act in the service of nature.

This piece is part of a series I did called 'Noah's Ark.' You see dogs in there. Birds fly high. Snakes crawl—they're the lowest. Then there are the fish in the sea. It's a universal statement about how all these things are essential in life and essential in the order of things.

Being black in America has a certain poignancy to it, especially if you happen to be on the lower end of things. I feel like if we all came together and treated each other with equal respect, things would be different.

I lived on a farm in South Carolina my first ten years. My family of sharecroppers was so busy trying to make a living that we didn't have time to think about philosophy. I didn't even know the word "art" at that time. Yet the experience I had there was tremendous. We'd go out in the woods and it would be so enlightening.

I see myself as a part of a puzzle. I try with my work to put these pieces together to make a composition that has a specific kind of order as defined by nature through me. The charge of each of us is to reveal who we are in relationship to the vastness of what's placed here.

CHARLES MCGEE
Detroit
August 1999

Good Thunder has 739 people and is about twelve miles from Mankato. The town is named for two Native Americans, both called Good Thunder. One was a Dakota Indian—a large portrait of him is at the upper right of the mural. The other Big Thunder was a Winnebago, but I don't have a picture of him. Instead under the portrait is an image of a Winnebago encampment, the first residents in the area.

The Dakota was the second resident, right before the big Indian Uprising in Minnesota. He became known for protecting white settlers. Later, when the people of the town were getting ready to change the town's name because they were angry over the uprising, a Bishop Whipple spoke up in Good Thunder's defense. They decided to keep the name.

Next to Good Thunder are some kids with a computer. Out of the computer come stalks of corn. I wanted to show what the future was going to be like for farm kids. They won't have to leave their farms. They just have to move up the technology.

The guy at the bottom left is a "gold star boy," the town's first casualty during World War I. Every town had one. There's an American Legion parade underneath him. The yellow building is a hotel that's gone now, and the two ghostly figures coming through it were its owners, the Grahams.

I put a lot of children in the mural to show that there's a generation of people, not just the Founding Fathers. There were women. There were children. When I do histories of Minnesota, there's no way I'll just do the first settlers. If I can't do the Native Americans as part of it, I don't do it at all.

There was once a black man that lived in the town. Nobody wanted to tell me about him. His name was Nigger Tom, and nobody wanted to say that. It took a hermit to reveal that information. I painted him on a singular dryer separate from the grain bins and the grain elevator, to show that this man was in his own world. They said he had saved a couple of people's lives, and then he'd gone to a poor farm and died there. He had an unmarked grave, but while I was painting, people raised money to put up a gravestone.

TA-COUMBA AIKEN
St. Paul
August 1999

Good Thunder, Ta-Coumba Aiken, 1987–88. Grain elevator, Good Thunder, Minnesota. Valspar acrylic on corrugated metal. Funded by Valspar Paint.

The Family: Pyramids of Power, Nina Smoot-Cain and John Yancey, 1988. Henry Booth House, 2328 South Dearborn Avenue, Chicago, Illinois. Ceramic mosaic, 10' x 17'. Sponsored by the Chicago Public Art Group and Urban Gateways: The Center for Arts in Education. Photograph courtesy of John Yancey.

Working in the projects, you're around mostly women and children all day long, but it's a myth that these children have no fathers. While working on this project, it became evident that you have to look beyond the forest to see the trees. Fathers in this community are clearly disenfranchised. The way welfare is set up, men have to stay away. It's a tragedy. The people who have power over these people's lives are mostly white Americans.

We wanted to make a joyful mural, celebrating the black family with men in the center. It makes a statement in support of men in the community to honor their presence. Some choose to disappear, others are there picking up glass, preparing formula, changing diapers— out hustling all day long—to bring something, maybe just chump change, at the end of the day. Their presence was not validated. They don't have skills to survive. They are in the community and need to be recognized.

NINA SMOOT-CAIN
Chicago
1993

Henry Booth House is nestled in the Dearborn Homes housing project. It's part of a strip of housing projects on the South Side that runs for about thirty-five blocks. The wall, instead of facing out toward driving traffic, faces the interior of the projects. The audience is entirely people that are walking or living in the project high-rise.

There is a preconception that there is no family structure in these areas. There is, but it's not the family structure people would expect. While so many of the men are dealing with incarceration and so on, you have this incredible effort by black women to keep families together.

There was a lot of idealism and a lot of optimism in this piece. Not so much to preach, but as a visual symbol of what that triad is between mother, father, children. The pointed peaks refer to that firm foundation the pyramid has always been used for and which it denotes.

Some murals speak of immediate reality in a nuts-and-bolts kind of way. This one is partially that, but it was also trying to celebrate the notion of the power of the family to serve as a symbol. Not so much to reflect what the present reality was, but to symbolize an ideal to strive for.

JOHN YANCEY
Austin
July 1999

Benu: Rebirth of South Shore, designed by Marcus Akinlana and Jeffrey Cook,
assisted by Joe Matunis, Kiela Songhay Smith, and fourteen youth apprentices, 1990.
71st and Jeffery, Chicago, Illinois. Acrylic and concrete bas relief.
Sponsored by Chicago Public Art Group, the Neighborhood Institute, and various funders

This project was part of the cultural, economic, and housing redevelopment of South Shore, a neighborhood on the far south side of Chicago. Benu was the second mural I was involved in during that wave of community activism. The first mural was called South Shore Rests on the Bosom of Oshun in 1989.

We had a community theme-planning meeting on what this mural was going to be about. One of the community members brought up Benu as an image and everybody loved it. Benu, more commonly known as the phoenix, is the bird that goes to its nest on a certain cycle and then is consumed in its own flames. From the ashes a new bird is born. Benu comes from the Khemetic or Egyptian culture.

As South Shore was one of the communities that was burned out in the riots in the late '60s and early '70s, the Benu was a fitting symbol of the community rising and rebuilding itself.

MARCUS AKINLANA
New Orleans
September 1999

In 1982 a 142-foot-long mural on the history of aviation was unveiled at the St. Louis Airport. It didn't include a single African American aviator. The next day a small local group of Tuskegee Airmen, their family, and friends began a drive to correct this oversight with another mural. The mayor questioned whether the airport needed a white mural and a black mural.

Black Americans in Flight, featuring seventy-five portraits (including a few supportive whites, such as Eleanor Roosevelt and Harry S. Truman), documents the involvement of African Americans in aviation. Beginning in the 1920s and early 1930s, African American aeronautic schools were started in Chicago and Los Angeles to train pilots and mechanics.

At the start of World War II, activists and the black press lobbied lawmakers for greater participation of African Americans in the war effort. The Civilian Pilot Training Act Program (CPTP) and Public Law 18 were designed to facilitate the entry of blacks into the Army Air Corps. However, longstanding segregationist policies, practices, and attitudes prevented this. As a compromise, a separate all-black air corps, known as the Tuskegee Experiment, was established near Tuskegee Institute (now Tuskegee University) in Alabama.

The Ninety-ninth Fighter Squadron was officially activated on March 21, 1941. Nearly a year later the first five graduates earned their wings. An imposed quota system restricted the number of pilots that could be trained. Later, various black squadrons were collectively organized into the 332nd Fighter Group, and the War Department began to train the 477th Bombardment Group. During their 1,578 missions, the Tuskegee Airmen never lost a bomber to enemy aircraft. The third panel of the mural features the twenty-three pilots and five ground crew members from St. Louis.

In 1948, President Truman signed the executive order integrating all the armed forces of the United States.

Black Americans in Flight
Spencer Taylor, assisted by
Solomon Thurman, 1990.
Lambert-St. Louis International
Airport, lower concourse east of
baggage claim, St. Louis, Missouri.
Oil on canvas, five panels, 8' x 51'.
Major funding by Anheuser-
Busch Companies, Inc.,
Emerson Electric Company, and
McDonnell Douglas Corporation.

did a four-year cycle of murals at Boulevard Arts Center that now go completely around the whole building. The main idea was to have a powerful explosion of color and activity, something dynamic that was very celebratory. To talk about the positive things that happen with bodies, with people, and with minds. I wanted color and patterns and movement to have a percussive sensibility when you came upon it.

When I do community murals I try to involve people who live in the area. I designed this mural, but when I develop a theme I want to do so with a lot of discussion and dialogue with the people that are going to have to look after it. Painted murals have a greater longevity if people feel a vested interest in protecting them.

It's important to me that anyone who participates in painting gets paid. I had a small crew that helped. My hope always is that they learn some of the technical points of working on that kind of a surface, what the issues are with a mural, and how to deal with the community. My goal is that they become not just helpers, but ambassadors for the mural. Hopefully, some of them will be able to execute murals on their own, keep the tradition expanding. I think this is important because I know that if people hadn't shared with me how to do a mural, I never would have learned.

Formative to my development as an artist was contact with William Walker, Mitchell Caton, Mark Rogovin, and later, John Pitman Weber. Through those artists I developed a sense of self. They were accessible, willing to talk and teach. They were available to younger artists. As young African American artists we realize we're in a hostile field. Art classes don't talk about African American art. We feel a sense of exclusion. These artists were a lifeline, not just mentors.

The lower panel was based on the idea of awakening, waking up and seeing beyond the game that's put in front of you. In many ways people who feel they are getting over, making a lot of money, are only pawns. There's a broader game, and a broader world, and so the world is shown inside the eyes. There's enormous power in that community and all communities like it. Powerful people, powerful ideas, powerful energy.

Each arch is half of an Ifa divination plate. In West Africa, particularly in Yoruba society, when you have a problem, you go to a diviner. The divining plates have positions around them. A cornmeal-based material is used to draw a crossroads. Then you throw shells and do a number of complex ritualistic processes that tell you what your problem is and how you can solve it.

JOHN YANCEY
Austin
July 1999

**Celebration of Arts,
Vibrations of Life**
John Yancey, 1991–92.
Boulevard Arts Center,
1531 West 60th Street,
Chicago, Illinois.
Acrylic, 8' x 32'.
Sponsored by the
Boulevard Arts Center.

The Cycle, Ras Ammar Nsoroma, 1993. 39th and North, Milwaukee, Wisconsin.

The male and female are in the center. Behind them are an Egyptian pharaoh and an ancient university. The different images in the mural show a balance between right- and left-brain thinking, between spiritual and creative on one hand and more scientific on the other. At the far left, under the baby, are the hands of a voodoo messenger. He's Pap Elegba, the guardian of the crossroads between life and death, also known as "the Trickster."

RAS AMMAR NSOROMA
Milwaukee
November 1999

The museum director asked me to show history from ancient Africa to today. He wanted to make the point that everyday people make history. I painted two teenagers, a male and a female, on a journey to different parts of history. The boy starts as a scribe on the far left and ends up a hip-hop rapper, a wordsmith of today, with a microphone in his hand. The girl is an artist. At the end she's on a scaffolding painting a mural.

RAS AMMAR NSOROMA
Milwaukee
November 1999

Untitled, Ras Ammar Nsoroma, 1994. Wisconsin Black Historical Society Museum, 27th and Center, Milwaukee, Wisconsin. Acrylic. Sponsored by the museum.

Go For Your Dream
Alexander Austin, 1994.
47th and Prospect Avenue,
Kansas City, Missouri.
Latex house paint.
Self-sponsored
with donations.
Photograph courtesy
of the artist.

After my first mural, Break the Chains, I came up with a slogan for myself: "Painting for Peace." There was so much violence in the inner city here in Kansas City. I wanted to go with something positive, something good for the community.

I went looking for another wall where there was gang graffiti. I found one and learned that it was owned by the city. There was supposed to be a highway coming through there, but they hadn't made any progress in almost ten years. So I decided to do some painting on it. I figured my mural would probably be up there for awhile.

I started with a couple of gallons of paint and an "Accepting Donations" sign, the same way I worked on my first mural. It was extraordinary the way people gave me money and paint. That's how I got off homelessness and became independent. I used to panhandle when I was homeless, but this was different. I was asking for donations, but I was giving something back at the same time. It was something special, getting people involved. I really enjoyed the concept.

The mural was a compilation of photographs I had collected of Martin Luther King giving his "I Have a Dream" speech. I wanted to capture a full range of his different expressions. Also, in the mural I told the story about my being homeless and not doing my artwork for all those years. It was time for me to be this artist that everyone told me I was all my life, or to go back to washing dishes at the local restaurant. The primary concept of the mural was to tell people that if you do have a dream, don't be afraid to take a chance and go for it.

I was out in a bar a few days after I finished the mural, and someone said he'd seen me on television. He just happened to be a member of the construction crew working on the highway. He told me the mural was going to be torn down in the next week or so. The strange thing was that the whole time I was out there painting, nobody came by to say anything to me. They had to have seen me out there.

There was a lot of media coverage all summer in regards to them tearing it down. There was talk about moving the mural to a different location, or the city paying me to paint another one somewhere else. Nothing prevailed. The community was really upset. We held rallies out in front of it, trying to keep them from tearing it down. Finally in about mid-August, they came with the wrecking ball and explosives.

ALEXANDER AUSTIN
Kansas City
July 1999

The sponsoring organization wanted the mural to celebrate the history of the porters as one of the first African American unions, and A. Philip Randolph as founder of that movement. It was a good bit of an education for me. There's also a big portrait of George Pullman, the railroad tycoon, opposite the portrait of A. Philip Randolph. The latter is a head painted the entire height of the mural, so it's very dramatic. It was inspired by popular culture imagery, like billboards. That's been a big influence on the work I've been doing.

BERNARD WILLIAMS
Chicago
July 1999

Tribute to the Pullman Porters
Bernard Williams, 1995.
103rd and Cottage Grove, Chicago, Illinois.
Acrylic on brick, two panels, each approximately 14' x 40'.
Sponsored by the Chicago Public Art Group.

I did this piece right after I restored the Calvin Jones and Mitchell Caton mural [Another Time's Voice Remembers My Passion's Humanity], *which had a big impact on this piece. I was very moved by Calvin's mural and enjoyed restoring it and interacting with him. It was a powerful experience and an altering one for my practice as an artist because that was the beginning of moving away from a more European style of putting images together. Calvin suggested I begin a study of African art. I did, and it was African art and the collage style of the mural that began a new direction for me.*

I feel a lot of connection to muralists Bill Walker, Calvin Jones, and Mitchell Caton. Bill Walker is originally from Alabama. My parents are from Alabama. Not only is he the father of the murals movement, but in some sense I see him as an artistic father, or even something deeper than that. As artists today we have to be more involved and more proactive in the same way the older artists were. I feel like the need is still the same—for images that empower and give voice to the community, that positively mark the space people live in.

This mural is a celebration of African and African American culture along with a big portrait of Ma Houston (right side, wearing a hat). She was active with Jesse Jackson and Operation Push. And she was very much recognized for her work with prisoners. The image of the guy behind bars addresses Ma Houston's work and also was meant as a visual deterrent for the kids who run around down there. It was a controversial image. A number of people walking by were unnerved that I was painting a negative image of the black male, but somehow I got away with it.

The gold mask represents the royal priesthood and is from Nigeria. It's called an Oba mask. The other mask is from Zaire and is associated with womanly strength. I've seen it repeatedly at the Art Institute of Chicago, and it's always been powerful for me.

BERNARD WILLIAMS
Chicago
July 1999

Feed Your Child the Truth
Bernard Williams, assisted by Stephanie George and Julia Sowles, 1994.
Ma Houston playlot, 50th and Cottage Grove, Chicago, Illinois.
Acrylic, 22' x 100'. Funded by AT&T.

The Great Migration (detail) Marcus Akinlana, assisted by Juan Angel Chavez, Stephanie George, Dorian Sylvain, Julia Sowles, Nyame Brown, Carrie Naumann, and other assistants, 1994–95. Elliot Donnelley Youth Center Art Playlot, 3947 South Michigan Avenue, Chicago, Illinois. Two panels, 28–31' x 120+'. Funded by Chicago Community Trust, Chicago Public Art Group, Chicago Youth Centers, Elliot Donnelley Center, and others.

This mural depicts the story of the Great Migration. It was done in conjunction with a BBC documentary and with a traveling exhibit called From Field to Factory put together by the Chicago Historical Society.

The mural shows you the glory days of "Bronzeville," what this area was called back in the '20s and '30s, when it was a thriving part of the black community. This was during the days of segregation. The music was there—the culture was being brought up North from the Deep South. It was an exciting time.

At that time Blacks had quite a few businesses in their community as compared to now. It was a big step up for you to come from being a sharecropper in Mississippi to being a working-class laborer in Chicago, or even possibly owning your own business. There was no welfare system at that time. Everybody was working; everybody had a hustle of one kind or another.

On the eastern side of the mural, there's a sharecropping family crossing a very idealistic representation of the Mississippi River (I painted it blue instead of brown). They're crossing the river and bringing the blues to Chicago.

At the corner of the wall is a train, which is symbolic of the Illinois Central that ran straight from New Orleans to Chicago—one of the major ways a lot of black folks moved from Texas, Louisiana, Arkansas, Alabama, and Mississippi up to Chicago.

On the next wall you've got a woman stitching a lampshade. They had a lot of cottage industries all over the South Side at one time, where people were working out of their own homes to produce things for larger companies.

MARCUS AKINLANA
New Orleans
September 1999

In 1980 I did my first mural on this wall. [William] Walker worked on it a little with me. It was called Dr. Martin Luther King, We Love You. *By 1995 it was getting old. I decided to paint something new over it. I took a survey from the community and they wanted something about Dr. King again, and so that's what I did.*

The mural has three large faces of Dr. King, each connected with a poem. The left side of the mural is about slavery and coming to this land. There are two or three types of people. There are the people on the boat. There are the people coming up from the ground, but they're also coming out of the water. They're coming from a cosmic dream. You can see them, but you can't see them. They're uplifting Dr. King with magical, unconscious, invisible support.

The last part is about the family and King as savior, as the Messiah. He's on the door with this Jesus look about him. Over that is the Lord's Prayer, which was on the earlier mural too. I decided to use the same prayer in the same place, just with a different background and a different face. I discovered that a lot of kids practice their reading by coming over and reading the poetry.

C. SIDDHA SILA WEBBER
Chicago
July 1999

Have a Dream, C. Siddha Sila Webber and Thomas Murdock, 1995. 40th and King, Chicago, Illinois.
Enamel, 45' x 12'. Sponsored by the Chicago Public Art Group and private donations.

The Memory Masks *project involved a unique method of completing community-involved public art. Three art groups and numerous private benefactors sponsored this project. There are ten Memory Masks inside the center, as well as the three on the outside. The Memory Masks on the outside are mine, and represent the three ethnic groups that are demographically dominant in the area and that use this art center. I was trying to say something, in a nontraditional way, about the intrinsic nature of these groups.*

The blue mask represents the African American. The standing figure is the deity Ausar (Osiris) from ancient Egypt (Khemit)—according to myth, he was so black that he looked blue.

The next mask is the Latino and it's based on St. Barbara or from Santeria, Sango, a deity with the qualities of fire, getting things done and achieving in life, qualities that remind me of the Latino people. There is also an indigenous woman holding a broken sword, which represents the resistance to colonization, land thievery, rape, pillage, etc.

The third mask is for European Americans that came to Chicago with the onset of the Industrial Revolution. A lot of them came as laborers and/or poor working-class people. They started May Day. The deity in this mask is Ogun, the god of iron and technology.

The masks on the inside were designed and painted by ten community members. After raising the money, we paid ten people fifty dollars each to take workshops that I designed and directed. The series was called "How to be an artist/How to market your talents and abilities." The concept was to teach people how to do for themselves. I shared the business knowledge that I had at the time and how to be an entrepreneur. Each student did a mask.

MARCUS AKINLANA
New Orleans
September 1999

The Inglewood area is one of the most dangerous neighborhoods in Chicago. The gang wars that occur there, especially in the summertime, result in at least three shootings a day, just in that one neighborhood. At the time I did this mural, there was a truce. The head of the Disciples was an older guy named Hoover, and he had various reasons for initiating a broader truce with other gangs. It held up for not more than four months, but that four months was a time when everybody was breathing a little bit.*

The truce stayed in effect during the whole mural painting process. The mural talks a lot about both the toll of the violence and the consequences. The symbol in the center—the handshake—is a somewhat trite symbol, but I thought it would be a direct way to lead people into the more complicated imagery.

There are figures that are facing off, about to have a chess game. Behind them are figures that are incarcerated. You also have the chessboard with the king turned over, a symbol of surrender. It's when you acknowledge that the game is over. The bodies floating along the bottom relate to a Congo tradition of bodies that exist in the land of the dead, moving along a river of time. In a lot of my murals, some West African philosophy is woven in.

Another part of this wall (not shown) was a quilt image, with hands as objects that are able to do more than wield guns and inflict violence. Artists, such as Jacob Lawrence, have used hands as great metaphors for doing things, building things, creating things.

All my murals have some sort of message, directed to that primary audience. When I do community-based murals, I am really considering who's looking at it and what are the real issues that they're dealing with and thinking about. This was one that everybody was thinking about. This was something that people had enormous hopes for. Even though they realistically knew the truce would not last forever, it was a time when people were celebrating that it had come into existence at all.

JOHN YANCEY
Austin, Texas
July 1999

Memory Masks, by Marcus Akinlana, 1995 (top). **Images of Reality: Building a More Unified Future,** by John Yancey, 1995 (bottom). Sponsored by Boulevard Arts Center, 6011 South Justine, Chicago, Illinois. Acrylic on masonry. Sponsored by Boulevard Arts Center and Chicago Public Art Group and WON Mural Society.

I had a chance to work with some young people, which is always a challenge and a good teaching opportunity. The painting is on a daycare school, and across from there, they are in the process of creating a senior citizen's home. The kids did practically all the drawing and painting. I didn't have to do much but teach and keep them safe.

It's a mentoring-type mural. There are two or three grandfathers with children, as well as mothers, fathers, children, and babies, teaching and learning. There's an underlay of Malcolm on one side and King on the other side. You can see them, but you can't see them. Along the bottom are African masks. They have relevance, but also there was a space to fill up.

C. SIDDHA SILA WEBBER
Chicago
July 1999

New Life, New Love
C. Siddha Sila Webber with
Bryant Jones, 1996.
Beth-Anne Life Center,
1140 North Lamon,
Chicago, Illinois.

Ta-Coumba and I met John in 1988 at a National Conference of Artists conference in Brazil. He was being honored. He'd seen an article in American Visions that same year about Ta-Coumba doing grain elevators. Since that time we'd been looking for a way that we could work together.

John is at a point now in his life where he doesn't want to be hanging off a wall. From the beginning, we wanted him to do the framework for the piece, to come up with the theme and then Ta-Coumba and I would execute it. He came up with the idea of using African stools as universal symbols, and then suggested concepts for us to work with.

We had funding for fifteen artists, but Ta-Coumba, John, and I decided to take a little less money so we could bring on two more really strong artists. None had done a mural before—that was one of the criteria. We were looking for emerging artists, and not just people in their twenties. Some were folks in their forties who had either switched careers or switched the emphasis in their lives and wanted to rededicate themselves to making art. They were all African American. Each artist had the opportunity to embellish John's idea, really superimpose his or her own vision on John's work.

SEITU JONES
St. Paul
August 1999

I was thinking in terms of ecology and the preservation of nature. I felt this was very timely.

The comb represents the spirit. I have a collection of 150 African combs. There are also Native American combs, very similar. I asked Ta-Coumba and Seitu to use one from a tribe in Minnesota.

Iron pots represent the source of life, birth. When I had an exhibit in Austin about twenty-five years ago, we included two iron pots. The teacher wanted to know what the children liked best in the exhibit. They liked the pots, because they said they represented their mamas' stomachs. That's very basic.

The stool is the throne of God. It is the mother's womb. The top of every stool is a boat. Where you sit, that's a boat. In the pyramids of Egypt every pharaoh had to have his boat. That meant he was going back to the womb. The stool is a universal symbol throughout Africa.

JOHN BIGGERS
Houston
August 1999

Celebration of Life
John Biggers, designer, Seitu Jones and Ta–Coumba
Aiken, lead artists, with fifteen other artists, 1996.
Olson Memorial Highway and Lyndale Avenue North,
North Minneapolis, Minnesota.
Cast stone, clay, and metal, 16' x 160'.
Funded by various city agencies, foundations,
corporations, and individuals.

We did extensive interviews with people in the community who are active and involved, including school principals and people from local business organizations, along with some of the students who work and play around there. It was our way of capturing the pulse of the community. Housing and education are two of the issues we showed. We had an image of a dump truck because Chicago Avenue is a route for the sanitation system, and there is a waste plant where they convert waste to energy in the area. Another image John worked up was a child in a box, which talks about kids feeling trapped or about the potential that's locked up.

We worked in a collage style, very much influenced by Romare Bearden, which is a little different from the collage style of Calvin Jones. There's more of a feeling of cut paper in this piece. Again, it relates to popular culture. I clipped images from magazines and constructed some of the large figures in this piece. We also laid in cut paper printed with decorative patterns.

BERNARD WILLIAMS
Chicago
July 1999

Urban World at the Crossroads
Bernard Williams and John Pitman Weber,
assisted by Lynn Edwards with teens from
the Youth Service Project, 1997.
Orr High School, Chicago and Pulaski
Streets, Chicago, Illinois.
17' x 100'.
Sponsored by the Chicago Public Art
Group, the Youth Service Project, and
Gallery 37.

The Life Works *series was about paying homage to people in Milwaukee who have made a difference, have had some involvement in the betterment of the community, or are well-known local figures with a positive reputation. The first two walls were painted at the House of Peace in 1995 and focused on local political figures and grassroots activists.*

This mural was a continuation of the Life Works *series because once again it highlights individuals dedicated to the community. It is a tribute to the staff that served at this community center over a twenty-five-year period.*

BRAD BERNARD
Milwaukee
July 1999

Life Works III:
Victory Over Violence
Brad Bernard, 1997.
Career Youth
Development Center,
Milwaukee, Wisconsin.
10' x 55'.
Photograph courtesy
of the artist.

Crossroads, Carole Byard and Marilyn Lindstrom with local youths, 1997. The Cultural Center of Minnesota, 3013 Lyndale Avenue South, Minneapolis, Minnesota. Latex on concrete block, 12' x 112'. Sponsored by Neighborhood Safe Art, the Cultural Center of Minnesota (owned and directed by African Americans), and the Lyndale Neighborhood Association. Photograph courtesy of Marilyn Lindstrom.

This mural is truly at a crossroads. It is a site where several neighborhoods begin and end and cultures converge. Crossroads *begins with Elegba from the Yoruba pantheon, an ancient guardian of the crossroads, entrances, beginnings and endings. Being at the crossroad is the point of deciding which road to take in the making and changing of our lives. The mural moves from the darkness to the light, from the past through the present and beyond. Roads as light intersect and fuse new creations untold as we choose the paths that shape and guide us. Marilyn Lindstrom of Neighborhood Safe Art, my collaborator, was already working with the young artists she had hired for the summer when I arrived from New York with a sketch for the design. We had a rainbow of wonderful young artists. I flew in from New York for five days every other week working with the design and getting to know our kids. We were all on the wall, drawing, painting, setting up, breaking down, cleaning up long hours and the kids were so faithful, so committed. The reality of Crossroads was not only the making of our mural, it was also a coming together of a mosaic of dedicated, inspired people who worked from the heart.*

CAROLE BYARD
New York City
January 2000

On the far left there's a portrait of a grandmother figure. I used my great aunt—I come from a very matriarchal family. I knew the area where the mural was placed. There are a lot of women who are the backbones of their families. While there are some fathers present, it isn't the norm. I wanted to show the strength and wisdom of older women. In one hand the figure is holding a folded flag, like you'd see at a military funeral. In her other hand she's holding an old photograph of my brother, who served in the armed forces and is no longer with us. I did that as a tribute to all the young men who served. They may be gone but they are remembered for their contributions.

I got a little flack for that flag while I was painting, but I get tired of hearing that African Americans are not patriotic. We do care about this country. I don't always feel that the country has cared about us.

The vines start behind her, interwoven through the whole mural, ending up in the hand of a young man. I did this to show knowledge and wisdom passing from the older to the younger generation.

We're so inundated with images. When you're doing public artwork, I think it's really important that the public image you put out there is a positive one. Even if you're talking about something that has some negativity, the overall message should be to find some kind of unity and common ground.

CARLA CARR
Joliet
October 1999

Visions from a Dream
Carla Carr, 1998.
Eliza Kelly School, 100
West McDonough Street,
Joliet, Illinois.
10' x 32'.
Sponsored by the City of
Joliet and the Friends of
Community Public Art.
Photograph courtesy of the
Friends of Community
Public Art.

The central theme of all the mosaics done in 1998 and 1999 is family: community as extended family and multigenerational family as community. Within this theme, numerous related themes circulate, overlap, harmonize, and inform each other, especially themes of caring, sharing, culture, traditions, and memory.

These themes and the images and compositions which express them were developed by local adolescents, more than thirty of them, during two summers. The young people were guided and encouraged in their design work, their discussions, their tile cutting, and their mosaic composition by master public artists Nina Smoot-Cain and John Pitman Weber, assisted by Tracy Van Duinen and Janet Gould.

Family Histories: *At the center are the family photos, largest of all Mama and next to her Papa. To the other side, a wedding picture in an oval frame. Above are grandparents with children; below find a pair of graduation pictures and a snapshot of a child on a tricycle. All these were translated into mosaic directly from the cut-paper versions of actual family photos done by our young apprentice artists.*

To the right of the family "photos" is a kitchen scene. The kitchen table was chosen by the young artists as symbolic of the center of home life, the place where we come together to make and to share food. The kitchen scene is a favorite of the artists, who love "home-cooking" both in the kitchen and in art.

Off to the right in a separate panel, a green crescent moon floats in a starry sky. The stars form the constellation the Big Dipper, also known as the Drinking Gourd (and to the ancients, the Big Bear). The last two stars in the cup of the Dipper / Gourd point to the North Star, which guided generations of fugitives from slavery in their nighttime journey to freedom.

She Is the Tree of Life to Them: *around the corner, adjacent to the collards and sunflowers. Two small children reach up toward a tall maternal figure. Above is a Morning Glory flower, its heart-shaped leaf made of stained glass.*

JOHN PITMAN WEBER
Chicago
1999

Peace by Piece: Family Histories and **She Is the Tree of Life to Them,** Nina Smoot-Cain and John Pitman Weber with Summer Youth Workers, 1998. Bethel New Life, Center for the Performing Arts, Chicago, Illinois. Mosaic. Sponsored by Gallery 37 and the Chicago Public Art Group in partnership with Bethel New Life Cultural Arts Program. Photograph courtesy of the artists.

One hundred and fifty-three vignettes of community activities are interspersed with portraits of well-known African Americans. Among those pictured is local hero and athlete Edwin Moses. Born in Dayton in 1955, he was a National Merit Scholar at Dayton Fairview High School. He graduated from Morehouse College with degrees in physics and engineering. Moses won the gold medal in the four-hundred-meter hurdles at the 1976 and 1984 Olympics. He also won the bronze at the 1988 games. From 1977 to 1987, he won 107 consecutive race finals.

In the Village (detail), James Pate, 1998. Riverview and Rosedale, Dayton, Ohio. Acrylic, approximately 5' x 200'. Sponsored by the City of Dayton Arts and Recreation Program.

Murals 1967–Present: Northeast

Africa Is the Beginning, Gary Rickson, 1969 (repainted in 1994). Roxbury YMCA, Boston, Massachusetts. Sponsored by Summerthing.

Thousands come into the city and thousands leave on a daily basis, so I put murals where the traffic is. My idea was to project family values and neighborhood values, morality, in a circumference that could expose and demonstrate to thousands of people coming and going. Once I did that, it was like an ongoing mural exhibition that happened for years and years. Africa Is the Beginning is a pyramid on a platform in space. To the left is the earth. In the upper-left corner is the sun eclipsed by the moon. The reason I eclipsed the sun is that one of my female friends, very spiritual, said that female power is coming. The moon is the woman. I had two comets, male and female, that were pointing at and coming to the point of the pyramid. The pyramid itself is a triangle of wisdom, knowledge, and understanding.

We had some older artists here that were teachers and they belonged to the National Conference of Artists: Marcus Mitchell, John Wilson, and Calvin Burnett. They were told to come back where they lived and start an art organization. I read the call in the local Bay State Banner and went to a meeting.

We formed the Boston African American Artists Association. At the time it was the Boston Negro Artists Association, because it was 1962. I was gung-ho, although at that time I couldn't paint. I could do some charcoal.

Being a writer and a poet, I was ready. I started collecting people's art, keeping them in my house and studying them daily. I wanted to learn how to paint, and I did. I've done about fifty murals, mostly inside. We kept busy. I did some main ones, maybe half a dozen. Between the years '68 and '74, about 150 murals were done in various neighborhoods in and around Boston and I was consultant to these. That was great.

GARY RICKSON
Boston
July 1999

Maternity
Sharon Dunn, 1970.
Yarmouth and
Columbus Avenue,
South Boston,
Massachusetts.
Sponsored by
Summerthing.

Among the first women's murals in the country, *Maternity* features a row of women, all of whom are pregnant or holding infants. Above them is another row of women, this time x-rayed with only their breasts and reproductive organs visible. The artist is said to have been pregnant at the time she painted this mural.

This large image shows a reclining child shooting up directly into his heart.

The Third Nail, James Brown, 1971. The Third Nail (drug rehabilitation center), Roxbury
Crossing, Boston, Massachusetts. Sponsored by Summerthing.

Smokehouse Project
William T. Williams, Melvin
Edwards, Guy Ciarcia, and
Billy Rose, 1969.
123rd Street, Harlem,
New York.
Funded by the National
Endowment for the Arts.
Photograph © Smokehouse
Associates, New York.

As this project developed, we agreed that the work would be abstract, and would dynamically dominate the spaces, but that we would make collective decisions about everything.

The word abstract for me deals not with style, but with concept. Historically most people saw the idea of a mural or wall painting as storytelling or message-giving in itself. The elimination of the storytelling aspect freed us to work with other things. It wasn't a rejection in that sense—opposition to a style—but rather a functional move that had to do with the idea of change, because the biggest need collectively seemed to be change.

We saw the work itself as being the actual change. You don't tell people to make things better, you make things better and people join you in making them better. I think the general idea of improving things was what we wanted to happen.

Smokehouse wasn't just painting, because we considered as many elements as possible, sometimes working in three dimensions and making alterations of the ground. A good example was the 123rd Street site where the little park there (Sylvan) had been literally taken over by addicts and other negative influences. When we renovated the walls, the Park Department said "This is a good idea," and so they renovated the seating. The people in the community, young and old, started to come back and use the park. The people who were using it for negative things just sort of floated away.

We started to realize that you could paint a place and start these aspects of change in motion, but then you couldn't give everybody in that ten-block-area a job and you couldn't give everybody ownership of their housing and couldn't take care of the public education and the health of everybody.

MELVIN EDWARDS
New York City
September 1999

A smokehouse is a place for storing the harvest during the long, tight winters. Mel had southern roots. I had southern roots. One of the other painters had southern roots. It's a term that's probably very rural. We were very aware that there was a certain kind of common man-ness about it. The smokehouse is really an international, universal symbol because everybody has rural roots.

There are many mural traditions to call upon that use geometry, use formal elements as a way of changing spaces. We were drawing as much upon those traditions as we were on the maybe more apparent traditions of the Mexican muralists. We can now look at murals painted by women in South Africa and see almost a direct connection between the things we were involved in and the way they went about changing one-story buildings, and the way one-story buildings functioned aesthetically and visually in relation to the environment.

We were not only interested in change, but in empowering people to realize they could change also. In a lot of cases that's what the walls did, kind of energize the community. Eventually we evolved into connecting with street festivals and other kinds of things.

The ideas that came out of that period certainly stayed with Mel, and certainly stayed with me, and evolved into other areas both nationally and internationally in terms of panels and discussions. Mel has gone on to make a number of large-scale public sculptures. The seed was planted there. Smokehouse has had a wide range of influences that seem to be invisible. It was a spirit about what artists can do in relation to humanity, and I think that spirit is very much alive.

WILLIAM WILLIAMS
New York City
September 1999

The Children's Art Carnival, located in Harlem, was founded in 1969 as a community outreach program of The Museum of Modern Art. In 1972 it became an independent, community-based nonprofit organization. For more than thirty years Children's Art Carnival has provided innovative visual and communication arts programming for young people ages four through twenty-one. Approximately 55 percent of its participants are African American.

This was the first mural that we did. We did lots of others after this one. For a good ten summers we did murals in the parks. For this one, I selected about seven children's paintings and was very true to what they had done, except that I did some color conversions so they flowed one to the other. The teenagers worked with project supervisor Sulvin Goldbourne, taking the dummy I had made and transferring it to the wall.

BETTY BLAYTON-TAYLOR
New York City
October 1999

Untitled, Betty Blayton, Sulvin Goldbourne, and teens from Children's Art Carnival, 1971. Lenox Avenue and 140th Street, Harlem, New York. Commissioned by the Reader's Digest Foundation.

Knowledge Is Power, Stay in School
Dana Chandler, 1972. Ziegler and Warren Streets, Roxbury, Boston, Massachusetts. Acrylic, approximately 15' x 35'. Sponsored by Summerthing.

I wanted to say something to young black children—teenagers—about staying in school. The two fists are coming out as flames from the mouth of Malcolm X and on the other side from this young black man whose hand is outstretched, pointing almost like the hand you see in the Sistine Chapel. The flame coming out of that finger and cracking open the egg has to do with the idea that we hold power to free ourselves from the egg of oppression and to spring out and be all that we can be. There's a godlike figure above the black man, which is a spiritual force allowing him to break the egg. Malcolm X, Martin Luther King Jr., and Medger Evers are the mentors of the African American male in particular.

I was directing much of the mural to African American males because even at that point in 1973—and long before 1973—I knew that we were an endangered species. It is still very true because we can be destroyed at any point, in any number of ways: physically, of course, which happens every day; psychologically; spiritually; and especially economically. . . . The streets and drugs were beginning to have too much sway. I wanted to see if I could visually encourage young people to stay in school and get an education, because developing the kind of resources necessary to lead our people to true freedom in the United States—as much freedom as one can get in the U.S.—would be impossible without a good sound education.

Education doesn't necessarily mean the kind you get just from the Eurocentric school system, which still today is highly extant in African American communities. But the process that begins and then leads you to do some research about our people and our own history so that you will have a fine understanding that our people are the beginning of all humanity. All cultures came out of the wellspring of our African forefathers and mothers.

DANA CHANDLER
Boston
October 1993

The Black Worker, Dana Chandler, 1973. United Community Construction Workers Labor Temple, Roxbury, Boston, Massachusetts.

In this mural I was trying to show the community that our skilled workers could build and rebuild anything our communities needed. Thus the fingers of this figure are tools of all kinds, ready, able, and willing to do the necessary tasks to make our community great. I was expressing the fact that we need our black workers, blue collar or otherwise, for they make us strong. I was also hoping to influence our black youths to stay off the corners and to work hard and grow into owning our own construction companies, etc. Just as the United Community Construction Workers Organization was doing at that time.

DANA CHANDLER
Boston
November 1999

We've got to start talking about the mural movement and public art in terms of nutrition, as vitamin supplements for the community. We fall into their trap by using their language when we talk about murals in terms of art and aesthetics. But if you start talking about the protective force of a mural to combat agents of ill health, I think that's the right way.

I love doing murals. Given my choice, I would paint murals as opposed to doing easel painting or working in my studio. One, because generally in my studio I work at night. I would much prefer to be outdoors. I like the physicalness. Also, there's the added thing of the input from all kinds of people going by. The whole idea of making art accessible is the notion.

Murals that we did were in the black community and therefore temporary, because the community's always being moved. It's called "Negro removal" or "urban renewal."

NELSON STEVENS
Springfield, Massachusetts
October 1993

Work to Unify African People
Nelson Stevens, 1973. United Community Construction Workers Labor Temple, Roxbury, Boston, Massachusetts.

In the Neighborhood
Vincent Smith, 1976.
Boys and Girls High School,
1700 Fulton, Brooklyn,
New York.
Oil and collage on canvas,
four panels, each 6'7" x 2'3⅜".
Sponsored by the Art
Commission of the City of
New York and the New York
City Board of Education.
Photograph courtesy of
the artist.

I was a little intimidated because it was the first time I'd ever done something public like this. The architect told me what he didn't want—anything sexual or about slavery (the latter being done by another artist). Just being given parameters cut into my vision.

I thought I'd do a community mural. The first panel showed the kids in the street playing basketball with some stores in the back. The second was a family scene with people in a house looking out the window, a man and woman with a baby in the street and some kids playing handball in the street. The third panel was another family scene. The father had on a dashiki, the mother was holding a baby, and there were some more children. The fourth panel was a vegetable market with a proprietor outside, and a woman and her daughter shopping.

VINCENT SMITH
New York City
January 1994

This portrait of the celebrated abolitionist is the artist's only known mural. Douglass was in Boston on the night that President Lincoln issued the Emancipation Proclamation, freeing all slaves in areas not held by Union troops. This act affected millions of African Americans. At the telegraph office, Douglass wrote, "We were waiting and listening as for a bolt from the sky. We were watching by the dim light of the stars for the dawn of a new day. We were longing for the answer to the agonizing prayers of centuries." Douglass next concentrated on winning blacks the right to fight for their freedom in the Union Army. The Massachusetts Fifty-fourth Regiment was the first all-black unit to be formed, and Douglass's two sons were among the first to enlist.

Frederick Douglass
Arnold Hurley, assisted by Gary Rickson,1976. Frederick Douglass Square, 1002 Tremont Street, Boston, Massachusetts. Photograph © Haskell Werlin.

Let There Be Life (detail), John Kendrick, 1976. Urban League Alexander E. Mapp Community Center (interior stairwell). Springfield, Massachusetts, funded by VISTA and ACTION.

One of more than thirty murals painted between 1974 and 1977 by summer session students at the University of Massachusetts, Amherst, under the supervision of artist and art professor Nelson Stevens. Kendrick did another mural at New Africa House on the Amherst campus.

Building the Community, 1976. New York City.

A CityArts project portraying members of the community proudly striding forward.
The prominence of a book and diploma emphasize the importance of education.

Martin Luther King: Remembering and Renewing the Dream, A. G. Joe Stephenson, assisted by local youths, 1981. Martin de Porres Community Service Center's Education Center, Astoria Houses Project, 4–25 Astoria Blvd., Long Island City, New York. Bulletin paint, 65'10" x 16'6". Sponsored by CityArts Workshop, Inc., Museums Collaborative, Inc., and the Brooklyn Museum.

This is not the original design. The only thing that remains is Dr. King with his fist up. There were images of people marching, buses burning, crosses and the KKK, and lots of flames—it really looked dynamic.

But some of the people in the neighborhood had a protest. We had to stop work and meet again with the community. They wanted more positive images. I had to go back and research family life. One woman said, "You wouldn't go painting swastikas in a Jewish neighborhood, or scenes of the Holocaust. That's what the KKK means to us." They said they didn't want their kids to see that kind of stuff. It was a learning experience for me as a muralist. It reinforced again that it's not easel painting—you can't just do what you want. You're working with people. So I went back and redesigned it, and this was the result. They liked it. It's tamer than it was.

A. G. JOE STEPHENSON
Albuquerque
December 1994

Untitled, Franklin "Franco" Gaskin, 125th Street, Harlem,
New York. Acrylic on metal security gate. Self-sponsored.

When I was about three years old, I fell from a three-story building and landed right on my head. As I got older, it became very noticeable that I couldn't articulate. I felt isolated so I began drawing cartoons, and those cartoons were my friends. I never played games with other kids. Drawing was my thing.

I came to the United States from Panama when I was in my early twenties. We moved to Harlem, because my father's mother, my grandmother, was here. I started to paint the gates in 1978. They are my contribution to Harlem. They serve as my calling card. When people see them, they want to get in touch with me, and that's how I make my money. It has opened a lot of doors for me. I have traveled to Japan, Europe, and Africa, all because I've done something that most artists wouldn't do. All of the gates I've done along 125th Street over the years were done for free.

People ask me why I stay in Harlem now that I have fame and money. Very simple, because when I first came to the States, I was planted right here in Harlem. I proved that you can go very far from exactly where you are. What I have done in the streets is for two reasons—for love and for beauty. I didn't have to go downtown or to other areas to be successful. I can be successful in my own neighborhood. This is one of the lessons I try to plant in youngsters I meet.

FRANCO THE GREAT
Harlem
June 1999

Noc, a master craftsman, created the "Style Wars" train in 1981. Every inch of the seventy-two-foot car was covered with spray paint "top to bottom." Windows, doors, the works. Trains were painted in the layups at night under exceedingly tense conditions and with little or no light. Coming into the '80s, getting one's name up in quantity was still a high priority, but style masters were constantly innovating to see who could create the most unusual forms, shapes, letter construction, characters, and backgrounds. This train was truly a "masterpiece," admired by all who came to the tracks to see the rolling stock go by. Noc paid deference to the different schools of style by painting "early" wildstyle letters for one word and straight letters for the other.

Quik, Linwood A. Felton (Quik), 1980. New York subway car, spraycan. Self-sponsored. Photograph courtesy of Henry Chalfant.

Style Wars, Melvyn Henry Samuels Jr. (Noc), 1981. New York subway car, spraycan. Self-sponsored. Photograph courtesy of Henry Chalfant.

My grandmother took me to the ballgame, and there I used to see the trains go by with the scrawls on them. I first dared to go out when I was twelve. I took the name Quik and started doing it all over the place.

The object of painting on the trains was to make beautiful things for people to see even if it was for a short time. You had to learn how to do the trains from a master. I did fifty or so little throw-ups every night and one or two nice ones. At my peak there was no one who did as many as I did. Nobody could keep up with me, not the police, not the writers.

The last time I got arrested was in 1987. I was twenty-eight or twenty-nine. I now do a piece once a year, for the kick of it, and I'll keep on doing that as long as I can.

I've had my peaks and my lows here in America, in New York, being an artist. I do 99 percent of my work businesswise in Europe. People there treat me as a professional. Here, when I say I'm an artist, it's incredible, like you must be kidding. It's not the thing to do in America. You can be a politician, a bank manager, a baseball player, a garbageman. I'm sure my mother would be much happier if I was a janitor with a stable job.

If the graffiti artists were all an army of blond-haired, blue-eyed American boys, we'd be the toast. But I like that discouragement, because it makes me paint harder.

QUIK

Wildstyle *was the coordinate style and then computer. That's what I brought out. Nobody else can get down with it 'cause it's too fifth-dimensional. I call it the fifth-dimensional step parallel staircase, 'cause it's like computer style in a step-formulated way. It's just sectioned off the way I want. Like if I take a knife and cut it, and slice, you know. I'll slice it to my own section and I'll call it computer style.*

KASE 2
From *Subway Art,* p. 71

Kase 2 El Kay, Kase 2, 1981. New York subway car. Spraycan. Self-sponsored. Photograph courtesy of Henry Chalfant.

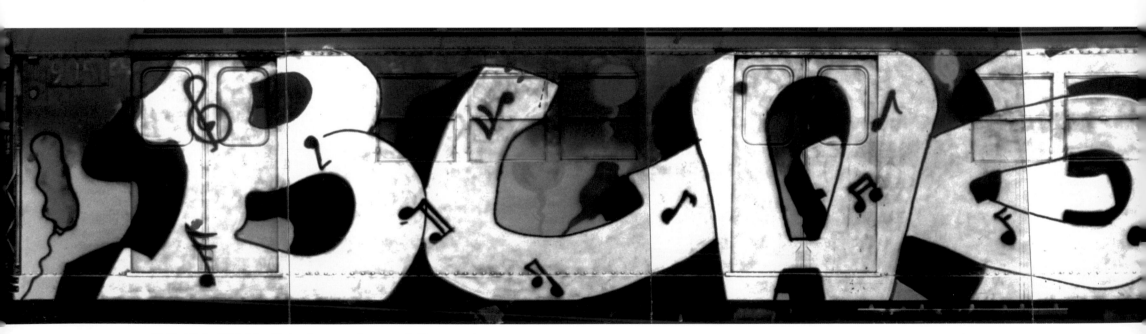

Blade, Blade, 1986. New York subway car. Spraycan. Self-sponsored. Photograph courtesy of Henry Chalfant.

I got started painting trains back in 1972. Lots of my friends were painting. It was just simple hits, what they call *tagging now*—we all got into it at that time for fun, just to be crazy kids. There were people before me, but I was one of the first people doing an actual "masterpiece" on a train. When I began writing, people didn't know how to make a piece at all. There was nothing on the trains, just scribble. I did five thousand trains between 1972 and 1984.

I did it on the trains for the danger, the rush of being out in the middle of the night in the train tunnels and the train yards. It was a Huck Finn–Tom Sawyer type of a life— every day was a real adventure!

Back then, putting up your name was the general idea of graf. Now people do these huge murals, but that wasn't graf. The stuff you see now is fantastic, but it looks more like graphic design stuff you learn in school.

When you went to the trains years ago, it was about bombing and seeing your name going from every borough in the city and tens of thousands of people knowing who you are. It was great! It was like this huge party going on for a decade and a half.

STEVE OGBURN (BLADE)
New York City
September 1999

This is a portrait of astronaut Ronald McNair, who was killed in the Challenger space disaster of 1986. Born in Lake City, South Carolina, in 1950, McNair received his Ph.D. from MIT, and was selected by NASA for its astronaut candidate program in 1978. He served as a mission specialist on a shuttle mission in 1984, logging 191 hours in space.

Dr. Ronald McNair, Kinrod Johnson, 1987. PS 5 (interior), 820 Hancock Street, Brooklyn, New York. Acrylic, 57" x 11'7". Sponsored by the New York Board of Education.

Untitled
Menelek, mid–1980s. PS 262, 500 Mecan Street, Brooklyn, New York. Sponsored by the New York Board of Education.

Portrait of Malcolm X with an Egyptian landscape behind him, painted as a mural inside a mural with children walking past.

Jonkonnu Festival Wid the Frizzly Rooster Band, Vincent Smith, 1988. Dempsey Multi-Service Center of Central Harlem, 127 West 127th Street, Harlem, New York. Sponsored by the New York City Department of Cultural Affairs. Photograph courtesy of the artist.

Thisᵀ mural was a great delight to me. What I tried to do was a combination of all the things I had been interested in over the years. I tried to get the ancestral in. I tried to get the musicians in. I tried to get a local aspect into the work. I wanted to create a broad sweep of all the little nuances and tricks and color schemes and shapes and forms that I'd played with in individual pieces that I'd done. I used a lot of fabric collage of various African designs in all three panels.

The Jonkonnu Festival is a Caribbean festival that originated in Jamaica and the Bahamas. It's one of the four or five major festivals. But the carnivals are all basically similar—some of them just have different meanings. Everyone invents masks to wear. It's not like there are particular masks worn in the different festivals. My masks are just how I feel as I go along. They also come out of various things that I've done over the last twenty years using an African motif. My first trip to Africa was 1972. I've been there about five times.

By painting a festival you're able to include all kinds of people wearing all kinds of clothes, and musicians, masks, and dancing. So what I did was incorporate all this. I had all the participants in with the carnival people, so that everyone was part of it. There were nine musicians and several dancers on stilts. To represent the community I had a church in one corner; next to it a big vegetable market; and then a small building with people looking out the windows.

Vincent Smith
New York City
January 1994

In the process of Mandela visiting, when I was working with the kids we talked about who Mandela was, what his release meant, and what was the ANC, so there was a little history that went on. We had maybe nine, ten days to do this.

PAUL GOODNIGHT
Boston
1993

Mandela
Paul Goodnight, 1990.
Madison Park High
School, Roxbury,
Boston, Massachusetts.
Self-sponsored.
Photograph courtesy
of the artist.

Untitled
A–One, 1990.
Graffiti Hall of Fame.
New York City.

When one thinks of a spraycan and its wide nozzle broadcast of paint, it is evident that artists who could control very skinny lines without dripping had special techniques. A–One is one of those who have mastered the art. This "piece" from the east wall of the Graffiti Hall of Fame probably didn't last too long and since has been covered by dozens of later images created by a myriad of other writers. There is some respect accorded those who "write" in this world-renowned Mecca, as the walls are a continuum of art. A–One created many mostly nonpermission New York City murals, but he wearied of making it as an artist in an inhospitable city and went off to live and work in Paris.

We designed Rivers *as a memorial tribute to Harlem Renaissance poet Langston Hughes; it covers the place where his cremated remains are interred, as well as marking the entrance to the theater that bears his name. The monument features a "cosmogram" that includes symbols and excerpts from Hughes's famous* Rivers *poem.*

HOUSTON CONWILL
New York City
February, 2000

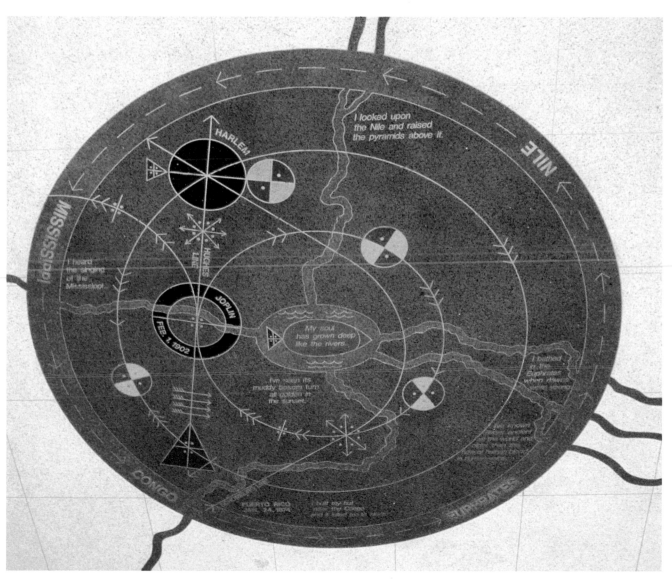

Rivers
Houston Conwill, Joseph DePace and Estella Conwill Majozo, 1991. Schomburg Center for Research in Black Culture, 515 Malcolm X Boulevard, Harlem.
Terrazzo floor with inlaid brass. Sponsored by the New York Public Library. Photograph courtesy of the New York Department of Cultural Affairs, Percent for Art program.

Vulcan lived in an apartment at 106th Street and Madison Avenue with a splendid view of the Graffiti Hall of Fame. The giant wall at the southeast corner was his most notable canvas. An early "king," he is credited with being one of the major innovators of wildstyle letters (letters that are camouflaged, shaped, bent, cut, and twisted so that they are hard to read).

Roughneck Reality, Vulcan and Spon, 1993. New York City. Self-sponsored.

E-Z One's outdoor public gallery is the bare walls surrounding 110th Street and Fifth Avenue in New York City. His figurative spraycan work often has political content, as he collaborates with A-One (now living in Europe).

Malcolm (2nd version), E-Z One, 1995. 110th Street, New York City. Self-sponsored.

"REPRESENT"

"I LEARN
I GO TO SCHOOL"

"I JUST TO MYSELF
WHAT PEOPLE THINK
ABOUT ME IS WHATEVER"

"DON'T COMPARE ME TO ANOTHER"

"I'M QUIET. I DON'T REALLY   NUTTIN'"

See What We Can See, Brett Cook (Dizney), 1996. Spray enamel, acrylic text on masonry, 15' x 50'.
Eldridge and Stanton Streets, Lower East Side, New York. Sponsored by the Abaca Project.

I was approached by a group of high school students through a gallery. The students were curating a show and they wanted to know if I wanted to be in it. They also offered to get me a wall. I said OK. They got me the wall next to their school, the Satellite Academy.

I said, "I'm going to do pictures of you. If you could tell the world one thing, what would you say?" They gave statements. I took photos of them. I knew the wall got really direct sun, so I lit them with these heavy cast shadows, then made a composition so it looks like they're standing in the sun with their quotes.

An artist should be a person who does more than just makes objects. One of the classic models is Diego Rivera, someone who was clearly an artist, yet he's thought of as an intellectual, he's thought of as an activist, he's thought of as a person who championed his cultural identity, and really can be talked about in all of these different ways. To me these things are connected. I am trying to be an artist, an educator, an activist, a writer, a person who speaks out about things, an advocate of social change.

BRETT COOK
Harlem
August 1999

I was at the Studio Museum in Harlem doing an exhibition. *I realized that the institution, even though it was in the center of Harlem, was really alienated from the community. I wanted to do something that built a bridge. I met with people in a nursing home, students from a school, and some miscellaneous residents from Harlem. In the installation at the museum I used drawings and writings—their writing, my writing, audio, video. Then I realized that none of these seventeen people had ever been to the museum. I did seven additional images of the people I'd interviewed and put them up in the neighborhood where they lived with quotes from our interviews. The exhibit was part of a residency at the museum, but I didn't get any type of support for the public work and did it on my own.*

BRETT COOK
Harlem
August 1999

Expressions of Harlem
Brett Cook (Dizney).
Harlem, New York.
Spray enamel, acrylic text
on acrylic and wood.
Self-sponsored.

Specialness
Brett Cook (Dizney), 1998.
Harlem, New York.
Spray enamel, acrylic text
on acrylic and wood.
Self-sponsored.

This one was not even loosely connected with an institution. This project was self-catalyzed. I met with the school around the corner from my studio. I met with students from the Hale House. I met with children from some of the businesses I had gone to. I asked them six questions about being special—what was special about them, something special that they do, some things about who they were, etc. From those six questions I had them pick out their four favorites and write them on four pieces of paper. On those four pieces of paper I helped them do a collage that represented whatever their statement was. From those four collages I picked one of the statements and put that text on an image of them and mounted that in the neighborhood where they lived.

Specialness addressed a lot of the same issues that my other works in the past have done in terms of empowering these people in their community. One of the most powerful things about that work, and my work in general, is that it's also about giving people a voice. In the history of Western art, the model seldom has a voice to speak, except usually through the filter of the artist.

BRETT COOK
Harlem
August 1999

Aband is a metaphor for the richness that comes about once we work and get along with each other. I chose bright, joyous colors to reflect the feeling of people getting along. The city calls it neighborhood renovation, but I think it's really about creating greater art appreciation in the community.

JIMMY JAMES GREENE
New York City
June 1999

New World Players
Jimmy James Greene, 1999.
Herbert Von King Park
amphitheater, Brooklyn,
New York.
Sign-painting enamel,
35' x 16'. Sponsored by the
City Parks Foundation.

Murals 1967–Present: West

This was one of six panels commissioned for the Third World Bicentennial Show. There was a big exhibition and then at the end of the show the murals went to different locations.

We built the mural on panels so it could be taken apart and put back together easily. I picked the theme and designed most of it. I wanted to investigate the historical aspect. When Attucks and the group he was with were shot in 1770, that was the beginning of the Revolutionary War. It was great to research all the material, the clothing, and the buildings from that time period, right down to the buttons and the lace. Caleb was really good at painting details.

We painted like crazy for about six months on it. Sometimes I would pull all-nighters doing cobblestones or bricks on the buildings.

HORACE WASHINGTON
San Francisco
1993

Crispus Attucks: The Boston Massacre
Horace Washington and Caleb Williams, 1976.
William De Avila School (interior auditorium), Haight and Masonic Streets, San Francisco, California.
Acrylic on masonite, 8' x 20'.
Funded by the San Francisco Museum of Modern Art.
Photograph courtesy of the San Francisco Museum of Modern Art.

Muralists are a special breed of people. You get up on walls sometimes fifty feet in the air and try to paint murals with people hollering at you all the time—What are you doing? How do you do that? What are you getting paid? You have to sometimes stop and spend a few hours talking to people.

I enjoy the freedom of working large. I did my first mural in the late 1960s at the Compton Communicative Arts Academy, just down the street from my house. Back then the only murals we were aware of were in the Mexican American community. I did go to see the murals in East L.A. in the early days. There weren't that many around the black community. I did a lot of study of the Mexican muralists.

ELLIOTT PINKNEY
Los Angeles
July 1993

Peace and Love
Elliott Pinkney, 1976 (repainted in 1991).
Watts Towers Arts Center, 1727 East 107th
Street, Watts, Los Angeles, California.
Acrylic, 3' x 6'.
Self-sponsored.

Blacks from Egypt to Now, Robert Gayton, 1976. Fillmore District, San Francisco, California. Photograph © Alan Barnett.

A panorama featuring large portraits of a sphinx, Queen Nefertiti, King Tutankhamen, and a field worker in overalls. Surrounding these figures, on a much smaller scale, are depictions from black history.

In 1966 the student wing of the Black Panther Party saw some murals in the hallways at Washington High by Victor Arnautoff. They didn't quite understand what he was doing, but they saw slaves in the murals and so they reacted violently—carving into the murals and throwing black ink on them. The city and the school became very upset and concerned because they didn't want these historic murals to be defaced. The black students said that if you want those murals saved then you better have somebody paint some murals that can go in the school that speak about the positive contributions and strengths of African Americans and not this slave stuff.

In fact, Victor Arnautoff was a communist, and was just simply trying to demonstrate that the Father of America owned slaves. He had studied in Mexico with Diego Rivera. The black students didn't want to hear none of that, and they put on a search for an artist. The students saw my work and related to it because it was very political. Therefore they said I had to be the one to paint the mural.

The school district went along with the students, but some members of the Art Commission said I was too young and inexperienced in painting murals. When they held up the process, I went all over the country studying murals. I was able to travel a lot, because my father worked for Pan-Am.

In 1968 I went to Detroit, Chicago, and New York. I went to Chicago to talk to Bill Walker. I went to look at all the murals they were doing. They made me feel that was not what I wanted to do. They were painting what was going on in the streets. I felt that they were too much like posters. I was more interested in something that had so much power that it would be like African American music, which speaks to right this moment but is really beyond time.

Starting in 1969 or 1970, I went on and off to Mexico for about two years, trying to study mural painting. Siqueiros for me was the greatest painter and the greatest muralist I ever saw. That was what I wanted to do in mural painting.

The murals at Washington High School did not just deal with African Americans. I and several students in the Black Panther Party felt the mural should be broader, even though none of the students from the other communities participated in forcing this issue.

DEWEY CRUMPLER
San Francisco
1993

Multi-Ethnic Heritage: Black, Asian, Native/Latin American (detail)
Dewey Crumpler, 1974.
George Washington High School (interior), 32nd Avenue and Anza, San Francisco, California.
Politec acrylic on masonite, three panels: 6' x 15', 12' x 16', 6' x 15'.
Sponsored by the San Francisco Unified School District.
Photograph courtesy of the artist.

This mural recalls the migration of African Americans to Portland and other parts of the Northwest during the 1940s from Texas, Oklahoma, and Arkansas. My family was among those coming north, except they didn't come willingly. My father was on the fly because he "broke the rules" and was what whites called "ornery." He didn't observe the tradition of calling whites "mister" and "miss." He called them whatever they called him. Also, he'd go in the front door to pay his bills when he was supposed to use the back door. They eventually tried to kill him, leaving him for dead, tied to a tree.

Six months later he sent for us, and that's how we came to Vanport, a housing project just outside Portland. Vanport City was the second-largest city in Oregon at the time. The merry-go-round shown in the mural was at Jansen Beach, which was a place of joy for us, but also a place that manifested live racism. Black folks couldn't swim in the public pool there after an incident where a white girl accused a black boy of fondling her under the water. It was important, too, because our black leadership at the time did absolutely nothing to protect our rights.

You can see bows of ships up at the top of the mural, referring to the importance of shipbuilding. Vanport was built for Kaiser shipyard workers during World War II. Portland was one of the big shipbuilding players. A ship was launched every day from the shipyards.

The portraits are mostly of family and friends and include a self-portrait.

ISAKA SHAMSUD-DIN
Portland
November 1999

Vanport: The Promise, Isaka Shamsud-Din, 1977–78. Vancouver and Alberta Streets, Portland, Oregon. Acrylic. Funded by CETA. Photograph © Alan Barnett.

Vanport: The Flood
Isaka Shamsud-Din, 1977-78.
Vancouver and Alberta Streets,
Portland, Oregon.
Acrylic.
Funded by CETA.
Photograph © Alan Barnett.

It was Memorial Day, a Sunday, in 1948, the year after we arrived, that the Columbia River broke through a dike. At least fourteen people died in Vanport City, plus forty-five in the Portland area. They didn't evacuate us—instead the authorities passed a note under people's doors the morning of the flood that said, "Don't panic, we will alert you when to evacuate." Within hours the river was coming down the street.

These two Vanport panels were part of a larger project called the Albina Mural Project involving six other adult artists: Charles Tatum, Henry Frison, Daryl Clegg, Chonitia Henderson, Larry Scott, and Jenny Harata [all but the last are African American]. Albina is the name of the neighborhood.

ISAKA SHAMSUD-DIN
Portland
November 1999

Mary McLeod Bethune
Charles White, 1978.
Los Angeles Public Library,
Exposition Park, 366 South
Vermont Avenue, Los Angeles,
California.
Oil on canvas, 10' x 14'.
Sponsored by the Los Angeles
Library Foundation. Use of this
mural courtesy of Heritage
Gallery, Los Angeles.

I*t is a glorious experience being an artist—to seek the meaning of truth, reality, beauty—in short to meet the challenge of life through one's sensitivities. For me, art is a very personal, intimate communicative affair—the most tangible means of establishing a rapport with my fellow man and relating to society with a oneness of thinking and feeling. My work takes shape around images and ideas that are centered within the vortex of the life experience of a black. I look to the life of my people as the fountainhead of challenging themes and monumental concepts. I strive to create an image that all mankind can personally relate to, seeing his dreams and ideas mirrored with hope and dignity.*

I'm not an editorialist in art. I'm too much of a romanticist. In Mexico I used to try to deal with specific issues in an almost political-cartoon way. I found myself uncomfortable with that specific, propagandistic way. In Europe I began to see more variances. I saw that if I got more involved more subjectively, it would be more meaningful than if it were objective.

CHARLES WHITE
From an interview in the *Chicago Daily News,* March 1976

This was my first mural. It led to two other high school projects—a portrait of Sojourner Truth and a California landscape. I was one of the coordinators of the Black Panther Party in Houston, Oakland, and finally in Los Angeles right before the demise of the Party. It was through that involvement that I began to see the importance of community activism. I felt that art was a vehicle for addressing issues and instilling a level of consciousness. One of my specialties was portraits of some of the Panther leaders.

CHARLES FREEMAN
Los Angeles
September 1993

Duke Ellington, Charles Freeman, c. 1976 (repainted in 1997). Duke Ellington Continuation High School, 1541 West 110th Street, Los Angeles, California. Acrylic. Sponsored by the school.

Games
Jacob Lawrence, 1979.
Originally installed in
Kingdome Stadium
100 level bridge at
Gate G, Seattle,
Washington.
Porcelain enamel on
ten steel panels,
approximately 9' x 17'.
Sponsored by King
County Arts
Commission.

T*he Kingdome mural was my first mural. I never thought of it, but evidently people thought my work would fit into the mural style. I could have refused, but I accepted the challenge.*

It's games. There are athletes in the foreground and of course it's interracial. I think there is a shot-putter, a diver, and in the background there are the spectators.

I like the mural form of painting because some people told me that my easel paintings are much like murals. I never studied the murals because I was encouraged to do a mural as you do your painting. Of course there are certain things you take into consideration. But the form is similar to my smaller works. An easel work you can move from one gallery to the next, but in a mural you think of it as permanently placed. So, therefore, I take into consideration the architecture. In content I take into consideration what the building or site is for.

I met Orozco in 1939—he was doing Dive Bomber *at the Museum of Modern Art (in New York). I actually saw him working on that piece. I was only with him about an hour. It was a wonderful experience.*

I was always taught that when you do a mural there are certain steps you take. First, you submit a design to the people who are commissioning you. And if that is accepted, the next step is to do a detailed drawing of the mural in color. And I asked him where his design was, where his sketch was, and he said he never used one. That was very impressive to me. In other words, he was working direct into fresco. I've never forgotten that. He had such control.

JACOB LAWRENCE
Seattle
February 1995

The symbols found in this abstract mural, as well as in others done by Alonzo Davis in Los Angeles during this period, represent themes in the artist's process of self-discovery. At the time this mural was painted, John Outterbridge, a long-time advocate for community arts and a mentor for many local artists, was the director of the Watts Towers Arts Center.

Homage to John Outterbridge
Alonzo Davis, 1980.
Watts Towers Arts Center,
1727 East 107th Street, Watts,
Los Angeles, California.
Acrylic on stucco, approximately 20' x 30'.
Self-sponsored.

I *presented some historical photographs [to my sponsor, civil rights attorney Walter Gordon], and we did a collage. He had certain scenes he wanted to see in the mural, so it was initially collaborative. Then I did a sketch, which he approved.*

I wanted the mural to have the effect of a time line. It starts in the upper-left-hand corner with an African mask. After that is a graphic scene from the period of slavery, including Roots's Kunta Kinte shackled and chained. There are two scenes of lynchings from an earlier part of American history when racism was so prevalent, especially in the South. The Klu Klux Klan is standing before a burning cross. An old slave stands in the foreground. There's an American flag with raggily ends. The red stripes are dripping blood and the blood drips through the streets. Also shown is an image of police brutality, which is always timely. I wanted to include the farm workers because I felt their struggle was linked to the overall struggle. You see Lady Justice in the upper right corner. She has a blindfold on (and a sign around her neck that reads "Out of Order") because justice is—in particular for black and poor people—a farce in a lot of instances. The black man in prison represents the injustice of so many being confined. Jail is a way of getting young black men off the streets, confined where they cannot develop. I look at it as part of a pattern or plan to control the community.

CHARLES FREEMAN
Los Angeles
September 1993

American Justice
Charles Freeman, 1981.
Law Office of Walter
Gordon III, 2822 South
Western Avenue, Los
Angeles, California.
Sponsored by Walter
Gordon III.

Olympic Series
Alonzo Davis, 1984.
Harbor Freeway (110) South 3rd Street onramp,
downtown Los Angeles, California.
Acrylic on concrete, approximately 20' x 200'.
Sponsored by the Los Angeles Olympics Organizing Committee.

This mural was one of ten painted on the freeways surrounding downtown Los Angeles in preparation for the 1984 Summer Olympic Games. Alonzo Davis had originally envisioned a project that would bring murals from downtown into South Los Angeles along Central Avenue, an economically depressed area that had once been the cultural hub of black L.A. However, Davis was unable to find funding for his original concept. Instead, he, along with fellow muralists Kent Twitchell and Glenna Boltuch (Avila), selected seven other veteran muralists to create a culturally and stylistically interesting diversity of images on downtown freeways.

Unity
Roderick Sykes, 1984.
Harbor Freeway at Figueroa
(destroyed), Los Angeles,
California.
Acrylic.
Sponsored by the Los
Angeles Olympics
Organizing Committee.

In the front panel is my face, me as a kid in St. Louis, where I'm from. I used to run track, and I always wanted to go to the Olympics. But as time went on, someone was always faster than I was. The mural's statement is all about getting rid of the generation gap and the color gap, as well as my joy at being involved with the Olympics.

One thing I do in most of my pieces, even in my paintings, is show the pain that I have. I reflect that in the faces and the imagery. The agony of the struggle in the faces, my culture, my race of people here in America, what it takes to be a warrior. I don't care what color the face is. I usually try to show the struggle. If you look into this human being, you'll find yourself. It's not all smiling faces, although smiling faces are wonderful too.

RODERICK SYKES
Los Angeles
April 1994

This mural is a continuation of my earlier one at the Recreation Center.

When I was in junior high school, teachers told me that there were no African American artists, so I took it that I was just a strange person. What led me to make murals was my need to record African American history. For me—a person who couldn't write in a way that would really work, the canvas and murals became a way of writing novels, writing the history that had not been written.

I felt it absolutely necessary to connect Africa with everything I did. By the early 1970s African Americans pretty well understood that Africa was a part of their thing completely. It's not that they ever didn't understand that. It's just that Africa was seen negatively and therefore real connection to it by the community was not embraced. This wasn't new territory—artists like Charles Alston, Woodruff, and all of them had already covered that territory. It's just that consistent reeducation has to take place. This sort of drumming of education was essential. In fact, that was what all the murals were about, about education, about thinking. Later white people began to take up the same cause. Out of this sprang a whole new consciousness of mural painting.

Even the Chicano mural movement owes a great debt to Chicago and the murals created by Walker, for example, one of the hallmarks of contemporary African American mural painting. Because the Walls of Respect that he and Jeff Donaldson and the others did, beginning in 1967, really lit the fire of mural painting all over the country. Those were the moments when mural painting was taken on a political journey that was designed to do what W. E. B. DuBois had called for earlier in the development of African American painting—that was to make paintings in the service of the struggle. For many years none of those works that related to the people were destroyed or defaced because they were like jewels in the community

DEWEY CRUMPLER
San Francisco
1993

The Fire Next Time II
Dewey Crumpler, 1984.
Joseph P. Lee Recreation Center gymnasium, 3rd and Newcomb Streets, Hunters Point, San Francisco, California.
Politec acrylic on concrete, 5,500 square feet.
Funded by the artist's uncle and the Mayor's Office of Community Development.

This mural is a celebration of African American culture. The arts are what make my blood circulate. I could take the images that are central to the highest achievement in cultural formation, like the Ife head—the Ife queen mother. That for me was clear. Then to go to music and take Louis Armstrong and Billie Holiday—two polarities that deal with the highest level of African American expression. And then to juxtapose Charlie Parker and Mahalia Jackson. And then to continue to do this up around this structure in a way that made these figures move through space and time. And then to place hard structural buildings next to an ancient African mud brick terracotta mosque. This polarity between the old and the new, between various aspects of these cultural offerings that this place (the cultural center) represented was at the heart of it. And to have Duke Ellington orchestrating the whole process is equivalent to Beethoven putting together the whole European high cultural thing. That was it.

DEWEY CRUMPLER
San Francisco
1993

A Celebration of African and African American Artists (also known as **Black and Tan Jam**), Dewey Crumpler, assisted by
Kermit Amenophis, Bonnie Long, and Sandra Roberts, 1984. Western Addition Cultural Center, 762 Fulton Street, San Francisco,
California. Politec acrylic on concrete, 45' x 131'. Sponsored by the Mayor's Office of Community Development.

Love, Peace and Unity, Eddie L. Edwards, 1985. Martin Luther King Jr. Elementary
School, Island and K Streets, San Diego, California. Acrylic.

Dr. King stands over an idealistic group of supporters, including a few that are
downright angelic. They are all assembled in Washington, D.C., in view of the
Washington Monument.

Bilalian Odyssey, Isaka Shamsud-Din, 1987. Portland Justice Center, Portland, Oregon. Commissioned by the Metropolitan Arts Commission. Photograph courtesy of the Regional Arts & Culture Council, Public Art Program, Portland, Oregon.

This mural deals with African American pioneers; early Portland; early Oregon; the first black woman lawyer in the state of Oregon; the Golden West Hotel (owned by blacks on Broadway in downtown Portland); Bill Pickett (the man who invented bulldogging); and Moses Harris, mountain man.

The main figure is York, who was the slave to William Clark and who traveled with the Lewis and Clark Expedition. He was an important member of the expedition, as it turned out.

ISAKA SHAMSUD-DIN
Portland
November 1999

This was the first piece that helped me realize the breadth of the audience for public work, that viewership was bigger than only the graffiti subculture, that a lot of people are looking at and considering these things being made in public spaces.

This piece was about some of the struggles and challenges that African Americans were facing, and continue to face, within their own culture, oftentimes related to compromising their identity for success or achievement. Two African American young men with haircut and clothing of the era are pulling on a crayon, trying to have ownership of a good idea or a representation that is clearly different from themselves. It's metaphorical for practices that not only African Americans but many people practice within corporate America, within academic institutions, and in daily existence, of compromising parts of who they are for the benefit of achieving a goal society sets up for us.

At the time, I was taking African American studies, beginning to consider the history and legacy of African Americans in America, starting to primitively investigate hegemony, starting to think about Western Christian patriarchal, white, capitalist society, and trying to do all that in a visual way.

At some point, while at college, I decided that I wanted to be a painter, a spray painter, and I wanted to redefine that medium. I wanted it to be recognized as a legitimate art medium. I'm still trying to continually expand the medium, not just conceptually but also technically.

I started spraypainting in '84. At the time in San Diego there really wasn't a subculture of spraypainting there. I had kinda heard about things going on in New York. I had seen the book Subway Art and I listened to the music, but it was still a pretty esoteric subculture. Hip-hop wasn't what it is now. And certainly graffiti wasn't what it is now where it's located throughout the world. I had always loved to draw, so I got the notion that I was going to start doing my drawings outside with spraypaint.

What was significant was that rather than going through the traditional tags and text-based apprenticeship, where you're doing styles, my things from the beginning were figurative. I was initially faced with defining my own imagery and practice, and even my own technical approach. There wasn't anyone there to tell me those things.

BRETT COOK
Harlem
August 1999

Why Fight for a Crayon That's Not Our Color?
Brett Cook (Dizney), 1988.
Psycho City, San Francisco, California.
Approximately 10' high.
Self-sponsored.

At Berkeley I was studying apartheid in southern Africa, considering the mass media both in America and in Africa and their portrayal of, or lack of, many of the issues and problems there, as well as the media's relationship to government. This piece was an attempt to explore and portray some of those relationships.

I've always been interested in the way text brings people into work. My work is affected by many different stimuli, and one is growing up in consumer America in the twentieth century. We all have a certain visual literacy regarding advertising and text and its relationship to imagery. I think that, being a teacher, I recognize that people have different learning styles, so text for me is another strategy to help viewers gain access to the ideas I'm dealing with.

It's oftentimes heard from graffiti writers that part of the attraction is that nonpermission aspect, that rush of being out in the middle of the night. That has never been a big draw for me. For me that was part of the price to pay to have that kind of viewership. In fact, I remember coming home in the morning from doing pieces really fatigued, physically and psychologically. It wasn't enjoyable for me. I was stressed and uncomfortable all night.

BRETT COOK

Harlem

August 1999

Apartheid, Brett Cook (Dizney), 1988. Psycho City, San Francisco, California. Approximately 10' high. Self-sponsored.

I did this piece of Cecil Fergerson because Cecil's been active for years in the community. When I was thirteen or fourteen years old, Cecil was one of the few people who was trying to get black artists exposure. He would show works in churches, libraries, people's homes—wherever. He tried to develop a support system during that period. He acquired some of my work and was real interested in it, and pushed me as well. He was very instrumental in my early development.

Anybody who knows him knows that Cecil always speaks what's on his mind, which is probably why he gets the respect he does. In 1948 he started working as a janitor at the Museum of Science and Industry, and at night he would go to the library and read books on art. A whole world opened up to him—impressionism, expressionism. In 1968 he cofounded the Black Arts Council with Claude Booker.

Cecil started as a janitor and wound up as a curatorial assistant when he retired in 1985. He was born and raised in Watts, so I did this piece at the Watts Towers Arts Center as a tribute to him.

RICHARD WYATT
Los Angeles
July 1993

Cecil, Richard Wyatt, assisted by Ian White, 1989. Watts Towers Arts Center, 1727 East 107th Street, Watts, Los Angeles, California. Acrylic on stucco. Sponsored by the Social and Public Art Resource Center. © 1989 Social and Public Art Resource Center.

Literacy
Roderick Sykes, 1989.
Los Angeles Unified
School District
Maintenance Building,
1406 South Highland
Avenue, Los Angeles,
California.
Acrylic, 10' x 20'.
Sponsored by the Social
and Public Art Resource
Center.
© 1989 Social and Public
Art Resource Center.

T*he faces are those of kids that live in the area: a Korean, a Latino, and an African American. Their faces are not happy, not sad. Beneath them is a kid sitting on the ground with a basketball. The basketball is between his legs, but he's reading a book. It's mainly to motivate the young men in this area to stop and think that they need to feed their minds.*

RODERICK SYKES
Los Angeles
April 1994

I wanted to create a project in public art that would provide training for young African American artists in this community. When I was growing up, I almost gave up becoming an artist because I had no role models. There are still almost no African American professionals being brought into the schools.

Two murals were painted involving six professional artists and four youth apprentices. This panel deals with education, self-knowledge, history, the African past, and the living Africa. The largest figure is Martin Luther King Jr. It was painted by Paul Odighizuwa, a Nigerian sculptor and painter. Among the other portraits are the Honorable Elijah Muhammed, Sister Clara Muhammad, Zora Neale Hurston, and Selaelo Maredi, a South African playwright who was living in town and visited with the youngsters on several occasions.

ISAKA SHAMSUD-DIN
Portland
November 1999

The Time Is Now, Now Is the Time (detail), Isaka Shamsud-Din and Paul Odighizuwa with youths, 1989. Martin Luther King Jr. Boulevard and Shaver, Portland, Oregon. Acrylic. Funded by the Portland Arts Commission and the Private Industry Council. Photograph courtesy of the Regional Arts & Culture Council, Public Art Program, Portland, Oregon.

Hollywood has a huge, legendary history of jazz. There have been a lot of jazz clubs as well as many artists who performed around that period of time. I couldn't put in all the artists, so in the background of the mural I created the illusion of etched names of some of the other artists, so everyone got some recognition.

RICHARD WYATT
Los Angeles
July 1993

From left to right: Chet Baker, Gerry Mulligan, Charlie (Bird) Parker, Tito Puente, Miles Davis, Ella Fitzgerald, Nat King Cole, Shelly Manne, Dizzy Gillespie, Billie Holiday, and Duke Ellington.

Hollywood Jazz 1945–1972, Richard Wyatt, 1990. Capitol Records, 1750 North Vine Street, Hollywood, California. Acrylic. Sponsored by the Los Angeles Jazz Society, City of Los Angeles Department of Cultural Affairs, and Capitol Records.

I *chose the theme. It's like the different walls of respect that are around the country in different communities. The building itself houses a swimming pool. The pool was there a long time before the building, and the community always complained about the fence around it. Finally, some kids snuck in there and drowned. Then the city came up with the money to build the building.*

For years people broke bottles against that wall, did all kinds of dumb things back there. So I wondered what could survive in that jungle. I thought of that theme and decided to see if the community would carry it. Once the work was up, nothing ever happened back there. No bottles, no graffiti, nothing. For years. Amazing.

We did it in tile instead of with paint, a slightly smaller scale, but appropriate to the architecture of the building. That's something I like to do, play with the architecture of a location, or the environment a public work goes in.

Public art is exciting because you get to jump around with different materials and different concepts. You're designing something for a specific site. They pay for it—you don't have to store it until you sell it. I put in a good twenty years doing studio stuff for galleries. I like to do that kind of stuff, too, but it's almost impossible in these times to continue in the studio. You'd be starving to death.

There's more opportunity now than there ever was. Wow. Things are jumping out there. Transit lines, Percent for Art things. All cities like tourists, and if you put art around it attracts tourism.

HORACE WASHINGTON
San Francisco
1993

Untitled (detail), Horace Washington, Seitu Din, and Kate Singleton, 1991. Martin Luther King Jr. Swimming Pool, 3rd and Carroll Streets, Bayview-Hunters Point, San Francisco, California. Ceramic tile, six panels, each 6' x 5'. Funded by the Mural Resource Program and the Mayor's Office of Community Development.

*N*ine larger-than-life African American women are rendered on a grand scale. Seated in front are educator Mary McLeod Bethune (wearing black and holding a cane), artist Alice Patrick (in the red dress), and Dr. Dorothy Height (then president of the National Council of Negro Women, wearing orange). Standing in back are Josephine Baker, Oprah Winfrey, Sarah Vaughan, and Florence Griffith-Joyner. The recent death of Florence magnifies the reason she was featured among the greatest. She showed us that black women are strong, that we can overcome obstacles, and that we can win.

ALICE PATRICK
Los Angeles
October 1999

Women Do Get Weary But They Don't Give Up
Alice Patrick, 1991. National Council of Negro Women, 3720 West 54th Street, Los Angeles, California. Acrylic on stucco, approximately 9' x 16'. Sponsored by the Social and Public Art Resource Center. © 1991 Social and Public Art Resource Center.

During the summer of 1991 the tobacco companies were targeting the black communities with billboards, television, newspaper, and magazine advertisements, as well as giving away free cigarettes. The above-mentioned agencies commissioned me to illustrate and depict the life-threatening health risks and results associated with cigarette smoking and tobacco use.

ELLIOTT PINKNEY
Compton
November 1999

Community Anti-Tobacco Mural
Elliott Pinkney, 1991. Watts Towers Arts Center, 1727 East 107th Street, Watts, Los Angeles, California. Acrylic, 40' x 8'. Commissioned by the California Department of Health Services, Tobacco Control Section, and the Los Angeles County Health Services Department Tobacco Control Program.

Most of my murals are basically about youth—trying to provide positive images and messages *in a clear way that they can understand. This one is a visual menagerie. There are African images as well as pictures of Martin Luther King Jr. and Malcolm X. There's also a TV screen split in half with one image showing people demonstrating in the 1960s and the other a little character of Arsenio Hall (a former late-night talk-show host). It is a quick little history, but in a playful and colorful enough way that kids want to spend time looking at it.*

KEITH WILLIAMS
California
May 1994

Becoming Conscious, Keith Williams, 1991. Martin Luther King Jr. Recreation Center, Orange Avenue and 19th Street, Long Beach, California. Acrylic, approximately 6' x 12'. Sponsored by the Public Corporation for the Arts.

Health Care Is a Right, Not a Privilege, A. G. Joe Stephenson, 1991. First Choice Community
Health, 1316 Broadway Boulevard SE (at Stadium), Albuquerque, New Mexico.

I bring in the Native American culture that's here because it's so rich. Most of the kids are so cut off from their heritage—all of them. That's why I try to resurrect all these images from the past. If you don't know where you came from, you don't know where you're going.

My politics and my art came together in mural painting. Working with people in their communities, all kinds of people. All I do is listen, allow them to bring something to it.

My personal philosophy is inclusive, internationalist; I look at things from a West Indian viewpoint. When I was growing up, Jamaica was still under British rule. I'd like to be considered for the color of my murals and my art rather than for the color of my skin.

JOE STEPHENSON
Albuquerque
December 1994

*took hundreds of photographs around Arizona,
from which I chose images of popular culture and ethnic diversity, education, business, transporta-
tion, and spiritual life. Included is the seal (yellow and black) for the Pima-Maricopa people as
well as various scenes from the Latino, Indigenous, African American, and European communities.*

HOWARDENA PINDELL
New York 1996

Memory: Arizona
Designed by Howardena
Pindell, fabricated by
Crovatto Mosaics of Venice,
Italy, 1991.
Sky Harbor International
Airport (Terminal 4, Level
2), Phoenix, Arizona.
Venetian smalti–glass mosaic,
10' x 14'.
Commissioned by the
Phoenix Arts Commission
through the Percent for Art
program of the City of
Phoenix Aviation
Department.
Photograph courtesy of the
Phoenix Arts Commission,
Percent for Art program,
Phoenix, Arizona.

Love Is For Everyone
Reginald LaRue Zachary
and Mary-Linn Hughes,
1992.
Minority AIDS Project,
5149 West Jefferson
Boulevard, Los Angeles,
California.
Acrylic.
Sponsored by the Social
and Public Art Resource
Center.
© 1992 Social and Public
Art Resource Center.
Photograph courtesy of
Mary-Linn Hughes.

We began work on the Minority AIDS Project (MAP) in 1990. After lengthy conversations and photo sessions with the MAP staff, clients, and community members, we designed a mural that reflected both the myriad of services provided by MAP and the "Love is for Everyone" spirit of the organization.

The most intriguing design challenge was the series of barred windows that ran through the middle of the wall. Only one window actually provided light or air to the building, and, after much discussion about security, we received permission to remove the bars and insert plywood panels. The figures in the mural, including those seen in silhouette, were drawn from black and white photos we made on site. The colorful background is inspired by "Afro traditional" quilts rooted in a distinct African American aesthetic of improvisation. Simple black line drawings within the white squares of the quilt represent MAP services: food, clothing, housing, education, counseling. Each of the quilt shapes bears the name, written in silver, of a community member who has died of AIDS. We wrote the text at the bottom of the mural to bring home the issue of AIDS on a personal level.

At the same time we were painting the mural, MAP shared the same building with the Unity Fellowship Church. Sundays were among our favorite days to paint because of the incredible gospel music and words of encouragement that would pour forth from the congregation. We are grateful to have had the opportunity to work with MAP, the church, and the community to design and paint this mural.

MARY-LINN HUGHES AND REGINALD ZACHARY
Los Angeles
1997

In August 1991, African American motorist Rodney King was videotaped being beaten by several Los Angeles policemen. The video was shown on news programs around the world. In April 1992, all four of the police officers involved were acquitted of wrongdoing by an all-white jury in Simi Valley, just outside L.A. Almost immediately, many sections of Los Angeles exploded in violence. Noni Olabisi's first mural captures the anguish, frustration, and impatience of the black community over the persistence of police brutality and injustice.

Freedom Won't Wait
Noni Olabisi, 1992. 54th Street and Western Avenue, Los Angeles, California. Acrylic, approximately 15' x 25'. Sponsored by the Social and Public Art Resource Center. © 1992 Social and Public Art Resource Center.

Marcus Garvey, Ivan Watkins with Carter, Frick, Roosevelt, Westlake, and Claremont students, 1992. Downtown Oakland, California. Sponsored by Project Yes of the East Bay Conservation Corps.

Ida B. Wells, Ivan Watkins with Carter, Frick, Roosevelt, Westlake, and Claremont students, 1992. Downtown Oakland, California. Sponsored by Project Yes of the East Bay Conservation Corps.

These two strong portraits (above) and others of Sojourner Truth and Malcolm X appeared on a bonded-up building targeted for redevelopment in downtown Oakland.

Marcus Garvey established the Universal Negro Improvement Association (UNIA) in Jamaica in 1914, moving to New York in 1916. The growth of UNIA, and the popularity of Garvey, were unparalleled in African American history. The organization's militant program protested the carving up of most of Africa by the European nations, and the brutal treatment of the African people. The strongest protest, however, was made against the oppression of blacks in the United States. This was during a period of hard economic conditions, mass migration to the North, brutal lynchings and race riots, and Klu Klux Klan terrorism. Garvey believed blacks would never find justice in countries where they constituted a minority of the population, hence UNIA's central slogan—"Back to Africa."

Born a slave in Mississippi, Ida B. Wells became one of the preeminent crusaders for African American rights and women's suffrage. In 1891, in Memphis, she cofounded *Free Speech,* a militant journal in which she denounced local whites for lynching black men. Her printing press was destroyed by a white mob while she was lecturing in the north. Her response was to launch an international campaign against lynching and to intensify her efforts against racial discrimination.

This is a motivational mural designed to encour- age young people. It depicts men and women who had visions to become great, then went about setting these dreams in motion.

ELLIOTT PINKNEY
Los Angeles
1997

Visions and Motion

Elliott Pinkney, assisted by Sam Barrow and Lloyd Godoy, 1993. Community Youth Sports and Arts Foundation, 4828 Crenshaw Boulevard, Los Angeles, California. Acrylic. Sponsored by the Social and Public Art Resource Center. © 1993 Social and Public Art Resource Center.

This project was done for the lobby of a new wing. There were two big arches, so I wanted to do a piece that reflected the architecture and also the people who live around there. If you stand at a certain angle, you get the illusion of looking through the building. Pictured in this panel—one of two—is artist May Sun. [In 1996 Wyatt collaborated with her on City of Dreams, River of History, a permanent installation at Union Train Station in downtown L.A.] The other people—the black family are friends of mine and typical of some of the people who use this center.

RICHARD WYATT
Los Angeles
July 1993

White Memorial Hospital Project
Richard Wyatt, 1994.
White Memorial
Medical Center (interior),
1720 Cesar Chavez Avenue,
Boyle Heights, Los Angeles,
California.
Acrylic, two panels.
Sponsored by White Memorial
Medical Center.

Return to the Light
Charles Freeman, 1994.
Carlota Boulevard and
Avenue 41, Highland Park,
Los Angeles, California.
Acrylic.
Sponsored by the Social and
Public Art Resource Center.
© 1994 Social and Public Art
Resource Center.

Realizing that our spiritual destiny is to Return to the Light, *I was inspired to reflect that in this work. We are captive in this material world for a brief time, and most of us become ensnared in the traps of those conditions of darkness (hatred, greed, envy, etc.). It becomes imperative that we work to unfold the powers of wisdom, purity, and goodness. Therefore, you see depicted two of the most prevalent social ills of our time—the senseless killing of our young people and the insensitivity to people without adequate shelter (young and old). The Shaman or Curandero in the center represents a healthy state of wholeness. Cesar Chavez represents vision or sole purpose. The elderly are symbols of rich experience and wisdom. The ethereal images of Pancho Villa and Emiliano Zapata signify strength and courage. All these characteristics become essential to our ultimate destination.*

CHARLES FREEMAN
Los Angeles
1997

I *found out through a friend of mine that some people were coming from Germany, and that they were going to do a mural. It was a group of eight or nine kids. They were staying in South Central and Compton. It was after everything had happened with the riots. We spent a lot of time with them before we did the mural. We took them around to show them the city.*

Those kids were full of energy. It was such a refreshing change from typical white people in California, or even Los Angeles. It would have been a whole different thing with people being more apprehensive. These guys were just following their hearts, I guess.

I came up with the theme of Los Angeles. I put in a downtown cityscape, Hollywood and South Central. I also did a helicopter shining down on a low rider. The piece was split into two sides with the guys from California doing one side and the guys from East Germany doing the other. We just blended them together. They came with their style and we came with our style. It merged really cool.

The direction I'm going in, I'm trying to take my graffiti art to another level. When a normal person looks at what we do, you see the letters and they're hard to read. It's like any other type of art. You have to study the history and know what it's all about so that you can understand it. When hip-hop and all that came into my life, it showed me that people involved in it basically had no boundaries. It's like a journey.

TOONS
California
1997

L.A.-Berlin Exchange
Tony Martin (Toons), DruOne,
A-One, Mith, Hex, and several
German youths, 1994.
Spraycan.
South Vermont Avenue at 88th
Street, Los Angeles, California.

We want an immediate end to POLICE BRUTALITY and MURDER OF BLACK people!
We want land, bread, housing, education, clothing, justice, and peace.
ALL POWER TO THE PEOPLE!

The statements above are taken from the Ten Point Program and Platform created by Dr. Huey P. Newton and Bobby Seale, founders in 1966 of the Black Panther Party for Self-Defense. This mural is dedicated to the fearless men and women who committed their lives and dared to be free. To protect, when lynching seemed to be the order of the day, the Black Panther Party armed themselves with law books and guns, reading their rights as citizens (including their Constitutional right to bear arms) and patrolling their neighborhoods against police brutality. And to serve, the Black Panther Party created and operated nationwide programs such as breakfasts for school children, free food programs, free medical clinics, and free clothing, and it set up independent schools for self-determination.

This mural commemorates the Black Panther Party and its unforgettable contribution to African American history. And the mural is dedicated to all political prisoners, as well as those who lost their lives fighting for truth, justice, and freedom. The spirit of these brothers and sisters cannot and will not die.

ALL POWER TO THE PEOPLE!

NONI OLABISI
Los Angeles
1997

To Protect and Serve
Noni Olabisi, 1996.
11th Avenue and Jefferson
Boulevard, South Los
Angeles, California.
Acrylic, approximately
40' x 12".
Funded through donations
and the Social and Public
Art Resource Center.

Portrait of My People #619, Willie Middlebrook, 1995. MetroRail Green Line Station, Avalon Boulevard at the 105 Freeway, Watts, Los Angeles, California. Computer-generated photo-mural on porcelain enamel tiles, 14' x 24'. Sponsored by Metropolitan Transit Authority Metro Art.

My specialty is mainly photography. I decided to do a mixture of photography and digital to achieve the piece, my first mural. I'd been using a computer for a long time—for basic layout and design, nothing photorealistic.

Right next to the mural is 118th Street in Watts. At 118th Street and Avalon is where the 1965 riots started. So it was very significant that the mural was there. I had a choice. I could either have made a very dark mural that talked about the things that went on back then, or do the type of piece I came up with.

There are thirty-three people in the mural, and they are all people who have been very involved in developing the arts in the community. Since I grew up in that area, I decided to put in people who motivated me when I was coming up as a young artist. There are people there who I absolutely love, and there are people there who I absolutely hate. In some way they all affected my life.

John Outterbridge, Stanley Wilson, and I did the station as a partnership. John did the pyramids and Stanley did the diamonds on the floor, the benches, and the metal reliefs. John and Stanley are both in the mural, and so are Cecil and Miriam Fergerson. I had always heard about the Fergersons, and then I got to work with them. They put on exhibitions. I also put in their son Kinte, because he had just curated his first show on hip-hop at Southwest College. Then you have people like singer Etta James, younger visual artists Tony Love and Cedric Adams, jazz greats Buddy Collette and Horace Tapscott. Charles White is there—when he came here from back east, he had a lot to do with developing younger artists. Others include Van Slater, who ran the art department at Compton College, Ivan Dixon, poet Wanda Coleman, Jepson Powell, Father Ouidee, writer/poet Kamau Daaood, Darnette Mitchum (a photography instructor at Compton College), painter Bill Pajaud, Betye Saar, Elliott Pinkney, Cora Bryant (a musician who has her own band), Ojenke, Rozzell and Roderick Sykes of St. Elmo Village, Pat Ward Williams, and Ruth Waddy, "godmother of African American artists." Ruth worked with Samella Lewis on the original book Black Artists on Art and she was influential in Art West, a group of African American artists that lasted almost twenty years. These are all people who did a lot for the community and in different ways affected my life.

WILLIE MIDDLEBROOK
Los Angeles
August 1999

The project began when Rafael Elementary School changed its name to Rosa Parks. Keith Jackson, San Francisco School Board president, was instrumental in the name change. He commissioned my center, Culture on the Corner, to do the mural.

It was a community effort. We just got anyone that wanted to participate, including students from the San Francisco Art Institute, the Academy of Art, and San Francisco State University.

The mural was a good tool for making the children aware of what Rosa Parks was about, what she stood for. She came and christened the finished mural.

Culture on the Corner is a group of artists that work in the Western Addition with kids. Everything we do we involves children. I take art and use it as a communication tool. This is Culture on the Corner's seventeenth year. Much respect to all the other artists involved.

MEL SIMMONS
San Francisco
October 1999

Now and Then
Mel Simmons, Zero Bey, Santie Hucklely, Searcey Ryles, and Culture on the Corner, 1996.
Rosa Parks Elementary School, Hollis at Ellis, San Francisco, California.
Acrylic on stucco, 20' x 26'.
Funded by the San Francisco School Board.

Evolution of the Spirit
Elliott Pinkney, 1997.
Los Angeles Southwest
College Library, 1600 West
Imperial Highway, Los
Angeles, California.
Sponsored by the Fox Hills
Mall Scholarship Fund,
LASC Associated Student
Organization, L.A. Southwest
Community Foundation,
LASC Academic Senate.

This mural was designed to do several things: to avoid dating the image by using abstract human figures, to show ethnic diversity, to celebrate thirty years of academic excellence in arts, music, literature.

ELLIOTT PINKNEY
Compton
November 1999

Portrait of reggae legend Bob Marley (1945–1981). The text is from *Uprising,* the last album released in Marley's lifetime. The album was an instant success and was followed by a major European tour.

Untitled
Senay Dennis (Refa), 1999. Spraycan. Haight-Ashbury, San Francisco, California. Self-sponsored.

For this particular project the sponsors wanted a work of public art that reflected the African American experience in Colorado, not necessarily a direct historical narrative.

In my mind, the two central figures in the mural are creative representations of Barney Ford and Aunt Clara Brown, founding members of the state of Colorado. They represent the male and female archetypes of excellence that African American pioneers brought to the Old West. They symbolize all those dynamic people who had the guts to make the move from the South to the West.

Barney Ford escaped from slavery and ended up a wealthy entrepreneur, owning hotels with his wife, first in Central America and then in Denver. In the late 1800s his Denver hotel was known as the number-one hotel in the West. The president used to stay there back then. Barney Ford was a stationmaster for the Underground Railroad. He and several of his colleagues agitated to have laws changed in Colorado so that Blacks could vote in the state.

Aunt Clara Brown was a slave too. When she was thirty-five, her husband and children were all sold to different places; she lost her entire family. She was fifty-five when she bought her way out of slavery. It took her another thirty years to finally locate her daughter, but she never found her husband and other children. Clara Brown paid her way West on one of those wagon trains by washing and cleaning for the prospectors. When she got to Colorado she started a laundry business. She also became instrumental in the church and owned a small hotel. She became wealthy; with her money she bought a lot of people out of slavery and brought them out West, including thirty-four of her relatives. She helped many families get set up, regardless of what race they were.

In order to do justice to the dynamic stories of the African American pioneers that immigrated to Colorado, I used several artistic techniques in the fabrication of this mural to make the piece entertaining. It is a combination of painted surfaces on aluminum and bulletproof glass, as well as cast bronze relief sculpture.

MARCUS AKINLANA
New Orleans
September 1999

Mile High and Rising
Marcus Akinlana, 1999.
Denver International Airport,
Jeppesen Terminal, Denver.
Mixed media.
Funded by the Mayor's Office of Art,
Culture and Film and administered
by ULOZI Arts Center.

I started looking at all the different crews, hanging out at different spots and checking out the scene in 1987, but I've actually been painting since '95. A lot of people from that time period give me respect because I was around then. They say I'm a new-school artist with an old-school feel. I try to have motion in my style, to have it fluid. I don't like styles where it's all contained within, hard-edged. My pieces have to have long lines, movement, interlocking. I'm taking sculpture classes, which is why I'm getting more into 3-D lettering. I want it to look more like a sculpture piece. At the same time, I like to go back and forth between 2-D and 3-D, not get too involved in one style.

RICARDO RICHEY
San Francisco
December 1999

Apex, Ricardo Richey (Apex), 1999. 5th and Folsom, San Francisco, California. Spraycan. Self-sponsored.

Getting to Know You
Elliott Pinkney, 1999.
Sativa Los Angeles
County Water District,
2015 East Hatchway
Street, Compton,
California.
Acrylic, 8' x 24'.
Commissioned by the
Sativa L.A. County
Water District.

This mural replaces an earlier mural I painted (Community Heroes) in 1990. The imagery and symbols in this one represent the black and Latino cultures, using words to create understanding and bridge the gap of misunderstanding.

ELLIOTT PINKNEY
Compton
November 1999

Murals 1967–Present: South

Portraits of more than two dozen artists, musicians, professionals, craftsmen, and politicians, including Louis Armstrong, Leadbelly, Mahalia Jackson, Clementine Hunter, Jelly Roll Morton, Dr. James Derham (the first recognized black physician in America), and Alexander Pierre Tureaud (a pioneering civil rights attorney). The mural also portrays significant events in Louisiana history.

I *was chair of the Fine Arts Department here at Southern and Professor Hubbard was chair of the Fine Arts Department at Baton Rouge. These are brother and sister institutions. Mr. Hubbard came up with the idea that we ought to do something on Louisiana. We thought that the impact would be far-reaching if the mural dealt with the different aspects of what were then called 'Negro Art' and 'The Negro Community.' We had to do a tremendous amount of research in order to do it.*

New Orleans might be considered the Cradle of Jazz, so we wanted that to be high-lighted. But we also wanted the public to realize that we do have people who have made other contributions, some of whom even today most people don't know.

For example, there's only been one black governor in these United States. Period. And it just so happens it was right here. Pinckney Benton Stewart Pinchback. He's represented in the center. He only was acting governor, between December 9, 1872 and January 13, 1873. Then we have Oscar Dunn, who is right next to the governor. Oscar Dunn was Lieutenant Governor for four years (1868–1871), the first black to hold an executive office in America.

That large central figure represents Freedom, Justice, and Self-Determination. He symbolizes the young blacks active in the Movement of the 1960s.

JACK JORDAN
New Orleans
June 1999

Contributions of Blacks to Louisiana History, Jack Jordan and Jean Paul Hubbard, 1975. Southern University, Education Building, 6400 Press Drive, New Orleans. Oil on canvas. Funded by grants.

The mural was done to commemorate the one-hundredth anniversary of the school. At the top are Tuskegee founder Booker T. Washington and three other former presidents. One large area is dedicated to the great scientist George Washington Carver and another section to the airmen of Tuskegee. During World War II the U.S. armed forces were still segregated and there were no black pilots. They had to be trained at Tuskegee Institute. There was a quota system such that the school was allowed to graduate 10 percent of the number of white pilots. Some of the airmen are still alive and meet to this day.

We used imagery to tell different kinds of stories. For example, there's a motif about the sculpture at Tuskegee that was commented on by writer Ralph Ellison. He considered whether the founder was lifting up or pulling down the shade of ignorance over his people.

NELSON STEVENS
Springfield, Massachusetts
October, 1993

Centennial Vision
Nelson Stevens, assisted
by John Kendrick and
John Sims, 1979–80.
Tuskegee University
Administration Building,
Tuskegee, Alabama.
12' x 30'.
Sponsored by Tuskegee
University.

From Montgomery to Memphis 1955–1968, John Feagin, assisted by Zakee Safeeullah Fishoe, 1980. Dexter Avenue King Memorial Baptist Church (interior), 454 Dexter Avenue, Montgomery, Alabama. Acrylic, 10' x 47'. Sponsored by the Dexter Avenue King Memorial Baptist Church.

I have been in Montgomery since 1954. I was fortunate enough to have been here when Martin Luther King was here. All through the civil rights movement and leading up to 1979, I had been thinking about doing a mural. I had never seen anyone do a mural, but I had read about the Mexican mural painters in college. This wall was always here, empty and fascinating. We wanted to commemorate Reverend King because this was his first church, his only church really.

We started out with a 10' x 10' area. When we put the first couple of figures on the wall, we realized that in order to tell the story as we wanted to tell it, we would have to use more space. We just moved down the wall as the ideas would come and the story unfolded. We had to stop because we ran out of wall!

I'm basically an abstract painter and I love the colors and the movement of the first section. Most people are fascinated by this section. They like seeing Reverend King at various stages of his career, first as a young man with no furls on his brow to the last picture, when he is about to go to Memphis. You can see how his expression changes.

I also love the last section with the children. We had to paint that section twice. I painted my son and some members of the church. The deacons did not approve because we didn't use all the children. They didn't want us to show favoritism. We painted that out and I painted my godchild in the center, where my son had been. I painted my niece and nephew on the bottom. They're not members of the church.

We had a lot of information, and we tried to pick the best possible to use. I guess that's why mural painting is a lot of work. They're fulfilling when you get them done. I have no inclination or desire to do another mural. I love painting and ceramics, but I want to keep it small.

JOHN FEAGIN
Montgomery
June 1999

This was the first community mural painted in Memphis. It traces the history of black music, especially the blues. The imagery includes an African tribal horn, a piano keyboard, guitar strings, and several portraits. Among those pictured are W. C. Handy, the Father of the blues, and Boss Crump, a notorious Memphis politician. William Christopher Handy was born in Florence, Alabama, in the late nineteenth century. In 1909 Handy wrote a campaign song for Boss Crump, which he then reworked and turned into the classic, *Memphis Blues*. He eventually wrote one hundred fifty songs, and performed at President Eisenhower's inaugural ball.

A Tribute to Beale Street, Charles Davis, George Hunt and forty art students from Shelby State Community College, 1980. Second and Beale Streets, Memphis, Tennessee. Funded by a federal summer youth program.

Christia Adair was a politician, an early leader of the women's suffrage movement. She served as president of the Houston NAACP for twelve years.

The Adair mural is involved with the shotgun houses because Mrs. Adair lived in the Third Ward—over in shotgun country. She worked to benefit young people. She encouraged a lot of kids to go to college, to get out of the ghetto. She was an inspiration.

So the Adair mural depicts aspects of her life. The role her grandparents played in inspiring her. You see the grandparents as ghosts. They are rising from the barn. Below the barn are the donkey and the cow. It was a farm atmosphere that she was born in. The well is there. The chopping block is there. The symbols of the rural are all there on the left.

Then there is the meaning for her of education. She became a teacher. On the right you see Mrs. Adair and a junior-high-school club cleaning an old cemetery. She's telling them who the people were. That was their research—to find out who these people in their community were.

Her church was built on the meaning of the morning star. So you see the church above her head and she rises out of that as a spirit.

JOHN BIGGERS
Houston
November 1994

The Adair Mural
John Biggers, 1982.
Christia V. Adair Park, 15107 Cullen
Boulevard, Houston, Texas.
Acrylic, 6' x 36'.

Voyage to Soulsville *is a metaphorical depiction of the African diaspora expressed through signs, symbols, and icons. These expressions signify the exuberance and reverence of a culture.*

JOHN FISHER
Austin
November 1999

Voyage to Soulsville (originally called **Sesquicentennial**), John Fisher, 1986 (restored in 1997–99). George Washington Carver Library, 1161 Angelina Street, Austin, Texas. Acrylic, 30' x 70'. Funded by the city of Austin. Photograph © BJ Smiley Goins.

Before Dawn, designed by Romare Bearden, 1989. Public Library of Charlotte and Mecklenburg County, 310 North Tryon Street, Charlotte, North Carolina. Italian mosaic tiles, 9' x 13'6". Funded by the Charlotte Observer and the library. Photograph courtesy of the Public Library of Charlotte and Mecklenburg County. © Romare Bearden/VAGA, New York/DACS, London, 2000.

The mural represents memories of life in Charlotte and Mecklenburg County, where Bearden lived as a child.

Triumphant Celebration, Calvin Jones, 1990. 321 Edgewood Avenue, Atlanta. 27' x 75'. Commissioned by the National Black Arts Festival.

The painting explores the relationship of pop, jazz, classical, and rap music as it relates to the visual arts. The bold colors reflect life, music, and the African influence on everyday society. We both like music a lot but listen to different types. We wanted to examine the impact of music on our culture.

KEVIN COLE
Atlanta
1994

The concept is in keeping with the theme of the National Black Arts Festival—the multifaceted contributions of African American arts to the world. The festival is held every two years. The mural was commissioned through a competition. That year William Walker was the juror.

I started with one of the most recognizable symbols, the American flag. Underneath all this other stuff you see traces of the stars and stripes and a ribbon of the red, white, and blue. Where it is white on the flag I painted strips of kente cloth. Where it's red on the flag, going all the way through, became the symbols and color of calabash. In African tradition the calabash, or what you may call the diamonds and pyramid shapes, are the symbols of life and death—both of them being positive. So that which was red on the flag, I changed to black and brown calabash, the colors of our pigmentation. I represented those contributions in music with the gospel, the blues, the classical dance, the traditional African dance, ceremonial dance, and the Ife deity of creativity and song.

For the visual or plastic arts I used the square mounted on the easel, because I am a painter. Also Elizabeth Catlett's mother and child to represent sculpture. Dealing with people of letters and writing, I just did a book. In the area where I sign it off, I put in the first passage of "Lift Every Voice and Sing," the Negro National Anthem of James Weldon Johnson.

CALVIN JONES
Chicago
1994

Rhythm Nation: The Near Future, Kevin Cole with high school student Norman Hill, 1990. Georgia State University, Urban Life Building, Atlanta, Georgia. 96" x 94" x 9". Sponsored by Georgia State University and Georgia Council for the Arts. Photograph courtesy of the artist.

Ascension (left) and **Origins** (right)
John Biggers and James Biggers Jr.,
1990–92.
Winston-Salem State University
O'Kelly Library (atrium).
Acrylic on canvas, each 30' x 15'.
Sponsored by Winston-Salem
Delta Fine Arts, Inc., partially
funded by the National
Endowment for the Arts and the
North Carolina Arts Council.

Ascension draws its imagery from the African American experience. The overall concept is of the family emerging from Dante's hell, ascending stairs toward the light without faltering. Biggers hoped to inspire students entering the library with a vision of ascending, rising above what had gone before.

Origins continues John Biggers's exploration of African myth with figures symbolizing the creation of day and night. At the top a phoenixlike form emerges from the darkness, creating pools of reflected light, representing the sun's daily appearance. Isis and Nephthys, two female Egyptian deities associated with the polarities of day and night respectively, frame the mural's lower half.

There were Indian people who were here (at Hampton) in the beginning. There were African people here in the beginning. And there was Armstrong who first built the church, which had all kinds of meaning. So I wanted to show the African mother, the Indian mother, and the church mother. These three became the trinity, the foundation of the Hampton mural.

Also, in my mind was this universal, ancient concept of the meaning of the rivers. Hampton is surrounded by water so I felt that one mural centered around the great tree growing out of the wetlands—the rivulets, the little creeks, the salt marshes and the rest—would be an ideal thing to give us a feeling of time and space. Now to transform the tree into a spiritual concept of growth and transition. The tree has always been a highway for the spirit. A symbol of the spirit. Where the limbs grow out like a cross is a crossroads into reality. And then, as you go above, you move toward the celestial. This is how I'm trying to use the tree that is actually the Emancipation Tree, where literally the first classes were taught on campus (and where residents of Hampton gathered to hear the reading of the Emancipation Proclamation).

Interiorly you see the Great Mother that represents the tree. I'm trying to show a mystery, the inner meaning of things with the mother in the tree. You have to look very, very carefully to see her inside the trunk. However, she's there. The tree of life is one of the oldest symbols in mythology. The fruit nourished us just as our mother nourished us.

JOHN BIGGERS
From *Stories of Illumination and Growth: John Biggers's Hampton Murals,* videocassette, 1992

House of the Turtle and **Tree House**
John Biggers, assisted by James Biggers Jr., 1990–92.
Hampton University, William R. and Norma B. Harvey Library, Hampton, Virginia.
Acrylic on canvas, each 20' x 10'.
Sponsored by Hampton University. In the collection of Hampton University Museum, Hampton, Virginia.

House of the Turtle

Tree House

This piece was designed to imitate the old shipbuilding technique of using multiple plates to create a complete surface. The grid pattern is the major unifying compositional element used throughout this work. The pattern is used aesthetically and symbolically because it is fundamental in the layout of a village, a city, a quilt, or a complex idea structure. The grid becomes symbolic of unity while allowing the possibility of diversity within its parts.

The mural is a visual narrative of the city's history in a progression from discovery to present-day references. The second panel makes reference to our musical heritage and the founding of the great form known as jazz, acknowledging the likes of Louis Armstrong, Buddy Bolden, and Danny Barker (a great musician and friend). It references "Storyville," the New Orleans Red Light District, the plantation system, and the spirit that survived in spite of that system.

The third and last panel refers to early river commerce and contemporary New Orleans. Cotton, coffee, the Super Dome, the Mardi Gras Indian, Saint Louis Cathedral, and the Twin Bridges across the river are all woven into the visual quilt of this panel.

The three panels that make up River Spirit are both two- and three-dimensional. The work is simultaneously narrative in its figuration and abstractly nonfigurative. If you are below the work parallel to its surface, what you will see is a totally abstract three-dimensional piece. When the mural is approached straight on, all the three-dimensional elements will disappear into the composition and allow the painted trompe l'oeil effects to dominate the visual field. Because of these visual contradictions, the viewer can become involved in a complex visual game of what is real and what is illusion.

Much of my work is based on the concepts of jazz improvisation. Not in imitation of the music, but to use the music's creative structural form to realize a visual idea. I replace the cacophony of auditory counterpoint with color, texture, pattern, and the other elements that constitute the visual language. I want my work to evoke the spiritual feel generated when one hears the jazz and spirituals constructed out of a culture of suffering/celebration.

JOHN SCOTT
New Orleans
August 1999

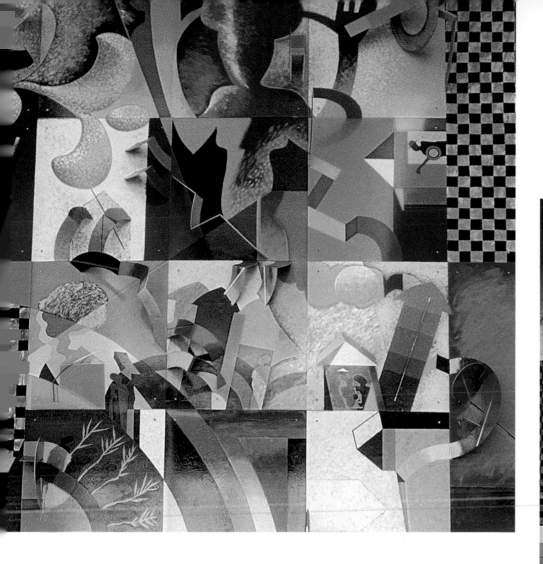

River Spirit
John Scott, 1996.
Port of New Orleans Administration Building, New Orleans.
Painted aluminum, three panels, 13' x 40'.
Sponsored by the City of New Orleans.

Louis Armstrong and His Heavenly All-Star Band
Richard C. Thomas, assisted by local art students, 1997.
New Orleans International Airport, Parabola Lobby, New Orleans, Louisiana.
28' x 41'.

Features twenty-seven local musicians, including Fats Domino, Professor Longhair, Louis Armstrong, Harry Connick Jr., and Jelly Roll Morton.

I wanted to understand jazz better, the whole concept of what was jazz. What I found was that religion and spirituality had a lot to do with the shaping of the music, not that it happened in a church necessarily. The church had an influence because it was about the celebration of life and death. It was music that expressed a yearning for freedom, the expression of African Americans who wanted to be free.

The fact that it was the first original art form in America, and that it happened here in New Orleans, really excites me. I fell in love with the whole idea of jazz. I went out and bought a horn and started to teach myself to play jazz.

In the 1920s and 1930s, there was a musician in every household, and certain individuals emerged. It's what I consider a purely African thing to challenge each other, to see who is the best or better. If you look at the Ashanti, the men show off to see who is the most handsome. In jazz it's about who can play louder or play higher notes.

Largely because of slavery, there was so much of our heritage and culture that we lost. In New Orleans we started developing new things. We started synthesizing ideas. It's like the whole idea of gumbo. Everything down here in New Orleans is pretty much like that. It's a mixture of a lot of different ingredients. But what you end up with is this awesome flavor, this awesome goodness. And that's what the music's like. That's what the food is like. And I'm trying to make the visual art like that.

RICHARD THOMAS
New Orleans
June 1999

The Museum had an exhibition called African Visions: Sacred Art and Ceremony of the Basotho, *featuring photographs by Gary Van Wyk. He lived among the Basotho people in Lesotho, South Africa, for many years, and, starting as a child, took photographs of their lifestyle. The exhibition was mainly dealing with the women, who paint murals as a way of praying to their ancestors. This mural was inspired by that exhibit.*

We started the mural program for many reasons: to make a difference in the community, to bridge the gap between African Americans and the museum, to try to knock down that negative image (thirty years ago blacks could only come to the museum on certain days and during certain hours), and to educate children about our collection.

It began in the summer of 1994 as an outreach program for the exhibition Jacob Lawrence: The Migration Series. *Although the exhibition itself did not include murals, Jacob Lawrence has completed many murals across the United States. The Museum in conjunction with the Birmingham Community Schools and P.I.N.G. (Partnership in Neighborhood Growth) sponsored an area youth mural project. The students, from elementary to high school, developed a concept and design for a mural based on their study of Jacob Lawrence. The murals were unveiled at a community reception. The overwhelmingly positive community response led us to continue the program.*

TOBY RICHARDS, MURAL PROGRAM DIRECTOR
Birmingham
June 1999

Untitled
Chris Clark and local youths, 1997. Tuxedo Community Center, 20th Place and Avenue Q, Birmingham, Alabama. Acrylic. Sponsored by the Birmingham Museum of Art Community Mural Project.

Murals 1967–Present: Mid-Atlantic

As a freshman art student at Howard University I was encouraged by Dr. James A. Porter, artist, scholar, and chairman of the art department. I was asked to be a member of a mural painting project which was coordinated by a visiting artist named Hughie Lee-Smith, a painter of the Harlem Renaissance era, and Dr. Jeff R. Donaldson of the art department. I painted four murals throughout the city.

The "style" that I used to paint the four murals was greatly influenced by renowned African American artist Jacob Lawrence. I selected my subject matter and constructed my compositions as a result of spiritual and personal experiences which provoked deep inner feelings of my heritage. The use of geometric patterns with an interplay of figures suggested movement without a realistic rendition. The color scheme of pure, vibrant colors with a mixture of monochromatic colors symbolized the subtle but complex environment that I attempted to depict. The murals also portray a blend of African patterns with a gentle touch of contemporary shapes and designs.

JAMES A. PADGETT
Wilberforce, Ohio
October 1999

Fine Arts, Art, Music, Drama, Past and Present (gone), James A. Padgett, 1968. Fine Arts Building (exterior), Howard University, Washington, D.C. 24' x 36'. Photograph courtesy of the artist.

The Aspects of Music
James A. Padgett, 1969. Anacostia Museum, Smithsonian Institute, Washington, D.C. 20' x 30'. Photograph courtesy of the artist.

The Church of the Advocate is in the heart of North Philadelphia. It used to be an upper-middle-class white community back in the 1940s until it changed over and became all black. The church is one of those monumental cathedrals, like a small-scale Notre Dame. When the civil rights movement came through, the rector then, Father Paul Washington—recognized around the country as an advocate of social change—decided to let the Black Power Conference (with Stokely Carmichael and H. Rap Brown) be held there. From that time on his church became an oasis for interactive minority experiences.

The church had these beautiful stained glass windows with traditional European figures. Father Washington asked himself how the church could represent its community in a way that would be beneficial to the religious aspect and the political aspect at the same time. We came up with the idea of a mural using verses from the Old Testament that would give credence to the goals of the civil rights movement.

This panel relates to Isaiah 40:3: "The voice cried, 'Prepare ye the way of the Lord.'" My parallel quote was: "The voices of Robeson, King, Malcolm, and Mohammad prepared the way."

RICHARD WATSON
Philadelphia
June 1999

Untitled, Clarence Wood and Gary Smalls, directors, with local youths and artists, 1971 (repainted in 1973). James Rhoads School, 50th and Parrish Streets, Philadelphia, Pennsylvania. Sponsored by the Philadelphia Museum of Art's Department of Urban Outreach.

A backdrop of black liberation colors with portraits of Marian Anderson, the Jackson Five, Shirley Chisholm, Adam Clayton Powell, Muhammad Ali, and others.

Untitled (panel 10)
Richard Watson, 1973–76.
One of fourteen panels by Richard
Watson and Walter Edmonds.
Church of the Advocate (interior),
18th and Diamond Streets,
North Philadelphia, Pennsylvania.
Acrylic on wood, one of
fourteen panels, materials
donated by the church.
Photograph courtesy of the artist.

A tribute to jazz, the people and music, which was a tradition on Baltimore's Pennsylvania Avenue fifty years ago.

Baltimore Uproar, Romare Bearden (designer), 1982. Upton subway station (mezzanine), Baltimore, Maryland. Venetian mosaic tile. Sponsored by the MTA. © Romare Bearden/VAGA, New York/DACS, London, 2000.

The King Mural
Don Miller, 1986.
Martin Luther King Jr.
Memorial Library,
901 G Street, NW,
Washington, D.C.
Oil on canvas, 7' x 56'.
Sponsored by the D.C.
Public Library
Board of Trustees.

The making of The King Mural *was the culmination of many things. At an early age I began taking satisfaction in depicting heroes who had made an impact on the life of black Americans, with particular attention to people who had gone against the status quo and tried to change things and make them better for our folks.*

The mural attempts to depict the origins of Dr. Martin Luther King Jr., starting out with his strong, loving family. Below them is depicted the church where his father was pastor, his grandfather was pastor, and where he later became copastor with his father. It takes him through his college years and depicts the major intellectual and political thinkers who influenced him, Dr. Benjamin Hayes and Mohandas Gandhi.

I approached this mural somewhat in the way Diego Rivera, Siqueiros, and Orozco approached a mural. Its purpose was to educate all levels of people, including those who might be illiterate and who can look at the events and hopefully draw knowledge from them.

The mural goes on to depict Dr. King in jail. He was jailed twenty-nine times and I show him in jail beside his close companion Ralph Abernathy. I show the leaders of the Southern Christian Leadership Conference who worked with him in the struggle to overcome segregation and to change the political balance in the south by registering black voters and encouraging them to vote.

The most tragic and emotional scene in the mural is a depiction of four little girls who were killed in a church bombing in 1963 in Birmingham just three weeks after the famous march on Washington where Dr. King gave his speech about equality, expressing his wish that people would judge his children by the content of their character, not by the color of their skin. I feel very strongly about that event and I have put that as one of the main episodes in the history of the struggle for racial justice. . . .

It shows some of the martyrs—there were many other martyrs in the struggle, but I have selected seven to paint in this mural in addition to the four girls and Dr. King himself. Another very important scene in the mural depicts three U.S. Marines having just torched a Vietnamese village and they are walking away from it. This exemplifies Dr. King's strong opposition to the U.S. participation in the Vietnam War.

DON MILLER
From an interview on Jamaican radio

This is a portrait of Philadelphia's celebrated death-row political prisoner, convicted of killing a policeman in 1982 in a trial marked by police misconduct, a judge notorious for his pro-prosecution bias, and an ineffective defense. Many famous people have publicly called for a new trial, from academic Cornel West to Hollywood personalities Oliver Stone, Paul Newman, and Mike Farrell, from Jesse Jackson to Nelson Mandela. In 1992, well-known trial lawyer Leonard Weinglass was recruited by Jamal's family and friends to take over as lead counsel. Rallies have been held in Mumia Abu-Jamal's behalf all over the world. His case has become a rallying cry for those opposed to injustice and the death penalty.

Before the incident in which Jamal interceded on his brother's behalf as he was being beaten by the police officer who ended up dead, Jamal had no criminal record. He was a politically active journalist who had been heard on National Public Radio, the National Black Network, and local Philadelphia stations. He had been elected chair of the Philadelphia chapter of the Association of Black Journalists. In 1969, at age fifteen, Jamal became a founding member of the local Black Panther Party after being beaten, threatened with a gun, kicked in the face, and called "nigger" by police in connection with various peaceful protest activities.

Mumia Abu-Jamal, Bennie, Paul, and Edna of Family Ethiopia, 1995. Allegheny and 21st Street, North Philadelphia, Pennsylvania.

Black Family Reunion 1991, Dietrich Adonis and Jane Golden, 1991. 33rd and Ridge Avenues, Philadelphia, Pennsylvania. Sponsored by the Philadelphia Anti-Graffiti Network.

*T*his was the second mural we did for the National Council of Negro Women. In order to get to the park, you have to pass this mural.

This is one of my favorites because the black man is the head of his house, the head of the family. A lot of families are run by black women—and they do a commendable job. But I think when the black man leads his family, like a shepherd leads his flock—he's not tyrannical, more like a facilitator—that's important.

DIETRICH ADONIS
Philadelphia
June 1999

Murals by Non–African American Artists

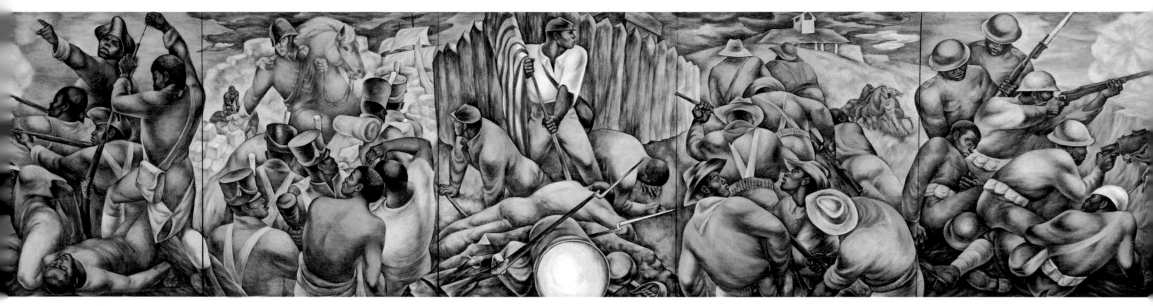

The Negro in America's Wars, Lew Davis, 1944. Fort Huachuca, Arizona. Oil on canvas, five panels, 20' x 4'. Commissioned by Fort Huachuca Post Commander Colonel Edwin N. Hardy and funded by the WPA. Photograph courtesy of the Howard University Gallery of Art, Washington, D.C.

Artist Lew Davis first visited Fort Huachuca, a black army base in Arizona, in 1943 to inspect the White Officers' Mess, where he had been commissioned to paint a mural by the post commander. While there, he observed the low morale of the black soldiers. He proposed setting up a silkscreen workshop to produce army posters featuring black soldiers to replace the unpopular official posters sent to every installation from Washington, D.C., that featured blond blue-eyed white men. Davis's silkscreen studio executed at least nine poster designs.

Davis also founded a workshop on the base for teaching mural painting. At least one of his students, Thurman Dillard, was inspired to become a muralist. After completing two murals for the White Officers' Mess, Davis painted *The Negro in America's Wars* for the Black Officers' Mess. Each panel depicts a scene from one of five major wars in which African American soldiers played a significant role, highlighting their contributions and sacrifices:

Panel 1 portrays the Battle of Monmouth, New Jersey (1778), during the Revolutionary War, in which more than seven hundred black soldiers fought alongside whites.

Panel 2 shows General Andrew Jackson giving a Call to Arms to blacks to join his campaign to drive the British from New Orleans during the War of 1812.

Panel 3 is of the Civil War battlefield at Fort Wagner, South Carolina, where the all-Black Fifty-fourth Massachusetts Regiment played a crucial role. These soldiers had enlisted after a speech from Frederick Douglass on the Boston Common.

Panel 4 is a scene from the Spanish–American-Cuban War showing eight men from the Tenth Cavalry charging up San Juan Hill to aid Lieutenant Colonel Teddy Roosevelt's Rough Riders at El Caney, Cuba.

Panel 5 features the soldiers of the 369th Regiment, formerly the New York National Guard, who served as the advance guard for the French Army. The 369th was the first Allied unit to reach the Rhine River, withstanding 191 days under fire without relief. The entire regiment received the Croix de Guerre, France's military medal for bravery.

When the U.S. Government deactivated Fort Huachuca in 1947 after World War II, this mural was sent to Howard University where it became part of the permanent collection of the Howard University Gallery of Art.

Leaders and Martyrs, Shirley Triest and David Salgado, 1969. Merritt College, Oakland, California.

Forebearers of Civil Rights (panel from **The Great Wall of Los Angeles**), Judith Baca (artistic director), Eric Alvarez, Eva Cockcroft, Mary-Linn Hughes, Patssi Valdez, and Matthew Wuerker with youths, 1983. Tujunga Wash flood control channel, Coldwater Canyon Avenue near Oxnard Street, Van Nuys, California. Acrylic. Sponsored by the Social and Public Art Resource Center. © 1983 Social and Public Art Resource Center.

The Black Panther Party was founded in Oakland in 1966. Founders Huey P. Newton and Bobby Seale attended Merritt College, a two-year community college, in the mid-1960s. When Newton was convicted and imprisoned in 1968 for killing an Oakland policeman the year before, many believed he had been framed in order to destroy the Panthers. A Free Huey campaign was launched and student supporters at Merritt set fires in trash cans and spraypainted walls.

In order to curb these militant actions on campus, Merritt's president made an agreement allowing students to paint murals. Art teacher Helen Dozier coordinated the project, soliciting designs from her students.

For this first mural (one of four done at the same time) the selection panel of student activists chose a composition by Shirley Triest, a young white woman, and David Salgado, a Filipino. Among those depicted were Huey P. Newton, Bobby Hutton (a young Panther killed by the police), Malcolm X, Martin Luther King Jr., Robert Kennedy, and H. Rap Brown.

The interior of a local bus with passengers Paul Robeson, Rosa Parks, Gwendolyn Brooks, Ralph Bunche, and Martin Luther King Jr.

The Great Wall of Los Angeles is a half-mile-long historical mural from the perspective of California ethnic groups, covering the era of the dinosaurs through the 1950s. Under the creative leadership of Judith Baca, the mural involved forty artists and two hundred fifteen youths over five summers.

By reading the black women writers, a new world was opened and I began to see things from a new perspective. The work of brilliant writers Gwendolyn Brooks, Toni Morrison, Maya Angelou, Patricia Parker, Audre Lorde, Alice Walker, Sonia Sanchez, Toni Cade Bambara, Nikki Giovanni, and Sojourner Truth touched me deeply. I want to honor and to publicize their work.

We have all been brainwashed to make judgments based on the white man's standard, which is not only limiting but also damaging to other peoples. My purpose for painting the mural is to promote the black aesthetic: to celebrate black endeavor at all levels, to portray the beauty, dignity, intelligence, creativity, love of life, and the unity of a beautiful people. If I can encourage a single person to be as turned on by the black writers as I am, I will feel gratified.

BROOKE FANCHER
From *Community Murals Magazine,* Summer 1987, p. 15

Tuzuri Watu (We Are a Beautiful People)
Brooke Fancher, 1987.
4900 Third Street, Palou,
Bayview-Hunters Point,
San Francisco, California.
Acrylic on stucco,
1100 square feet.
Funded by the Office of
Community Development.

Portrait of "Dr. J," the famed basketball star of the Philadelphia 76ers. He introduced a style of play featuring airborne maneuvers and slam-dunks that redefined the game of basketball. Erving led the New York Nets to two American Basketball Association championships before joining the 76ers in 1976. He was named the NBA's most valuable player in 1981, led the team to the NBA title in 1983, and was an All-Star nine times. Erving retired in 1987 and was elected to the Basketball Hall of Fame in 1992. Muralist Kent Twitchell is well known in his hometown of Los Angeles for the many gigantic portraits he has painted on walls throughout the city, mostly of artists and character actors—no athletes.

Julius Erving
Kent Twitchell, 1988.
Philadelphia, Pennsylvania.
Acrylic.
Sponsored by the
Philadelphia Anti-Graffiti
Network.

Monochrome portrait of the well-known rapper, film actor, and producer. Ice Cube was a founding member of N.W.A. in the late 1980s, one of the most important rap groups of the time. He launched his solo career in 1990 with the recording of "AmeriKKKa's Most Wanted." In 1991 he made his acting debut in John Singleton's *Boyz in the Hood.*

Psycho City was a centrally located practice yard that lasted ten years. It started with tagging in 1984, getting its name from a piece done there by Dug in 1986. Although Psycho City wasn't a permission location, no one hassled the writers who did pieces there until a 1992 incident with the police—some kids tagged a squad car—led to arrests and the eventual fencing up of the site.

Ice Cube, Booker, 1992. Psycho City, San Francisco, California. Spraycan. Self-sponsored.

Singing in the Dark Times (detail), designed by David Fichter, painted by David Fichter and Darryl Johnson, 1992. Seven Stages
Theatre, Atlanta, Georgia. Acrylic, 22' x 145'. Sponsored by Seven Stages Theatre, the Alliance for Cultural Democracy, and others.

Singing in the Dark Times *celebrates performing artists, playwrights, and theatrical traditions from around the world that are strongly based in the political or social issues of their times. The design of the mural features a series of large-scale portraits within overlapping circles. Shown in this detail are Paul Robeson and Lorraine Hansberry (author of* Raisin in the Sun*). Among those also in the mural are Bertolt Brecht, a Kubuki actor from Japan, a Native American mask, puppets from the Bread and Puppet Theater, Teatro Campesino (Luis Valdes), the San Francisco Mime Troupe, the Dance Brigade, and Italian playwright/performer Dario Fo. The title is based on a quote by playwright Bertolt Brecht: "In the dark times, will there be singing? Yes, there will be singing about the dark times." The mural was created as part of a large national conference of the Alliance for Cultural Democracy, with participants in the conference assisting in the painting process.*

DAVID FICHTER
Cambridge, Massachusetts
December 1999

Faces of Dudley
Mike Womble and
the Boston Youth
Cleanup Corps,
1995.
Dudley Square,
Boston,
Massachusetts.

Our program began in 1991 in Codman Square in the Boston neighborhood of Dorchester as an initiative in the city to stop tagging. I was hired to run the mural painting part of this giant city job program for teenagers. I was given a very small budget and eight teenagers, who were randomly selected from the neighborhood. Half of them weren't interested in painting murals—it was too messy! But we forged ahead for that first year.

From 1991 to 1993 it was just a summer program. Those first few years I was working, it was me working with only African American kids, not really artists. They were kids from that particular part of Boston. I was the white lady coming and doing this work as an outsider. I didn't know that part of Boston. Now I know it like the back of my hand.

We don't always do a sketch before we start to paint. We like to see what happens and who shows up, because the majority of our work incorporates real people's stories or portraits of people who are in the neighborhood. We go there with a basic idea and that can evolve into something that is genuine to the community.

I think we've done sixty-some murals. Not all of them are still up. A lot of them were subject to buildings being renovated. One fell off a building and we've had a fire or two. Things change. The murals are ephemeral, but the impressions they make are definitely permanent. We've brought public art to neighborhoods in Boston for the first time ever, where no art had ever gone.

One of the philosophies behind our program is to bring kids out of the neighborhoods where they live and take them to other parts of the city so they are able to be real citizens of Boston, able to travel from one neighborhood to another and feel comfortable and feel they can be part of a place that is not their home.

HEIDI SCHORK
Director, Boston Youth Cleanup Corps, Boston
September 1999

Frederick Douglass Mural, G. Byron Peck, 1995. 12th Street and Massachusetts Avenue, NW, Washington, D.C. 45' x 35'. Sponsored by McDonald's restaurant franchises in the Washington, D.C., area. Photograph © Steven Cummings Photography.

Scenes from the life of abolitionist and orator Frederick Douglass in commemoration of the one hundredth anniversary of his death.

Painted as an advertisement for men's clothier Bigsby & Kruthers, the over-size, glowering face of Dennis Rodman—with a five-foot removable cutout of his dyed hair—attracted so much gawking from passing motorists as to be a traffic hazard. In addition to Rodman, the mural-sign also featured an elegant Michael Jordan (left) and Cubs second baseman Ryne Sandberg (unfinished on the right).

After a little over two weeks of snarling traffic, Rodman was painted out at the request of traffic officials.

Untitled, Armando Martinez and Jesse Carrizales of Billboards, Inc., 1996. Ashland Avenue facing the Kennedy Expressway, Chicago, Illinois. 32' x 75'. Sponsored by Bigsby & Kruthers.

Tupac Shakur
student Manuel Valdivia
under the supervision
of teacher Gary
Graham, 1997.
Balboa High School, San
Francisco, California.

Balboa High School was "reconstituted," which means the entire staff was kicked out, including the principal. The school district was looking for different people to come there and try to make it work. I came from the community college system and brought in my idea of community art, public art.

In the same hallway as Tupac Shakur, we did quite a few murals while I was there. This was the most successful in terms of its cultural impact.

Manuel happened to be taking my class. He came up with the project. It was all his work. All I did was teach him traditional technique with monochrome underpainting and the style of photorealism.

The students couldn't believe a student did it. They loved the mural. Not only was Manuel streetwise, but he was also politically savvy. By doing this mural, he started to unite all the different cultures on campus. He brought the school together.

GARY GRAHAM
Grass Valley, California
December 1999

The artist, selected from a national search, worked with the Malcolm X Commission and others in developing the mural's content and design. The mural utilizes images from print, film, and television to weave a panorama of events in the life of Malcolm X against a backdrop of the civil rights struggles of the 1950s and 1960s, culminating in his role as a spokesperson, leader and martyr in American society.

The mural was created with a black and white underpainting that was overlaid with subtle hues of glazes of oil color, leaving some areas in black and white. This technique was developed to give the mural a resonance of the past while bringing the message to a contemporary audience. Individuals from the past were integrated with present-day individuals as well to underline the significance and meaning Malcolm X's words still hold today.

The Audubon Ballroom, site of Malcolm X's assassination in 1965, was saved from the wrecking ball by Manhattan Borough President Ruth Messinger and a number of community groups. It underwent a $7 million restoration as part of Columbia University's new Audubon Biomedical Science and Technology Park project.

Homage to Malcolm X (detail), Daniel Galvez, 1997. Audubon Ballroom, 3940 Broadway, Harlem, New York. Oil on canvas, 12' x 64'. Commissioned by the New York City Cultural Affairs Department Percent for Art program and the New York City Economic Development Corporation. (Photograph taken in Galvez's studio prior to installation.)

ROBESON SINGS
CIO 1941 VOTE

UAW

**Paul Robeson and the
CIO-UAW Struggle 1940**
Kathleen Farrell, 1998.
United Auto Workers Hall,
Dearborn, Michigan.
Acrylic on canvas, 6' x 11'.
Commissioned by the
Labor Heritage
Foundation.
Photograph © Ron Molk.

I have been involved in doing labor murals since 1974. For many years the Labor Heritage Foundation has been holding annual labor arts festivals in Washington, D.C. At some point I was invited to do a canvas mural with people at the festival. I did this from 1993–1998. It evolved.

The Foundation would find a union with a particular issue that related to the theme of the festival/conference. I would design and paint a mural on that theme and bring it to the event two-thirds complete. Then I would do educational workshops in which participants would paint and learn about how murals were done.

The year 1998 was the centennial of Robeson's birth, so his role in union struggles was the theme. I researched his connection with organized labor. Robeson's crucial contribution was speaking to the workers at the Rouge Plant in Dearborn, Michigan, the night before the election to have the United Auto Workers (UAW) represent the workers there. He spoke specifically on the race issue because the black workers had been brought in and were supported by the company, and so didn't always have a great relationship with the white workers. Robeson did his pitch on the importance of black and white workers joining together to get their rights and be victorious. The next day the election went for the UAW.

We contacted the people representing the workers at the Rouge Plant. They paid for supplies and shipping, and I donated my labor in painting the mural. My union, the United Scenic Artists Union Local 829, donated my expenses for the trip to Washington, D.C.

KATHLEEN FARRELL
Joliet, Illinois
October 1999

In 1991 a burial ground was unearthed when construction began on a new federal building. If it weren't for the organized protests in the black community, I don't think the government would have even stopped construction.

In the course of the archaeological dig that they set up on the site, it was estimated that twenty thousand African slaves were buried in a five-block radius. The fact that there were slaves in New York as late as 1827 is not something most people, including me, ever learned. At the time of its discovery, the African burial ground was recognized as the largest pre-Revolutionary cemetery in America.

When I was doing my research, I found that a lot of the imagery of African Americans, especially before there was photography, was very stereotypical, racist, and offensive. I wanted to focus on images of labor because I think people aren't aware of the contributions that African Americans made to the building of colonial New York City. They were not only manual laborers, but also blacksmiths, printers, and even some doctors and teachers.

The celebratory images are in gold. On the far left is a portrait of Sojourner Truth. Above her is the first African American church built in New York City, the AME Church. It was one of the first places gospel was sung, symbolic of the building of an African American culture.

The images that deal more with the history of slavery are in red, such as those of the slave auctions on Wall Street. There's an image of the slaughtering of the Lenape Indians, who lived in Manhattan before the Dutch came.

The image of a mountain is sacred in many cultures. Showing the mountain coming out of the water represented to me the city being built on the backs of so many different people and cultures. I set it off by the two vertical panels, which also represent portals—New York as a port of entry. The column on the right includes an image of one of the prisons in Africa that was used as a holding center for slaves, and a slave ship. I also make reference to the millions of slaves that were drowned during the Middle Passage.

In the center of the mural is a divination board, which in the Yoruba religion was used to communicate with ancestors. Inside the divination board are some of the artifacts that were dug up during the excavation. A tragic byproduct of slavery was that people were totally cut off from their past. One of the reasons the Burial Ground project was so emotionally charged was that it had to do with discovering one's ancestors, reestablishing a connection with a lost past.

TOMIE ARAI
New York City
From a September 1999 interview

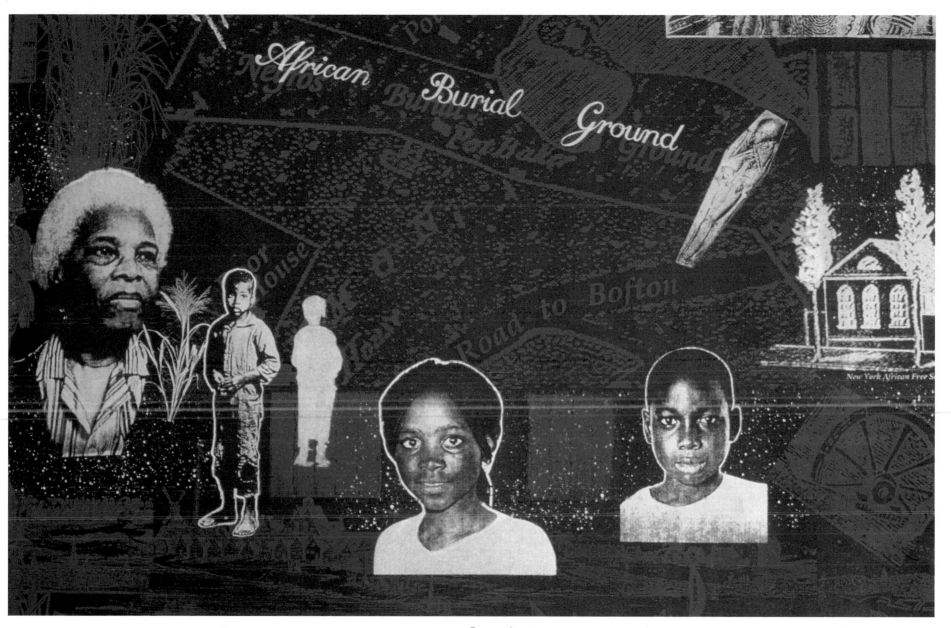

Renewal
Tomie Arai, 1998. Foley Square Federal Office Building, 290 Broadway, New York City.
Silkscreen on canvas, 7' x 38'. Sponsored by the General Services Administration's Art-in-Architecture Program.
Photograph courtesy of GSA Art-in-Architecture.

People of Point Breeze, A. David McShane, 1998. 541 South 22nd Street,
South Philadelphia, Pennsylvania. Sponsored by the Mural Arts Program.

Famous people of South Philadelphia who grew up in the Point Breeze area: a
young Marian Anderson; the Heath Brothers, jazz group; and Mamie Nichols, local
community activist.

Duke Ellington's portrait overlooks the Cardozo Metro Plaza across from the Lincoln Theater in the heart of Washington's historic black entertainment area, the neighborhood in which Ellington was born.

City Arts Inc. was founded in 1998 by muralist G. Byron Peck to continue the work he had begun under the auspices of DC Artworks. DC Artworks, a nonprofit arts organization that supervised the Mayor's Summer Youth Program for the arts, closed down in 1996. City Arts Inc. works with school and government agencies in hiring urban youths to participate in murals, mosaics, and traditional arts projects.

Duke Ellington Mural, G. Byron Peck, assisted by nine students, 1999. 13th Street and U, Washington, D.C. Sponsored by City Arts Inc. Photograph © Steven Cummings Photography.

Geographic Listing of Major Murals by African American Artists

ALABAMA

The Amistad Mural, Hale Woodruff and Robert Neal, 1939, Talladega College, Savery Library, Talladega.

Centennial Vision, Nelson Stevens, John Kendrick, and John Sims, 1979, Tuskegee University Administration Building, Tuskegee.

Civil Rights Mural, John Feagin, 1980, Dexter Avenue Martin Luther King Memorial Baptist Church, 454 Dexter Avenue, Montgomery.

The Founding of Savery Library, Hale Woodruff, 1939, Talladega College, Savery Library, Talladega.

Function in the Junction, 1995, Birmingham.

Highways of Life, Toby Richards and youth, 1994, Robert E. Lee School, 18th Street S.W. and Pearson Avenue, Birmingham.

Untitled (based on *Basotho* exhibit at Birmingham Museum of Art), Chris Clark with youth, Tuxedo Community Center, 20th Place and Avenue Q, Birmingham.

Untitled (history of the school), Willie Cook, early 1960s, Alabama A & M University, Learning Resources Center, Normal.

A World Without Violence, Toby Richards with high school students, 1996, Harrison Park Recreation Center, 1615 McMillian Avenue S.W., Birmingham.

A World Without Violence, Toby Richards, John Sims and Elizabeth Mansour with youths, 1998, YWCA, Birmingham.

ARIZONA

Memory Arizona, Howardena Pindell, 1991, Sky Harbor International Airport (Terminal 4, Level 2), Phoenix.

CALIFORNIA

[Abstract], Jean Cornwell, 1995, Malcolm X Library, 51st Street and Market, San Diego.

African American Life, Peter Macon, Momar Clemons, Michael Mills, 1996, African American Cultural Center, 762 Fulton, Western Addition, San Francisco.

African Mask, Caleb Williams, 1976, Plaza East Housing Project (interior staircases), Laguna Street near Eddy, Fillmore, San Francisco.

[African Scenes], Horace Washington and Caleb Williams, 1973, Plaza East Housing Project, Laguna Street and Eddy, plus Buchanan Street and Eddy, Fillmore, San Frrancisco.

Afro-American Historical and Cultural Society Mural, Arthur Monroe, 1974, Afro-American Historical and Cultural Society, 680 McAllister Street, Civic Center, San Francisco.

Alice Griffith Mural, Horace Washington with Ray Patlán, 1990, 2555 Griffith at Gilman Street, Hunters Point, San Francisco.

All That You Can Be, Elliott Pinkney, 1990, 8601 South Broadway, Los Angeles.

American Black History, Horace Washington, 1984, Martin Luther King Jr. Swimming Pool, 3rd and Carroll Streets, Bayview, San Francisco.

American Justice, Charles Freeman, 1981, Law Office of Walter Gordon III, 2822 South Western Avenue, Los Angeles.

Apartheid (destroyed), Brett Cook (Dizney), 1988, Psycho City, San Francisco.

Aspiration, Aaron Douglas, 1936, (one of four panels originally painted for the Hall of Negro Life, Texas Centennial Exposition in Dallas, Texas), DeYoung Museum, Golden Gate Park, San Francisco.

Becoming Conscious, Keith Williams, 1991, Martin Luther King Jr. Recreation Center, Orange Avenue and 19th Street, Long Beach.

Black Culture, Alonzo Davis, Joseph Sims and Porter, 1974–76, Crenshaw Boulevard, South Los Angeles.

Black Seeds, David Mosley, Eddie Orr, Norman Maxwell, Michael McKenzie, Marvin Hunt, 1991, 2301 West Jefferson Boulevard, South Los Angeles.

Blacks From Egypt to Now, Robert Gayton, 1976, Fillmore District, San Francisco.

California Moments, Richard Wyatt, 1991, Gas Company Tower, Second-floor cafeteria, 555 South 5th Street, downtown Los Angeles.

Cecil, Richard Wyatt and Ian White, 1989, Watts Tower Arts Center, 1727 East 107th Street, Watts, Los Angeles.

A Celebration of African and African American Artists (also known as *Black and Tan Jam*), Dewey Crumpler, Kermit Amenophis, Bonnie Long, and Sandra Roberts, 1984, Western Addition Cultural Center, 762 Fulton Street, Western Addition, San Francisco

The Children of San Francisco, Dewey Crumpler, 1968, San Francisco Public Health Center #2, Steiner and Ellis Streets, Fillmore, San Francisco.

City of Dreams/River of History, Richard Wyatt, 1996, Union Station East Portal, Alameda at Cesar Chavez, downtown Los Angeles.

Commemoration, Elliott Pinkney, 1977–78, 818 West Alondra Boulevard, Compton.

Community Heroes (replaced with newer mural), Elliott Pinkney, 1990, 2015 East Hatchaway Street, Compton.

Confused, Frustrated, Vandalized, Misguided, Active, Poor, Need Love, Gato, Desolate (destroyed), Brett Cook (Dizney), 1993, 509 Cultural Center, Howard Street near 6th, South of Market, San Francisco.

Crispus Attucks: The Boston Massacre, Horace Washington and Caleb Williams, 1976, William De Avila School (interior auditorium), Haight and Masonic Streets, Haight-Ashbury, San Francisco.

Cultural Black Folks (destroyed), Robert Gayton, 1972, condemned warehouse wall, Fillmore, San Francisco.

Dial 900 Society, Ian White, 1992, Crenshaw High School, 5010 11th Avenue, South Los Angeles.

Diversity, Synthia Saint James, 1998, Ontario International Airport Terminal 2 (baggage area), Ontario.

Duke Ellington, Charles Freeman, 1976 (repainted in 1997), Duke Ellington Continuation High School, 1541 West 110th Street, South Los Angeles.

Education, Akinsanya Kambon, 1994, Burnett Library, 560 East Hill Street, Long Beach.

Education is a Right, Noni Olabisi with Alma Lopez, 1998, Los Angeles Public Library, 2700 West 52nd Street, South Los Angeles.

Encanto lamppost project, Eddie L. Edwards, Imperial Avenue between 61st and 69th Streets, Encanto, San Diego County.

Ethnic Simplicity, Elliott Pinkney, 1977–78, 126th Street and Alameda, Compton.

Evolution of the Spirit, Elliott Pinkney, 1997, Southwest College library, 1600 West Imperial Highway, South Los Angeles.

The Fire Next Time I, Dewey Crumpler, 1977, Joseph P. Lee Recreation Center, 3rd and Oakdale, Hunters Point, San Francisco.

The Fire Next Time II, Dewey Crumpler, 1984, Joseph P. Lee Recreation Center, 3rd and Newcomb, Hunters Point, San Francisco.

Four Great Moments, Charles Freeman, 1995, Magic Johnson Theatres, Baldwin Hills Shopping Plaza, Crenshaw and Martin Luther King Jr. Boulevards, South Los Angeles.

Freedom Won't Wait, Noni Olabisi, 1992, 54th Street and Western Avenue, South Los Angeles.

Genocidal Tendencies, Ian White, 1990, 2526 West Jefferson Boulevard, South Los Angeles.

Getting To Know You (replaces *Community Heroes*), Elliott Pinkney, 1999, Sativa L.A. County Water District, 2015 East Hatchway Street, Compton.

God and Us, Eddie L. Edwards, 1986, First A.M.E. Church (sanctuary), 25th Street and Harvard Boulevard, South Los Angeles.

He, She and It (destroyed), Brockman Gallery with Mark Greenfield, Varnette Honeywood, and Houston Conwill, 1976, Crenshaw Boulevard, South Los Angeles.

Hollywood Jazz 1945–1972, Richard Wyatt, 1990, Capitol Records, 1750 North Vine Street, Hollywood.

Homage to John Outterbridge, Alonzo Davis, 1980, Watts Towers Arts Center, 1727 East 107th Street, Watts, Los Angeles.

The Inglewood Project, Richard Wyatt, 1987, Inglewood High School, 231 South Grevillea Avenue, Inglewood.

Institutions, Brett Cook (Dizney), 1990, Balmy Alley, Mission District, San Francisco.

The Insurance Man, Richard Wyatt, 1985, Golden State Mutual Life Insurance Company (auditorium), 1999 West Adams Boulevard, South Los Angeles.

In the Spirit of Contribution, Bernard Hoyes, 1990, La Salle Avenue near 23rd Street, South Los Angeles.

International Friendship, Eddie L. Edwards, Rowan Elementary School, San Diego.

It Takes a Whole Village to Raise a Child, Elliott Pinkney with youth, 1999, Orizaba Park, Long Beach.

L.A.-Berlin Exchange, Tony Martin (Toons) with others, 1994, South Vermont Avenue at 88th Street, South Los Angeles.

Lake with Pyramid, Horace Washington, 1977, 590 Francisco Street at Taylor, North Beach, San Francisco.

Literacy, Roderick Sykes, 1989, Los Angeles Unified School District Maintenance Building, 1406 South Highland Avenue, Los Angeles.

Lives, Brett Cook (Dizney), 1994, Cohen Alley, between Ellis and Leavenworth, Polk Gulch, San Francisco.

Los Angeles Community Anti-Tobacco Mural, Elliott Pinkney, 1991, Watts Towers Arts Center, 1727 East 107th Street, Watts, Los Angeles.

Love is for Everyone, Reginald LaRue Zachary and Mary-Linn Hughes, 1992, 5149 West Jefferson Boulevard, Los Angeles.

Love, Peace and Unity, Eddie L. Edwards, 1985, Martin Luther King Jr. Elementary School, Island and K Streets, San Diego.

Mary McLeod Bethune, Charles White, 1978, Los Angeles Public Library, 3665 South Vermont Avenue, Exposition Park, South Los Angeles.

Medicare 78, Elliott Pinkney, 1977, 920 South Alameda Street, Compton.

Mother Watts, Anthony Cox, 1988, Watts Towers Arts Center, 1727 East 107th Street, Watts, Los Angeles.

Multi-Ethnic Heritage: Black, Asian, Native/Latin American, Dewey Crumpler, 1974, George Washington High School, 32nd Avenue and Anza, Outer Richmond, San Francisco.

The Muralists, Richard Wyatt, 1989, 6542 Hollywood Boulevard, Hollywood.

The Negro in California History, Charles Alston and Hale Woodruff, 1949, Golden State Mutual Life Insurance Company, 1999 West Adams Boulevard, Los Angeles.

New Worlds, Elliott Pinkney, 1977, 423 East Rosecrans Avenue, Compton.

Not Somewhere Else, But Here, Daryl Elaine Wells, 1993, National Council of Jewish Women, 543 North Fairfax Avenue, West Hollywood.

Now and Then, Mel Simmons and Zero Bey, Santie Hucklely, Searcey Ryles, Culture on the Corner, 1996, Rosa Parks Elementary School, 1601 O'Farrell Street, Japantown, San Francisco.

Oh, Speak, Speak, Dale Davis, Charles Dickson, Nate Ferance, John Outterbridge, Elliott Pinkney, and Tom Little, early 1970s, Watts, Los Angeles.

Olympic Series, Alonzo Davis, 1984, Harbor Freeway (110) south at 3rd Street on-ramp, downtown Los Angeles.

The Ones We Love; We Remember, Edythe Boone, 1997, Balmy Alley, Mission District, San Francisco.

Peace and Love, Elliott Pinkney, 1976, Watts Towers Arts Center, 1727 East 107th Street, Watts, Los Angeles.

People Coming, People Going, Richard Wyatt, 1996, MetroRail Red Line station, Wilshire Boulevard at Western Avenue, Los Angeles.

People's Park, Bob Gayton, 1979, 6th Street between Mission and Minna, South of Market, San Francisco.

The People's Park, Edythe Boone, Elvijo Dougherty, and Trish Tripp, 1997, Haste Street and Telegraph Avenue, Berkeley.

Performing To Be, Keith Williams, 1990, Long Beach.

Portrait of My People #619, Willie Middlebrook, 1995, MetroRail Green Line Station, Avalon Boulevard at the 105 Freeway, Watts, Los Angeles.

[Portraits], Charles Freeman, 1993, Billiard center, Crenshaw Boulevard, South Los Angeles.

[Portraits of heroes], Charles Freeman, 1993, Korean restaurant, Figueroa, Los Angeles.

Rainbow Community, Eddie L. Edwards, Encanto, San Diego.

Reach Out, Alonzo Davis and Joseph Sims, 1970s, La Brea Avenue underpass, Santa Monica Freeway, Los Angeles.

Return to the Light, Charles Freeman, 1994, Carlota Boulevard and Avenue 41, Highland Park, Los Angeles.

The Right of Education/The Seed of Freedom, Arch Williams with others, 1987, Francisco Middle School, Stockton and Francisco Streets, North Beach, San Francisco.

St. Vincent Project, Richard Wyatt, 1995, St. Vincent Institute Plaza, 2200 West 3rd Street, Los Angeles.

[A Salute to Artists], Dewey Crumpler and the Neighborhood Youth Corps, 1975, Beidman Minipark, O'Farrell near Divisadero and Scott, Fillmore, San Francisco.

Samuel Fryer Project, Richard Wyatt, 1988, Fryer Hebrew Academy (interior chapel), 7353 Beverly Boulevard, West Hollywood.

Sgt. Henderson Park (destroyed), Sondra Chirlton, Doug Huntley, Craig Moline, Milton Schueler, and Mark Soetaert, 1973, Divisadero and Eddy Streets, Fillmore, San Francisco.

Sharing Ourselves, Jacqueline Alexander, 1999, 4600 Main Street, South Los Angeles.

Shut 'Em Down (destroyed), Brett Cook (Dizney) and Aaron Wade, 1992, Market and 6th Streets, San Francisco.

Slaying of the Dragon, Elliott Pinkney, 1977–78, 423 East Rosecrans, Compton.

Sojourner Truth, Charles Freeman, late 1970s, Locke High School, South Los Angeles.

Something From Nothing (door relief), John Outterbridge, early 1970s, Communicative Arts Academy, Compton.

Spike Lee (destroyed), Richard Wyatt, 1993, 7267 Melrose Avenue, Hollywood.

Spirits of America, Elliott Pinkney, 1977, Dollarhide Neighborhood Center (interior), 1108 North Oleander Avenue, Compton.

Sports World of Fun, Elliott Pinkney with youth, 1999, Orizaba Park, Long Beach.

Stations of the Cross (twelve panels destroyed in 1974, two in storage), Aaron Miller, 1952, Emmanuel Church of God in Christ, Post Street, Fillmore, San Francisco.

Success, Elliott Pinkney, 1990, Long Beach School for Adults, 1794 Cedar Street, Long Beach.

Summer Fun, Elliott and Arnold Pinkney, 1977–78, Santa Fe and Rosecrans, Compton.

Sunflowers of Nature, James Phillips, assisted by Sara Williams and Todd Duncan, 1985, Hunters Point Housing, 1033 Oakdale, Hunters Point, San Francisco.

Sunrise on Central Avenue, Richard Wyatt, 1999, Broadway Federal Bank, Figueroa and Martin Luther King Boulevard, Los Angeles.

Tapestry of Spirit, ongoing, Roderick Sykes and Jacqueline Alexander, St. Elmo Village, 4830 St. Elmo Drive, Mid-City Los Angeles.

Third World, Eddie L. Edwards, Educational Cultural Complex, Oceanview Boulevard and 43rd, San Diego.

The Time is Now (destroyed), Elliott Pinkney, 1976, Watts, Los Angeles.

Together We Dance, Elliott Pinkney, 1991, Anaheim Street and Walnut Avenue, Long Beach.

To Protect and Serve, Noni Olabisi, 1996, 11th Avenue and Jefferson Boulevard, South Los Angeles.

Tribute to the People of Lompoc, Richard Wyatt, 1991, Lompoc County Courthouse, 115 Civic Center Plaza, Lompoc.

Tribute to the Workers, Elliott Pinkney, 1977–78, Rose Avenue and Compton Boulevard, Compton.

Truth and Education, Dewey Crumpler, 1970, Hunters Point School, San Francisco.

Unity (destroyed), Roderick Sykes, 1984, Harbor Freeway at Figueroa, downtown Los Angeles.

Untitled, Camille Breeze and David Mora, 1972, Black Light Explosion (cultural center), Fillmore, San Francisco.

Untitled, Robert Curry with students from Lake Junior High School, 1974, Watts, Los Angeles.

Untitled, Bob Gayton, 1977, Booker T. Washington Community Center, 800 Presidio Drive, Fillmore, San Francisco.

Untitled, Elliott Pinkney, 1984, Los Angeles Sentinel, 4300 Central Avenue, South Los Angeles.

Untitled, Elliott Pinkney, 1998, Orizaba Park, Orizaba Avenue at Spaulding, Long Beach.

Untitled, Richard Wyatt, 1996, Los Angeles Public Library, 10205 Compton Avenue, Watts, Los Angeles.

The Urban Village, Nzinga Kianga, 1987, 4401 Telegraph Avenue, Berkeley.

Vision and Motion, Elliott Pinkney, 1993, Community Youth Sports and Arts Foundation, 4828 Crenshaw Boulevard, South Los Angeles.

Wake Up, Noni Olabisi, 1996, 621 Fifth Street (interior), downtown Los Angeles.

Wall of Visions, Alonzo Davis, director, with Rudolph Porter, Joe Sims, Jonathan Clark, Audubon Lucas, and others, 1974–79, Crenshaw Boulevard, South Los Angeles.

WAPAC Mural, David Bradford, 1977, WAPAC Building, 1956 Sutter Street, Fillmore District, San Francisco.

We Know Who We Are, June Edmonds, 1995, MetroRail Blue Line station, Pacific Avenue near 5th Street, downtown Long Beach.

White Memorial Project, Richard Wyatt, 1994, White Memorial Medical Center, 1720 Cesar Chavez Avenue, Boyle Heights, Los Angeles.

Why Fight for a Crayon That's Not Our Color? (destroyed), Brett Cook (Dizney), 1988, Psycho City, San Francisco.

The Willowbrook Project, Richard Wyatt, 1979, Willowbrook Middle School, Wilmington Avenue and El Segundo Boulevard, Compton.

Women Do Get Weary But They Don't Give Up, Alice Patrick, 1991, National Council of Negro Women, 3720 West 54th Street, South Los Angeles.

World Harvest, Jacqueline Alexander, 1993, 8773 Venice Boulevard, West Los Angeles.

COLORADO

Mile High and Rising, Marcus Akinlana, 1999, Denver International Airport, Jeppesen Terminal, Denver.

Street Scene, Darrell Anderson, Oye Oginga, and Carlos Fresquez, 1996, Five Points Media Center Corporation, 2900 Welton Street, Denver.

Subcore Floors, Darrell Anderson and Barb McKee, Denver International Airport (Concourse A), Denver.

FLORIDA

Time, Space, Energy, 1988, Jacob Lawrence, Florida International Airport, Orlando.

GEORGIA

Art of the Negro, Hale Woodruff, 1950–51, Clark-Atlanta University, Trevor Arnett Library, Atlanta.

City Dance in Three Movements, John Scott, Hartsfield Atlanta International Airport, Concourse, Atlanta.

Coca-Cola Olympic Centennial Mural, Kevin Cole, 1996, Atlanta.

The Daily Agenda, Kevin Cole, 1989–90, Atlanta City Hall, Atlanta.

Education of the Colored Man, Aaron Douglas, 1938, Atlanta City Housing Project, Atlanta.

Flight, Benny Andrews, 1980, Atlanta Mid-Field Airport (Eastern Airlines Terminal), Atlanta.

From Africa to America, Wilfrid Stroud, 1988, Harriet Tubman Historical and Cultural Museum, Macon.

From the Outside, Kevin Cole.

Jammin' on the Ceiling, Kevin Cole.

The Near Future, Kevin Cole, 1999, Georgia State University, Urban Life Building, Atlanta.

The Negro in Modern American Life: Literature, Music and Art, Hale Woodruff, assisted by Wilmer Jennings, 1933–34, David T. Howard High School, Atlanta.

Saints, Radcliffe Bailey, Hartsfield Atlanta International Airport, Concourse E

School Watch Intimate, North Springs High School students under the direction of Kevin Cole, 1999, My Sister's House, Atlanta.

Triumphant Celebration, Calvin Jones, 1990, 321 Edgewood Avenue, Atlanta.

Untitled, Amos and Truman Johnson, David Hammons, and Steven Seaberg, 1977, Neighborhood Arts Center, Atlanta.

Untitled, Ashanti Johnson, 1970s, Eagan Homes, Atlanta.

Untitled, John Riddle, 1975 and 1976, Shrine of the Black Madonna, Atlanta.

Untitled, Lawrence A. Jones, Fort Valley State College, Fort Valley.

Untitled, Michael Harris, 1970s, Prize High School, Atlanta.

Wall of Respect, Amos Johnson, Vera Parks and Nathan Hoskins, 1976, downtown Atlanta.

ILLINOIS

All of Mankind (Why Were They Martyred?), William Walker, 1971–73, Strangers Home Missionary Church, 617 West Evergreen Avenue (at Clybourn), Chicago.

All Power to the People, African American youth with John Pitman Weber, Chicago.

Another Time's Voice Remembers My Passion's Humanity, Calvin Jones and Mitchell Caton, 1979, Elliott Donnelley Youth Center, 3947 South Michigan Avenue, Chicago.

Band Playing, Archibald Motley Jr., c. 1936, Nicholas Elementary School (music room), Evanston.

Benu: Rebirth of the South Side, Marcus Akinlana and Jeffrey Cook, 1990, 71st and Jeffery, Chicago.

Black Love, William Walker, 1971, 515 West Oak Street, Chicago.

Black Man's Dilemma, Don McIlvaine, 1970, Chicago.

Black Women Emerging, Justine DeVan and Mitchell Caton, 1977, 4120 South Cottage Grove Avenue, Chicago.

Bright Moments, Memories of the Future, Calvin Jones and Mitchell Caton, 1987, New Regal Theater, 79th and Stony Island, Chicago.

The Builders, Eugene Wade (Eda), 1981, Chicago State University, Chicago.

Builders of the Cultural Present, Calvin Jones and Mitchell Caton, 1981, Chicago.

Celebration of the Arts, Vibrations of Life, John Yancey, 1991–92, Boulevard Arts Center, 1531 West 60th Street, Chicago.

Ceremonies for Heritage Now, Calvin Jones and Mitchell Caton, 1980, Westside Association for Community Action, Chicago.

Children Are the Future (Childhood Is Without Prejudice), William Walker, 1977, 56th Street and Stony Island Avenue, Chicago (restored by Bernard Williams and Olivia Gude).

The Circle Journey, Patrice Santiago, Ras Ammar Nsoroma, and Stephanie George, c. 1991, 53rd Street Viaduct, Hyde Park, Chicago.

Commerce, William Edouard Scott, 1909, Lane Technical High School, Chicago.

Corporate State: 1984, John Yancey, 1982, Springfield.

[Dance] (destroyed), Aaron Douglas, 1929, Sherman Hotel College Inn Room, Chicago.

Dance Scene, Archibald Motley Jr., c. 1936, Nicholas Elementary School (music room), Evanston.

Dare to Dream, Paul Minnehan, 1995, Chicago Public Library, 3353 West 13th Street, Chicago.

Earth is Not Our Home, C. Siddha Sila Webber, 1981, Martin Luther King Jr. Boulevard, Chicago.

[Egyptian doors], Eugene Wade (Eda), 1972–73, Malcolm X College, Chicago.

Es Tiempo Recordar (Time to Remember), Marcus Akinlana, Sondra Antongiorgi, and Rolf Mueller, 1992, Chicago.

Events in the Life of Harold Washington, Jacob Lawrence, 1991, Harold Washington Library Center (1st floor), downtown Chicago.

Feed the People: Paul Robeson, C. Siddha Sila Webber, 1997, Chicago.

Feed Your Child the Truth, Bernard Williams, 1994, Ma Houston playlot, 50th and Cottage Grove, Chicago.

Founding of the First Presbyterian Church of Old Fort Dearborn in 1833, William Edouard Scott, c.1920, First Presbyterian Church, Chicago.

Freedom Now (carved wood relief), Robert Witt Ames, 1965, DuSable Museum of African American History, Chicago.

Gift to the World's Children, William Walker, 1978, 47th Street and Martin Luther King Drive, Chicago.

The Great Migration, Marcus Akinlana, assisted by youth, 1994–95, Elliott Donnelley Youth Center Art Playlot, 3947 South Michigan Avenue, Chicago.

Have a Dream, C. Siddha Sila Webber and Thomas Murdock, 1995, 40th and King, Chicago.

History of the Negro Press (destroyed), Charles White, 1940, Chicago Coliseum.

History of the Packinghouse Worker, William Walker, 1974, Amalgamated Meat Cutters Union Hall, 4859 South Wabash Avenue, Chicago.

In Defense of Ignorance, Calvin Jones and Mitchell Caton, 1977, 8350 South Ashland, Chicago.

Into the Mainstream, Don McIlvaine, 1970, Chicago.

Joliet's History, Our History, Carla Carr, 1997, East Washington Street and Eastern Avenue, Joliet.

Journey into Indigo, Mitchell Caton, 1983, Pride Community Center (interior), Chicago.

Justice Speaks: Delbert Tibbs/New Trial or Freedom, William Walker, 1977, 57th Street at Lake Park Avenue, Chicago

King Memorial Wall, Eugene Wade (Eda), 1982, 43rd and Langley, Chicago.

Knowledge and Wonder, Kerry James Marshall, 1995, Legler Branch Library, 115 South Pulaski Road, Chicago.

Learning to Look, Eugene Wade (Eda), 1986, Kennedy-King College (interior lobby), Chicago.

Legacy, Eugene Eda, 1996, Kinsey and Laramie, Chicago.

Legends of Tobacco Road (destroyed), Bernard Williams, 1993, Chicago.

Man's Inhumanity to Man, William Walker and Mitchell Caton, 1978, Chicago.

Memory Masks, Marcus Akinlana, 1995, Boulevard Arts Center, 6011 South Justine, Chicago.

Nation Time, Mitchell Caton, 1971, Chicago

Negro Children, Archibald Motley, c.1939, Nicholas Elementary School (music room), Evanston.

Our Time Has Come, John Yancey, 1984, Springfield.

Peace and Salvation, Wall of Understanding, William Walker, 1970, 872 North Orleans Avenue, Chicago.

Peace, Peace, William Walker, 1984, Chicago.

Prescription for Good Health, Mitchell Caton, Justine DeVan, Caryl Yasko, 1975, Chicago.

Putting Power Into the Future, Jeffrey Cook, 1991, 1628 Drexel, Ford Heights, Chicago.

Reaganomics, William Walker, 1982, Chicago.

Recreation, Archibald Motley Jr., c.1940, Doolittle School (auditorium), Chicago.

St. Martin Luther King, William Walker, 1977, 40th Street, Oakwood Boulevard and Martin Luther King Drive, Chicago.

[Signing of the treaty between the Indians and Governor Edwards in 1819], William Edouard Scott, c. 1920, bank, Edwardsville.

South Africa Exposed, Mitchell Caton and Nii-Oti Zambezi, 1985, Chicago Defender Building, 2400 South Michigan, Chicago.

South Shore Rests at the Bosom of Oshun, Marcus Akinlana and Ivan Watkins, 1989, Chicago.

Stagecoach and Mail (also known as *United States Mail*), Archibald Motley, 1937, Wood River Post Office, Wood River.

A Time to Unite, Justine DeVan, Mitchell Caton, Calvin Jones, 1976, 41st Street and Drexel Boulevard, Chicago.

Tribute to the Pullman Porters, Bernard Williams, 1995, 103rd and Cottage, Chicago.

Universal Alley/Rip-Off, Mitchell Caton and C. Siddha Sila Webber, 1974, Chicago.

Untitled, Frederick D. Jones Jr., 1946 (repainted in 1992), First Church of Deliverance, 43rd and Wabash, Chicago.

Urban World at the Crossroads, Bernard Williams and John Pitman Weber, 1997, Orr High School, Chicago.

Visions from a Dream, Carla Carr, 1998, Eliza Kelly School, 100 W. McDonough Street, Joliet.

Visitation Realization, Bernard Williams and Derrick Holey, 1999, Visitation Elementary School, 900 West Garfield, Chicago.

Wall of Daydreaming/Man's Inhumanity to Man, William Walker, Mitchell Caton, and Santi Isrowuthukal, 1975, 47th Street and Calumet Avenue, Chicago.

The Wall of Family Love, William Walker, 1971, Southside Community Art Center, 3831 S. Michigan Avenue, Chicago.

Wall of Meditation, Eugene Wade (Eda), 1979, Olivet Community Center, Chicago.

The Wall of Peace and Understanding, William Walker, 1970, Chicago.

Wall of Respect (destroyed), William Walker and OBAC, 1967, Chicago.

Wall of Struggle and Dreams, Kiela Songhay Smith with the community, 1993, Clyde Park, Evanston.

Wall of Truth, Eugene Wade (Eda), 1969, Chicago.

Where There is Discord, Harmony; the Power of Art, Olivia Gude, Marcus Akinlana, and Ivan Watkins, 1991, Chicago.

Why Were They Martyred?, William Walker, 1972, Chicago.

Working Hands, Eugene Wade (Eda) and William Walker, 1985, Kennedy-King College, Chicago.

You Are as Good as Anyone, William Walker, 1980, 47th Street, Chicago.

INDIANA

[Egyptian designs], William Edouard Scott, c.1920, First National Bank, Fort Wayne.

The Fountain of Knowledge, William Edouard Scott, 1913, Public School #23, Indianapolis.

The Four Seasons, The Life of Christ, Nations Coming to Light, William Edouard Scott, 1915, Wishard Memorial Hospital, Indianapolis.

[The Life of Jesus], William Edouard Scott, 1914, Wishard Memorial Hospital, Indianapolis.

The Old Woman Who Lived in a Shoe, William Edouard Scott, 1913, Public School #26, Martindale Avenue, Indianapolis.

LOUISIANA

The Assumption of Mary, Frederick J. Brown, 1993, Xavier University Library, New Orleans.

Contributions of Blacks to Louisiana History, Jack Jordan and Jean Paul Hubbard, 1975, Southern University, Education Building, 6400 Press Drive, New Orleans.

The Journey, Terrance Osborne, Xavier University Student Center, New Orleans.

Louis Armstrong and His Heavenly All-Star Band, Richard C. Thomas, 1997, New Orleans International Airport, Parabola Lobby, New Orleans.

Louis Ouis Lou, Richard C. Thomas, 1979, Treme Community Center, Armstrong Park, 1400 St. Philip Street, New Orleans.

Mystical, Magical New Orleans, Marcus Akinlana, 1993, Dillard University, New Orleans.

River Spirit, John Scott, 1996, Port of New Orleans Administration Building, New Orleans.

Untitled [neighborhood demolition], Bruce Brice, 1971, Treme, New Orleans.

Untitled [plantation life], Clementine Hunter, mid-1950s, African House, Melrose Plantation, Natchitoches.

Untitled [police brutality and the slave trade], Bruce Brice, 1971, Desire, New Orleans.

MARYLAND

[Abstract lines and curves], Pontella Mason and Avon Martin, 1976, Cumberland and Carey Streets, Baltimore.

Baltimore Uproar, Romare Bearden, 1982, Upton Metro Station, Baltimore.

[Children on trikes], James Voshell and Pontella Mason, 1975, Lombard and Mount Streets, Baltimore.

[Men playing checkers], James Voshell and Pontella Mason, 1975, Edmondson and Franklin Streets, Baltimore.

[People engaged in daily life], James Voshell and Pontella Mason, 1975, Department of Social Services (interior), Olver and Greenmount Avenues, Baltimore.

Some Aspects of the Evolution of Negro Colleges in America, Charles W. Stallings, 1954, Morgan State University, Baltimore.

MASSACHUSETTS

The Black Worker, Dana Chandler, 1973, United Community Construction Workers Labor Temple, Roxbury, Boston.

Build Senior Power, James Reed, 1987, Cambridge Committee Elders, Inc., 15 Pearl Street, Cambridge.

Drum Major for Justice, James Reed, 1988, Massachusetts Housing Project, 280 Martin Luther King Boulevard, Roxbury, Boston

Geome-A-Tree, Paul Goodnight with Elayna Yoneoka assisted by E. Genovese, 1991, Ruggles Street MTA Station, Roxbury, Boston.

I've Been to the Mountain Top, Dana Chandler, 1981, Martin Luther King Middle School, Roxbury, Boston.

Knowledge is Power, Stay in School, Dana Chandler, 1972, Ziegler and Warren Streets, Roxbury, Boston.

Let There Be Life, John Kendrick, 1976, Urban League Alexander E. Mapp Community Center, Springfield.

Shelter, Alonzo Davis, 1994–96, Revere Beach Station, MBT Blue Line Subway, Boston.

South End Honor Roll, K. Jameel Parker with youth, 1999, Boston.

We're All in the Same Gang, K. Jameel Parker, 1992, Floyd Street at Blue Hill Avenue, Boston.

Work to Unify African People, Nelson Stevens, 1973, United Community Construction Workers Labor Temple, Roxbury, Boston.

MICHIGAN

Harriet Tubman Memorial Wall (also known as *Let My People Go*), Eugene Wade (Eda) and William Walker, 1968, St. Bernard's Church, 11031 Mack Avenue (at Lillibridge), Detroit.

Continuity: Our Heritage Great, Our Destiny Even Greater, Calvin Jones, Kwasi Asante, Dana Chandler, Nelson Stevens, and Napoleon Jones-Henderson, Campbell Elementary School, Detroit.

Continuum, Jon Onye Lockard, 1980, Wayne State University, Manoogian Hall, Detroit.

[*Fourteen Stations of the Cross*], Allan Rohan Crite, c. 1953, Chapel of Our Lady of Victory, Detroit.

Hot Pursuit, Allie McGhee, 1982, Martin Luther King Homes Community Center, St. Aubin and Larned Streets, Detroit (other murals there by Charles McGee, Lester Johnson, MacArthur Binton, and others).

Kaleidoscope, Leroy Foster, Southwestern Hospital, Detroit.

Life and Times of Frederick Douglass, Leroy Foster, 1973, Detroit Public Library, 3666 Grand River Avenue, Detroit.

Message to Demar and Lauri (destroyed), designed by Alvin Loving Jr., 1971, First National Bank, Woodward Avenue and Cadillac Square, Detroit.

Paul Robeson, Leroy Foster, Institute of African American Arts, Detroit.

Renaissance City: The Rebirth of Detroit, Leroy Foster, Cass Technical High School, Detroit.

Untitled [abstract planes of color], Charles McGee, 1974, Pontchartrain Wine Cellars, 234 West Larned Street, Detroit.

Voyage, Allie McGhee, 1987, Michigan-Cass People Mover Station, Detroit.

Wall of Dignity (destroyed), Eugene Wade (Eda) and William Walker, 1968, across the street from St. Bernard's Church, Mack Avenue and Lillibridge, Detroit.

MINNESOTA

All About Hair, Alvin Carter, 1984, 710 East Lake Street, Minneapolis.

Birds For Peace, Seitu Jones and others, 1984, 1624 Chicago Avenue South, Minneapolis.

Celebration of Life, John Biggers, Ta-Coumba Aiken, Seitu Jones, lead artists, with fifteen other artists, 1996, Olson Memorial Highway and Lyndale Avenue North, Minneapolis.

Children Are the World, Ta-Coumba Aiken, 1978, Pilot City Regional Center, 1315 Penn Avenue North, Minneapolis.

Crossroads, Carole Byard and Marilyn Lindstrom, 1997, The Cultural Center of Minnesota, 3013 Lyndale Avenue South, Minneapolis.

Good Thunder, Ta-Coumba Aiken, 1987–88, grain elevator, Good Thunder.

A Healthy Community, Seitu Jones and Ta-Coumba Aiken, 1981, Southside Community Clinic, 4243 4th Avenue South, Minneapolis.

Jimmy Lee the Coach, Seitu Jones and others, 1982, Jimmy Lee Recreation Center, 1063 Iglehart Street, St. Paul.

Lambert Landing, Seitu Jones, Ta-Coumba Aiken and Sticks and Stones, Inc., 1986, Lambert Landing, Warner Road, St. Paul.

Recreation, Alvin Carter, 1977, Oxford Playground, 1063 Iglehart Street, St. Paul.

Untitled, Alvin Carter, 1977, Inner City Youth League, 175 North Victoria, St. Paul.

Untitled, Alvin Carter, 1986, School of Communication Arts, Inc., 2526 27th Avenue South, Minneapolis.

Untitled [bird], Seitu Jones, Denise Mayotte and children, 1986, Aldine Park, Iglehart and Aldine Streets, St. Paul.

Untitled [Egyptian imagery], Alvin Carter, 1982, People's Choice, 920 Selby Avenue, St. Paul.

Welcome to Elliot Park Neighborhood, Ta-Coumba and others, 1985, 812 Park Avenue, Minneapolis.

MISSISSIPPI

Adoration, Baptism, Resurrection, Lawrence A. Jones, 1953, Northside Baptist Church, Jackson.

Black Monopoly Enterprises, Abie's Creations, Lynch Street at Lucedale, Jackson.

The Carver Mural, Vertis Hayes, 1945, Johnson Hall, Jackson State University, Jackson.

Centennial Mural, Lawrence A. Jones, 1978, F. D. Hall Music Center (2nd floor), Jackson State University, Jackson.

Untitled, Lawrence A. Jones, College Hill Baptist Church, Jackson.

MISSOURI

Black Americans in Flight, Spencer Taylor and Solomon Thurman, 1990, Lambert-St. Louis International Airport, lower concourse east of baggage claim, St. Louis.

Break the Chains of Ignorance: Educate, Alexander Austin, 58th Street and Troost Avenue, Kansas City.

A Brush of Time, Alexander Austin, 1995, Kiddie Campus Daycare Center, 3217 Troost Avenue, Kansas City.

Go For Your Dream (destroyed), Alexander Austin, 1993, 47th and Prospect Avenue, Kansas City.

Malcolm X, Alexander Austin, 1992, 25th and Prospect, Kansas City.

The Origin of Freemasonry, Jessie Housley Holliman, 1941, Masonic Temple Association of St. Louis, 3681 Lindell Boulevard, St. Louis.

Up You Mighty Race, 1968, Seven artists, 2600 Dr. Martin Luther King Jr. Drive, St. Louis.

Wall of Respect, Leroy White and six others, 1968, St. Louis.

NEBRASKA

Jazz Griots: A Pictorial History from Africa to America, Warrior Richardson with youth, 1997, Omaha.

NEW MEXICO

Health Care Is a Right, Not a Privilege, A. G. Joe Stephenson, 1991, First Choice Community Health, 1316 Broadway Boulevard SE (at Stadium), Albuquerque.

Peace and Love, A. G. Joe Stephenson, 1994, 1025 Lomas (at 11th St. NW), Albuquerque.

Route 66 Mural, A. G. Joe Stephenson, 1989, 3701 Central Avennue NW, Albuquerque.

Sin Un Pasado, No Hay Futuro (Without a Past We Have No Future), A. G. Joe Stephenson, 1994, 115 2nd Street (at Gold), Albuquerque.

Untitled, Thurman Dillard, 13 West Colorado Ave., Santa Fe.

Untitled, Thurman Dillard, 1790 St. Michaels Drive,1972, Santa Fe.

NEW YORK

Abstract, Fern Stanford, 1976, Boys and Girls High School, Brooklyn.

Abstract, Norman Lewis, 1976, Boys and Girls High School, Brooklyn.

African Market, Nafissa Camara, 1995, Fulton and Tompkins, Brooklyn.

Afro American History and Literature, Ernest Crichlow, 1976, Boys and Girls High School, Brooklyn.

Art and Music, Eldzior Cortor, 1976, Boys and Girls High School, Brooklyn.

Aspects of Negro Life, Aaron Douglas, 1934, New York Public Library, 135th Street branch, Harlem.

The Children's Cathedral, Jimmy James Greene, 1996, ceramic mosaic, Utica Avenue Subway Station.

City of God (destroyed by fire, 1972), Allan Rohan Crite, c. 1946, St. Augustine's Church, Brooklyn.

CommUnion, Emmett Wigglesworth, 1994, Union Street Station, New York City.

Community, Jacob Lawrence, 1989, Addabbo Federal Building, South Jamaica, Queens.

A Decoration (destroyed), Vertis Hayes, late 1930s, Bayard Rustin High School (formerly Straubenmuller Textile High School), 351 West 18th Street, New York City.

El and El, Michael Kelly Williams, 1992, glass mosaic, Intervale Avenue Station, Bronx.

Environs, Howardena Pindell, 1993–94, mosaic, Lehman College, Bronx.

Equal Justice Under the Law, Charles Alston, 1973–75, Family and Criminal Courts Building, East 161st Street, Bronx.

Evolution of the Negro Dance, Aaron Douglas, 1933, YMCA, Harlem.

Family, Romare Bearden, 1989, Addabbo Federal Building, South Jamaica, Queens.

The Family of Man, Charles Alston, 1973–75, Family and Criminal Courts Building, East 161st Street, Bronx.

Fire!, Aaron Douglas, 1927, Club Ebony, Harlem.

First in the Heart is the Dream, Carole Byard, 1997, P.S. 233, 9301 Avenue B, Brooklyn.

Flying Home: Harlem Heroes and Heroines, Faith Ringgold assisted by Tim Tait Designs, 1996, mosaic, 125th Street Subway Station, Harlem.

For the Women's House, Faith Ringgold, 1972, Women's House of Detention, Riker's Island.

Grafton Street Conquest, Alvin McCray, 1981, Grafton Street, Brooklyn.

Harlem Timeline, Willie Birch, 1995, glass mosaic, 135th Street subway station, New York City.

In the Neighborhood, Vincent Smith, 1976, Boys and Girls High School, 1700 Fulton, Brooklyn.

Jonkonnu Festival wid the Frizzly Rooster Band, Vincent Smith, 1988, Dempsey Multi-Service Center of Central Harlem, 127 West 127th Street, Harlem.

Jungle Tales, Sara Murrell, 1936, Harlem Hospital, children's ward, Harlem.

Life and Times of Jesus Christ, Alvin McCray, 1985, Risen Christ Lutheran Church, Blake Avenue, Brooklyn.

Lincoln and FDR (two panels), Charles Alston, 1955, Lincoln High School, New York City.

Madison Square World, Alvin McCray, 1990, Madison Square Post Office (interior), New York City.

Man on the Threshold of Space, Charles Alston, 1964, P.S. 154, West 127th Street, Manhattan.

Minton's Playhouse, Vincent Smith, 1999, 116th Street Subway Station, New York City.

Mother Goose Rhymes, Selma Day, 1936, Harlem Hospital, children's ward, Harlem.

The Movers and Shakers, Vincent Smith, 1999, 116th Street Station.

Mystery and Magic and *Modern Medicine,* Charles Alston, 1936, Harlem Hospital, entrance to women's pavilion, Harlem.

New World Players, Jimmy James Greene, 1999, Herbert Von King Park amphitheater, Brooklyn.

New York in Transit, Jacob Lawrence, 1991, Times Square Subway Complex, New York City.

Ode to Zimbabwe, Vincent Smith, c. 1979, Crotona Social Service Agency, Tremont Street, Bronx.

Pride and Joy, A. G. Joe Stephenson and Leslie Bender, 1985, Linden Boulevard and 180th Street, St. Albans.

Pursuit of Happiness, Vertis Hayes, 1936, Harlem Hospital, west corridor of Nurses' Residence, Harlem.

Queens: Festival, Howardena Pindell, 1989, Addabbo Federal Building, Parsons Boulevard and Jamaica Avenue, South Jamaica, Queens.

Recreation in Harlem, Georgette Seabrooke, 1936, Harlem Hospital, Nurses' Recreation Room, Harlem.

Rivers, Houston Conwill, Estella Conwill Majozo, and Joseph DePace, 1988, Schomburg Center for Research in Black Culture, 515 Malcolm X Boulevard, Harlem.

St. Alban's Greatest Hits, A. G. Joe Stephenson, 1983, underpass, Linden Boulevard and Newberg Street, St. Albans.

Savoy, Richard Yarde, 1989, Addabbo Federal Building, South Jamaica, Queens.

Toy Parade, Elba Lightfoot, 1936, Harlem Hospital, children's ward, Harlem.

Tradition: For Romare Bearden and Jacob Lawrence, Frank Smith, 1989, Addabbo Federal Building, South Jamaica, Queens.

Untitled, Alvin McCray, 1986, Gospel Baptist Church, Brooklyn.

Untitled, Alvin McCray, 1987, Greater Crossroad Baptist Church, Brooklyn.

Untitled, Alvin McCray, 1986, T. Anthony Baptist Church, Utica and East New York Avenues, Brooklyn.

Untitled, artist unknown, Fulton and Verona, Brooklyn.

Untitled [history and education], Kinrod, 1970, P.S. 167K, New York City.

Untitled, Nafissa Camara, c. 1995, Fulton and Throop, Brooklyn.

NORTH CAROLINA

Ascension and *Origins,* John Biggers and James Biggers, 1990–92, Winston-Salem State University O'Kelly Library (atrium), Winston-Salem.

Before Dawn, designed by Romare Bearden, 1989, Public Library of Charlotte and Mecklenburg County, Charlotte.

Harriet Tubman, Aaron Douglas, 1932, Bennett College, Greensboro.

OHIO

Bugaloo Beat: All Dressed Up and No Place to Go, Terrence Corbin, 1997, Central State University (library), Wilberforce.

Crucifixion, William Walker, 1953, Zion Church of God in Christ, Columbus.

Freedom of Expression, Elmer W. Brown, 1942, Men's City Club, Cleveland.

[Historical Cleveland scene], Elmer W. Brown, 1940, Valleyview Homes Community Center, Cleveland.

In the Village, James Pate, 1998, Riverview and Rosedale, Dayton.

Outhwaite, Charles Sallée, 1940, Outhwaite Homes Management Office, Cleveland.

The Tallest Tree in the Forest, Jon Onye Lockard, 1982, Central State University, Robeson Center for the Performing Arts, Wilberforce.

World Deluxe, Sano1, 1997, Cleveland.

OREGON

Albina Mural Project, Isaka Shamsud-Din, Charles Tatum, Henry Frison, Darryl Clegg, Chonita Henderson, Larry Scott, and Jenny Harata, 1977–1978, Portland.

Bilalian Odyssey, Isaka Shamsud-Din, Portland Justice Center, Portland.

Children of Humanity, Charlotte Lewis, 1995.

Untitled, Adriene Cruz, 1998, Northeast Health Center, Portland.

PENNSYLVANIA

Adventure in Reading, Walter Edmonds, 1989, Philadelphia Regional Library, 57th and Sansome, Philadelphia.

Black Family Reunion 1991, Dietrich Adonis and Jane Golden, 1991, 33rd and Ridge Avenues, Philadelphia.

Celebration, Charles R. Searles, assisted by James Phillips and others, 1976, William J. Green Jr. Federal Building (second floor), 600 Arch Street, Philadelphia.

Church of the Advocate Mural, Walter Edmonds and Richard Watson, 1973–76, 18th and Diamond Streets, North Philadelphia.

Homage to Diego Rivera, Dietrich Adonis, 1989, 17th and Wallace Streets, Philadelphia.

Night of the Poor, Day of the Harvest, Sharecropper, 1946, John Biggers, Pennsylvania State University, Burows Education Building, State College.

Pittsburgh Recollections, designed by Romare Bearden, 1984, Gateway Center Station, Allegheny County's Light Rail Transit, Pittsburgh.

Tribute to [Henri] Rousseau, Dietrich Adonis, 1988, Philadelphia.

RHODE ISLAND

Procession of the Ancients, Napoleon Jones-Henderson, 1996, Providence.

Shaping Things to Come, Munir Mohammad and Michael Sandoval with youth, 1991, Elmwood Community Center, 155 Niagara Street, Providence.

TENNESSEE

Alley B, William Walker, 1954, Flamingo Club, near Beale Street, Memphis.

Black Music, Dana Chandler with students, 1971, Knoxville College.

Building More Stately Mansions, Aaron Douglas, 1943, Fisk University International Student Center, Nashville.

Jamming the Blues, William Walker, 1954, Flamingo Club, near Beale Street, Memphis.

Library Murals, Aaron Douglas, assisted by Edwin A. Harleston, 1929–30, Fisk University Cravath Library, Nashville.

[Sports murals](gone), William Edouard Scott, 1915, Fisk University gymnasium and Student Union, Nashville.

Street Scene, William Walker, 1954, Flamingo Club, near Beale Street, Memphis.

A Tribute to Beale Street, Charles Davis and George Hunt with forty art students from Shelby State Community College, 1980, 2nd and Beale Streets, Memphis.

TEXAS

At the Park, Arleen R. Polite, 1992, Holly Street Power Plant/Menz Park, Austin.

Birth from the Sea, John Biggers, 1964–66, Houston Public Library, Houston.

The Contribution of Negro Women to American Life and Education, John Biggers, 1953, YWCA (Blue Triangle Branch), 3005 McGowen, Houston.

Evolution of the Carver High School, John Biggers, 1955, Naples.

Gleaners and Harvesters, John Biggers, 1951, Eliza Johnson Home for Aged Negroes, Houston.

Local 872 Longshoremen, John Biggers, 1957, Houston.

Monkeys Reaching for the Moon, Carroll Simms, 1960, Dowling Veterinary Clinic, Houston.

Red Barn Farm, John Biggers, 1960, Dowling Veterinary Clinic, Houston.

Riffs & Rhythms, John Yancey and Steven Bernard Jones, 1996, Austin Convention Center, Austin.

Scott Joplin, unknown artist, Texarkana.

Stations of the Cross, Arleen R. Polite, 1997, St. James Episcopal Church, Austin.

Untitled, Arleen R. Polite, 1988, Wheatsville Food Co-op, 3101 Guadalupe, Austin.

Untitled, Theodore Stevens, 1997, 1157 Chicon Street on Studio 22, Austin.

Voyage to Soulsville (originally called *Sesquicentennial*), John Fisher, 1986 (restored 1997–99), George Washington Carver Library, 1161 Angelina Street, Austin.

Web of Life, John Biggers, 1966, Texas Southern University Science Bldg., Houston.

VIRGINIA

The Contribution of the Negro to Democracy in America, Charles White with students, 1943, Hampton University, Hampton.

House of the Turtle and *Tree House,* John Biggers and James Biggers Jr., 1990–92, Hampton University, Hampton.

WASHINGTON

Games, Jacob Lawrence, 1979, originally in Kingdome Stadium, 100 level bridge at Gate G, Seattle.

Theatre, Jacob Lawrence, 1985, University of Washington, Meany Theatre lobby, Seattle.

WASHINGTON, D.C.

The Aspects of Music, James A. Padgett, 1969, Anacostia Museum, Smithsonian Institute.

Community Rhythms, Alfred J. Smith with Howard University students, 1994, U Street Metro Station.

Equal Justice Under Law, DC Youth, 1994.

Exploration, Jacob Lawrence, 1979–80, Howard University Armour J. Blackburn University Center.

Fine Arts, Art, Music, Drama, Past and Present (gone), James A. Padgett, 1968, Howard University Fine Arts Building (exterior).

Five Great American Negroes (Progress of the American Negro), Charles White, 1939–40, Collection of Howard University Gallery of Art.

Frederick Douglass (destroyed), Archibald Motley Jr., 1935, Howard University, Douglass Memorial Hall.

Frederick Douglass Appeals to President Lincoln, William Edouard Scott, 1943, Recorder of Deeds Building.

Into Bondage, Aaron Douglas, 1936 (one of four panels originally painted for the Hall of Negro Life, Texas Centennial Exposition in Dallas, Texas), Corcoran Gallery.

The King Mural, Don Miller, 1986, Martin Luther King Jr. Memorial Library, 901 G Street, NW.

Origins, Jacob Lawrence, 1982–84, Howard University Armour J. Blackburn University Center.

Progress of the American Negro (also known as *Five Great American Negroes*), Charles White, 1939–40, Howard University Gallery of Art.

The Role of the Health Center, James A. Padgett, 1973, Shaw Community Health Center.

The Role of the Social Worker, James A. Padgett, 1970, Howard University School of Social Work.

WISCONSIN

The Cycle, Ras Ammar Nsoroma, 1993, 39th and North, Milwaukee.

Life Works I: Community Service, Brad Bernard, 1995, House of Peace, Milwaukee.

Life Works II: Political Activists, Brad Bernard, 1995, House of Peace, Milwaukee.

Life Works III: Victory Over Violence, Brad Bernard, 1997, Career Youth Development Center, Milwaukee.

Patterns of Life: Years of Color (gone), Brad Bernard, 1993, Bethesda Community Center, Milwaukee.

Untitled, Ras Ammar Nsoroma, 1994, 27th and Center, Milwaukee.

Untitled, Milwaukee Arts Center, Milwaukee.

Artist Biographies

A-One (Anthony Clark) (b.1964)

Born in New York City and raised in the Bronx, A-One was one of the youngest spraycan artists to have his work selected for exhibit at the Venice Biennale. He credits friend Jean-Michel Basquiat as an important source of inspiration and guidance. He has lived and worked in several European countries.

Adonis, Dietrich

Born in the Virgin Islands, he studied at the Philadelphia College of Art (BFA in illustration, 1980) and Temple University–Tyler School of Art (M.Ed. in art education, 1997). In addition to being an accomplished muralist, he has been the assistant art director of the Mural Arts Program for the Philadelphia Department of Recreation since 1996. Before that he was assistant artistic director of the Philadelphia Anti-Graffiti Network's mural program, 1985–96.

Aiken, Ta-Coumba

He graduated from the Minneapolis College of Art and Design, majoring in design and printmaking. He has lectured widely, including presentations in Nigeria. Aiken has directed the Minneapolis Arts Commission, the African American Cultural Center, the Minnesota Citizens for the Arts, and the St. Paul Art Collective.

Akinlana, Marcus (Mark Jefferson)

Born and raised in Washington, D.C., he has traced his ancestry to the Yoruba people of Benin and Nigeria. By age six, Akinlana knew he wanted to be a public artist, and at fourteen he joined Washington's Public Art Works, Inc. as an apprentice muralist. Attracted by Chicago's reputation as a mural center, he moved there in 1984. He studied at the School of the Art Institute of Chicago. After graduating he taught art at several community art centers and public schools. In 1987 he joined the Chicago Public Art Group. In 1989 *Ebony* magazine named him one of fifty future African American leaders of America. Since 1991 Akinlana has divided his time between Chicago and New Orleans.

Alston, Charles (1907–1977)

Born in Charlottesville, North Carolina, he moved to New York City at age seven. His father was an Episcopal minister who died when Charles was three years old. His mother's second husband was artist Romare Bearden's uncle. After finishing college he got a job working at a community center in Harlem called Utopia House, where one of his students

was ten-year-old Jacob Lawrence. Between 1935 and 1938 he was New York City mural painting supervisor for the Federal Art Project. He watched Diego Rivera paint his Rockefeller Center mural. Alston graduated from Columbia University, and he was a teacher and magazine illustrator as well as a muralist. In the early 1970s he was an artist-member of the New York Arts Commission.

Anderson, Darrell

He studied at the Art Students League of Denver and the University of Colorado. Anderson has been commissioned to create numerous painted and mosaic murals throughout Colorado, as well as one in Brest, France. His personal work has been exhibited in close to thirty solo shows in Colorado and California.

Apex (Ricardo Richey) (b. 1978)

A native of San Francisco, Apex has been a spraycan artist since 1995, although his interest in graffiti art began when he was in the third grade. He began hanging around with graffiti writers in 1987, studying the various styles and techniques. In 1999 he attended San Francisco City College with plans to transfer to California College of Arts and Crafts in 2000. His major is graphic arts.

Austin, Alexander (b. 1961)

A native of Tallahassee, Florida, Austin studied billboard painting for three years and commercial art for a year before moving to Kansas City, Missouri, in 1988. During a period of homelessness, he turned to mural painting, using an "Accepting Donations" sign to earn enough to get off the streets. In addition to his many self-sponsored murals, he has also been commissioned to do murals for the Kansas City Zoo as well as local churches and schools.

Basquiat, Jean-Michel (1960–1989)

Born in New York to Haitian and Puerto Rican parents, Basquiat, also known as SAMO, was active in the local hip-hop, street culture, beginning in the late 1970s with spraycanned poetry on subway walls and trains. In 1981 he had his first solo show of mixed-media paintings in Italy, and the following year in New York City at the Annina Nosei Gallery.

Bearden, Romare (1911–1988)

Born in Charlotte, North Carolina, Bearden was raised in Pittsburgh and Harlem. He studied mathematics at New York University (BS in 1935) and at the Art Students League (1935–36). He was a social worker in New York for twenty years. Best known for his collages, his work is in major museum and private collections throughout the world.

Bernard, Brad (b. 1967)

Born and raised in Madison, Wisconsin, Bernard moved to Milwaukee in 1988. He studied commercial art illustration before receiving his BFA from the Milwaukee Institute of Art and Design. Before painting his first mural in 1993, Bernard assisted George Gist on several Milwaukee murals. He has been teaching art at community centers and alternative schools since 1992.

Biggers, John (b. 1924)

Biggers, one of this country's foremost muralists, was born in Gastonia, North Carolina. He studied at Hampton Institute (now University) (BS and MS in 1948) and Pennsylvania State University (Ph.D. in 1954). He founded the Art Department at Texas Southern University in 1949, and was its chair until his retirement in 1983. A major retrospective of his work, organized by the Houston Museum of Fine Arts, began an extensive tour of museums around the United States beginning in 1995.

Birch, Willie (b. 1942)

Born in New Orleans, he studied at Southern University (BA) and Maryland Institute College of Art in Baltimore (MFA). In 1984 he was a cofounder of Artmakers, Inc., a nonprofit multiethnic organization of professional public artists who worked on community-based projects. He also created murals for the New York subway's Intervale Station in the Bronx and at Philadelphia International Airport. His work has been widely exhibited in the United States, as well as in Mexico City, Havana, Moscow, Paris, and Bologna.

Blade (Steve Ogburn) (b. 1957)

A native of New York, he did his first "piece" in 1972, and over the next twelve years he spraypainted five thousand trains in the New York City area. Since 1981, he has participated in numerous exhibits of spraycan art throughout Europe and in New York.

Blayton, Betty (b. 1938)

Born in Williamsburg, Virginia, she received her BFA from Syracuse University in 1959. She also studied at the Art Students League and the Brooklyn Museum Art School. In 1968 Blayton became executive director of the Children's Art Carnival, an art program started by Victor D'Amico of the Museum of Modern Art. A teacher as well as a fine artist, she created a visual arts curriculum at the Children's Art Carnival in Harlem.

Borders, Michael (b. c. 1948)

He studied at Fisk University (AA) and Howard University College of Fine Arts (MFA). In 1974 his mural proposal for downtown Hartford, Connecticut, became the subject of controversy. Members of the local Fine Arts Commission opposed his design, which showed a black presence in the building of Connecticut's capital city.

Bradford, David (b. 1937)

Born in Chicago, he studied at the Art Institute of Chicago, Otis Art Institute in Los Angeles, Lincoln University (BS, 1963), and the University of California at Berkeley (MS). Bradford worked briefly on the *Wall of Respect*. He taught graphic arts at the East Oakland Development Center (later, Merritt College Community Educational Center) in the early 1970s.

Brice, Bruce

Brice is a self-taught New Orleans muralist who documented the demolition of his neighborhood, Treme, through murals during the early 1970s. His work inspired other local artists, including muralist Richard Thomas.

Brown, Elmer W. (b. 1909)

He was born in Pittsburgh, moving to Cleveland in 1929 where he almost immediately became involved with other artists at Karamu House, a local community arts center. He did murals for the Cleveland Federal Art Project and one at the Cleveland City Club.

Byard, Carole (b. 1941)

Byard is a painter and installation artist as well as a creator of art for publication. She has received two fellowships from the National Endowment for the Arts (drawing in 1986 and sculpture in 1994), a travel grant to five African countries in 1972 from Ford Motor Company and the Institute of International Education, five Coretta Scott King awards, and a Caldecott Honor Medal for children's book illustration. Byard lectures and exhibits throughout the country and abroad.

Carr, Carla (b. 1971)

A native of Joliet, Illinois, she studied at Creighton University (BA) and Governors State University (MFA in painting, 1999). She has worked with the Friends of Community Public Art in Joliet and the Chicago Public Art Group since 1995.

Carter, Alvin

Born in Bogalusa, Louisiana, Carter came to Minnesota in 1968 after serving in the Navy. Primarily a self-taught artist, he took classes at the Minneapolis College of Art and Design. He has worked as an artist-in-the-schools and has painted murals for St. Paul's public agency COMPAS (Community Programs in the Arts and Sciences).

Caton, Mitchell (c. 1930–1998)

Born Theodore Burns Mitchell in Hot Springs, Arkansas, he was raised in Chicago. Shortly after graduating from high school, Caton received a commission to paint a portrait of then Arkansas governor Sidney McMath. That led to a scholarship to study art at the University of Little Rock. He also studied at the School of the Art Institute of Chicago and the Art Students League in New York. He met William Walker while working as a mail sorter at the downtown Chicago post office during the 1960s. In 1969 he joined a group of artists in repainting sections of the *Wall of Respect*. In 1970 he joined the Chicago Mural Group. His mural collaboration with Calvin Jones began in 1976 when they got together with Justine DeVan to paint *A Time to Unite*.

Chandler, Dana (aka Akin Duro) (b. 1941)

Born in Lynn, Massachusetts, Chandler studied at the Massachusetts College of Art (BS in 1967). He was a leading figure in the mural movement in Boston during the late 1960s and early 1970s. He started AAMARP (the African American Master Artists in Residency Program) at Northeastern University, where he taught for many years. He has also been teaching at Simmons University since 1971. A major retrospective of his work was held at Northeastern and the Massachusetts College of Art in 1987. In 1998 his work was again featured when the AAMARP Galleries at Northeastern celebrated *34 Years of Outsider Art*. Professor Chandler exhibits and lectures widely at colleges and universities across America.

Chisolm, Ayumi (*see* Sano1)

Clark, Chris

Born and raised in Birmingham, Alabama, Clark identifies himself as a "visionary folk artist." He became an artist after attending Livingston University and spending time in the army. In addition to working on mural projects with youth through the Birmingham Museum of Art, he also creates story quilts, furniture, and ceremonial staffs.

Clark, Melvin W.

Born in Detroit, he moved to New York City in 1986. He created his first public mural in 1996, two mosaic panels for a school in Brooklyn. His work has been exhibited in New York, Detroit, Amsterdam, Paris, Copenhagen, and Stockholm.

Cole, Kevin E.

Born in Pine Bluff, Arkansas, Cole attended the University of Arkansas at Pine Bluff (BS in art education), the University of Illinois, Champaign, (MA in art education and painting), and Northern Illinois University (MFA in drawing). Of the more than a dozen public artworks he has created, many with children, the best known is the fifteen-story-tall mural he did when the Olympics came to Atlanta in 1996. It features portraits of thirty-five significant Georgians and the silhouette of a giant Coke bottle. Cole currently is Chairman of the Visual Arts Magnet Program at North Springs High School in Atlanta.

Conwill, Houston (b. 1947)

Born in Louisville, Kentucky, Conwill is a sculptor and public artist. He studied at Howard University (BFA, 1973) and the University of Southern California (MFA, 1976). While living in California in the late 1970s, he gave performances with his wife, Kinshasha Holman Conwill, and other participants, incorporating music, dance, and the spoken word in his shows. In the late 1980s Conwill began collaborating with his sister, poet Estella Conwill Majozo, and architect Joseph DePace to do site-specific public art monuments that incorporate Kongo/Yoruba-inspired cosmograms—these are commonly marked on the ground in traditional and New World African cultures as emblems of empowerment. Conwill, Majozo, and DePace built several major monuments in cities across the country, including Miami, Chicago, San Francisco, and New York City, and they recently completed a memorial tribute to the African burial ground in Manhattan.

Cook, Brett (*see* Dizney)

Cox, Anthony (b. 1954)

Cox grew up in Watts, Los Angeles. He studied animation and commercial art at Otis Art Institute (1972) in a program for inner-city youth that was started after the Watts Rebellion. Between 1975 and 1979 he painted murals with the Citywide Mural Project in Los Angeles. He has done freelance animation for Hanna-Barbera, and has taught art at the Watts Towers Arts Center.

Crumpler, Dewey (b. 1949)

Born in Magnolia, Arkansas, he studied at the San Francisco Art Institute (BFA in 1974) and San Francisco State University (MFA in 1989). He currently teaches at the University of California at Berkeley, San Francisco State University, and the San Francisco Art Institute. A major force in the San Francisco Bay Area mural movement, Crumpler was influenced by his travels to Mexico to study *Los Tres Grandes*.

Cruz, Adriene

A nationally known quilt maker, Cruz was selected by the Portland, Oregon, Percent for Art program to decorate the exterior of the Northeast Health Center with patterns from her quilts and African *adinkra* symbols.

Davis, Alonzo (b. 1942)

Born at Tuskegee Institute (now Tuskegee University), he studied art in Los Angeles at Pepperdine College (BFA in 1964) and Otis Art Institute (BFA in 1971 and MFA in 1973). He established Brockman Gallery in the Leimert Park neighborhood in South Los Angeles in 1967. During the 1970s, Davis and his Brockman Gallery Productions received numerous grants to offer art and art history classes and to paint murals throughout the city of Los Angeles. After leaving L.A., Davis spent time teaching art in Sacramento and San Antonio before becoming affiliated with the Memphis College of Art; he is currently the dean and director of Graduate Studies. His paintings and mixed media works have been exhibited in solo shows throughout the United States as well as in Scandinavia.

Davis, Charles

Davis created his first mural, *Afro-Occidental Projections,* in Miami in 1974, and later painted others at the University of Miami and the Model Cities Cultural Arts Center. His best-known work, painted with students and George Hunt, was *A Tribute to Beale Street* in Memphis in 1980.

Davis, Charles (b. 1912)

Born in Evanston, Illinois, he studied at the School of the Art Institute of Chicago with George C. Neal. He was active in the Chicago WPA, painting a mural for the Hall Library. He also executed a six-panel mural called *Progress of American Industry for Sea View Hospital on Staten Island, New York* in 1938.

Dennis, Senay (*see* Refa)

DeVan, Justine (b. 1936)

A native of Philadelphia, DeVan worked on her first mural in 1968. From 1973 to 1977, while on sabbatical from teaching art in the Philadelphia public schools, she lived in Chicago in order to study at the School of the Art Institute of Chicago. She also studied at Cheney and Temple Universities in Pennsylvania. During her stay in Chicago, she worked with the Chicago Mural Group, doing her first Chicago mural in a school in 1974. In 1976, she collaborated with Calvin Jones and Mitchell Caton on *Time to Unite,* the latter two's first mural together. She is retired from teaching, and lives in Philadelphia.

Dillard, Thurman

Originally from St. Louis, Dillard studied mural painting while in the army at Fort Huachuca, Arizona. There he participated in a workshop founded by white artist Lew Davis to teach black soldiers how to paint murals. After his discharge in 1946, he studied art and music at Colorado College (BA, 1949, and MA in 1952). Mexican muralist Jean Charlot was on his thesis committee. Upon completing his education, Dillard set up a

studio in Santa Fe. His two known Santa Fe murals appear to have been destroyed. In addition to painting, he also wrote poetry and completed an opera, *Navajo Night Song.*

Dizney (Brett Cook) (b. 1970)

Born and raised in San Diego, Dizney began spraypainting in 1984. He moved to the San Francisco Bay Area in 1986, where he studied art and education at the University of California, Berkeley (BA 1991), and created numerous nonpermission aerosol pieces on the streets of San Francisco. After graduating he did some teaching before moving to the East Coast in 1994. He has lived in Harlem since 1997, and his aerosol work continues to reflect his commitment to making art that empowers and challenges both museumgoers and people in the streets.

Donaldson, Jeff (b. 1932)

Donaldson was born in Pine Bluff, Arkansas, and grew up in Chicago. He studied at Arkansas A.M.&N. College (BA), Illinois Institute of Technology (MS), and Northwestern University (Ph.D.). He first painted murals in 1960 in Pine Bluff at Arkansas A.M.&N. College (now the University of Arkansas, Pine Bluff). In 1967 he helped organize OBAC (Organization of Black American Cultures), a group of Chicago artists, musicians, and dancers who wanted to participate in the black power and pride movement. Bill Walker, the group's oldest member, suggested they do a mural, which became the now-famous *Wall of Respect.* After completing that mural, the group broke up, but several of its members, led by Donaldson, formed AfriCobra (African Commune of Bad Relevant Artists) in 1968. Donaldson began teaching at Howard University in 1970. Murals by members of his social painting course were installed on campus during the 1970s. At various times Donaldson was director of Howard's art gallery, chair of the art department, and associate dean of the College of Fine Arts.

Douglas, Aaron (1899–1979)

The leading painter and illustrator of the Harlem Renaissance, Douglas received a BFA from the University of Nebraska in 1922, and an MA from Columbia University. After moving to Harlem in 1925, he studied with Winold Reiss, a painter who greatly influenced his work. Douglas became the first president of the Harlem Artists Guild when it was formed in the mid-1930s. He illustrated James Weldon Johnson's *God's Trombones,* as well as issues of *Crisis* and *Opportunity* magazines. In 1939 he became founding chair of the Fisk University art department. He taught there until his retirement in 1966.

Duncanson, Robert Scott (1821–1872)

Born in Fayette, New York, his parents were of Scottish and African American ancestry. In 1838 Duncanson began working as a glazier and house painter. By 1841, he had opened a studio in Cincinnati, specializing in landscape, genre, and portrait painting. His mural series for the Cincinnati home of abolitionist attorney and art patron Nicholas Longworth became the historical starting point for African American murals.

Dunn, Sharon

She is known for her mural of women, *Maternity,* painted in the Roxbury area of Boston in 1970.

Duro, Akin (*see* Chandler, Dana)

Eda, Eugene (Eugene Wade) (b. 1939)

Born in Baton Rouge, Louisiana, he earned a BS from Southern University and an MA from Howard University, where he studied with Hughie Lee-Smith. Eda also received a scholarship to Skowhegan School of Art in Maine, where he worked under Jacob Lawrence. He has been creating murals since the 1960s. Eda worked on later versions of the *Wall of Respect,* and in 1971 he was one of the four original artists for the *Murals for the People* show and its accompanying Artists' Statement. He has been artist-in-residence at Malcolm X College (where he painted many stairwell doors with Egyptian motifs), at the DuSable Museum, and for the City of Chicago. He teaches at Kennedy-King College in Chicago.

Edwards, Eddie L.

Born in Pineville, Louisiana, Edwards came to California as a child in 1950. In 1969 he opened the first culturally oriented art gallery in San Diego. He has lectured and exhibited throughout the United States.

Edwards, Melvin

Born in Texas, Edwards received his BFA from the University of Southern California. Primarily a sculptor, he was one of the Smokehouse artists in Harlem from 1968 to 1971. Since then Edwards's large abstract stainless-steel constructions have appeared at the Wadsworth Atheneum in Hartford, Connecticut, the Los Angeles County Museum of Art, the Museum of Modern Art in New York, and the Whitney Museum of American Art. In 1993 the Neuberger Museum of Art in Purchase, New York, presented a thirty-year retrospective of his work.

Feagin, John W.

A native of Birmingham, Alabama, Feagin studied at Alabama State University (BS and MA in fine arts and history). He did an additional two-year art course at the University of Alabama. For thirty-four years he taught fine art and creative drawing at George Washington Carver High School in Montgomery, where he has lived since 1957. His work at Dexter Avenue King Memorial Church is his only mural.

Fisher, John (b. 1962)

A native of Austin, Texas, he apprenticed with artist Amado Peña Jr., then studied with John Biggers at Texas Southern University. He has done several murals in the Austin area, but most of them are no longer in existence. He recently restored his major public work *Voyage to Soulsville,* originally painted in 1986 at Carver Library.

Foster, Leroy

He was born in Detroit and studied at Cass Technical High School (where he later did a mural), the Society of Arts and Crafts under Sarkis Sarkisian, the Academie de la Grande Chaumiere in Paris, and the Heatherley School of Art in London. He painted several murals in the Detroit area.

Franco (Franklin Gaskin) (b. c. 1929)

Franco's father was a U.S. Marine. Born in Panama, Franco studied art at the Fine Arts School in Panama, and apprenticed with two local artists. He moved to New York in 1960, initially supporting himself by painting murals for restaurants and bars. In 1980, Franco began painting colorful imagery on the steel pull-down security gates lining Harlem's 125th Street. The recognition he's achieved from his free "murals" in Harlem has brought opportunities to travel to and paint murals in Japan, Europe, and Africa.

Freeman, Charles (b. 1951)

Born and raised in Houston, Texas, Freeman is a self-taught artist. He moved to Los Angeles in 1974 while active in the Black Panther Party as an organizer. He has painted close to a dozen murals over the past twenty years, and operates his own sign-painting business.

Gaskin, Franklin (*see* Franco)

Gayton, Robert

He is a former boxer who painted the first outdoor mural in San Francisco's Fillmore district in 1972, a *Wall of Respect*-type image featuring portraits of prominent African Americans. During the late 1970s he was employed by CETA to paint murals in Juvenile Hall in San Francisco.

George, Stephanie

Active with the Chicago Public Art Group, George has participated in creating murals at the Forever Free Women and Children's Shelter (1994), Nicholson School (with Julia Sowles, 1995), and Harper High School (with Nina Smoot-Cain, 1997). She also collaborated with Marcus Akinlana on *The Great Migration* (1995) and with Juan Chávez on *The Cameron Transformation Mosaic* (1996).

Gist, George

A student of Jon Onye Lockard, he painted several murals in Milwaukee. He moved to Pittsburgh in the mid-1990s.

Goodnight, Paul (b. 1946)

Born in Chicago, he was raised in New London, Connecticut, and Boston. He was so damaged by military service in Vietnam that he returned unable to speak. Using drawing to communicate the horrors of war, he healed himself. In 1976, he received his BA from Massachusetts College of Art. He has traveled extensively, living in Russia, China, Haiti, Nicaragua, Brazil, and Africa.

Goss, Bernard (b. 1913)

Born in Sedalia, Missouri, Goss studied at the University of Iowa (BA, 1935) and the Art Institute of Chicago (1935–37). He did murals for New Crusader's Negro History Hall of Fame at the Chicago Coliseum from 1960 to 1962.

Greene, Jimmy James

A collagist and a painter, he studied at the Rhode Island School of Design. He apprenticed with Jon Onye Lockard, assisting him on murals in Detroit and Wilberforce, Ohio, before moving to Brooklyn.

Harleston, Edwin (Augustus) (1882–1931)

Born in Charleston, South Carolina, he studied at Atlanta University (BA, 1904), Boston Museum of Fine Arts School and Harvard University. He is best known for his collaboration with Aaron Douglas on the murals at Fisk University.

Harris, Michael D. (b. 1948)

Harris studied at Bowling Green State University (BS, 1971), Howard University (MFA in painting, 1979), and Yale University (MA in African and African American Studies, 1989; MA in the history of art, 1990; M.Phil. in the history of art, 1991; and Ph.D., 1996). He has been a member of AfriCobra visual arts group since 1979. Harris painted murals in Cleveland and Atlanta during the mid-1970s and the early 1980s. An accomplished painter, Harris recently curated the *Transatlantic Dialogue* show that traveled to the Smithsonian in Washington, D.C., in 2000. He is currently assistant professor of African and African American art history at the University of North Carolina, Chapel Hill.

Hayes, Vertis (b. 1911)

Born in Atlanta, Georgia, Hayes studied with Mexican muralist Jean Charlot in Chicago before moving to New York in the mid-1930s. He worked for the Federal Art Project's mural division in New York City (1935–39). In addition to his mural at Harlem Hospital, he also painted *The Chelsea Story* (1934) for a New York high school and *The Carver Mural* (1942) at Jackson State University. He became chair of the LeMoyne College Art Department in Memphis, where he taught from 1938 to 1940. He founded the Hayes Academy of Art in Tennessee in 1947, serving as its director until 1952. Later, in the 1970s, he was a lecturer at Immaculate Heart College in California.

Holliman, Jessie H. (c. 1905–84)

She studied at the Art Institute of Chicago, Columbia University, and the Washington University of Fine Arts, and graduated from Harris-Stowe State College in St. Louis. She taught art for thirty-nine years at the Divoll School in St. Louis. Holliman was also a freelance fashion illustrator. She painted three murals in St. Louis, of which only one, *The Origin of Freemasonry,* remains at the Masonic Temple Association. That mural was dedicated by then Senator Harry Truman in 1941. Her first mural, *Racial and Industrial Harmony,* was painted in the old Urban League building. *Christ's Fellowship* was in the Central Baptist Church.

Howard, John

He assisted Hale Woodruff on his murals at Talladega College and Atlanta University. He taught mural painting at what is now the University of Arkansas in Pine Bluff. One of his students was Jeff Donaldson, who painted his first mural in 1960 while in Howard's class.

Hubbard, Jean Paul

Born in Bedford, Virginia, he studied at Wilberforce University (BS) and Ohio State University (MFA), Dayton Art Institute, University of California at Berkeley and Tulane University. He served as chair of the Fine Art Department at Southern University in Baton Rouge.

Hudson, Henry (b. 1908)

Born in Georgia, Hudson studied at Yale University's School of Fine Arts and at Howard University. While a student at Howard, he and Elizabeth Catlett were selected to do murals under the federally sponsored Public Works of Art Project in 1934. Catlett never completed hers, but Hudson painted two murals.

Hunter, Clementine (b. c. 1886)

Born on Hidden Hill Plantation in Cloutierville, Louisiana, she worked as a farm laborer and domestic servant. She is believed to have done her first painting, on a window shade, at age fifty-five. However, before starting to paint, Hunter found other ways to express her creativity, including quilting, basket weaving, sewing clothes, hand-tying lace, and cooking. During the mid-1950s, she painted a mural depicting plantation life in Cane County, Louisiana, for a room in "African House" on Melrose Plantation.

Jarrell, Wadsworth A. (b. 1931)

Born in Albany, Georgia, he studied at the Art Institute of Chicago. He was a professor for many years at Howard University as well as at the University of Georgia. His early artistic influences included Archibald Motley and Eldzior Cortor. A participant in the original *Wall of Respect* in Chicago, he was a founding member of OBAC and AfriCobra. After retiring from teaching, he moved to New York City in 1993.

Jefferson, Mark (*see* Akinlana, Marcus)

Johnson, Jerome

He studied art at North Carolina A & T State University and Federal City College in Washington, D.C. (BA in Art Education). After doing a number of small murals, he won his first major commission in 1983 in a contest through the Cultural Arts Center in Newport News, Virginia, where he was on the staff. He has painted ten to fifteen murals, including several temporary backdrops for large church holiday productions. He has lived in Washington, D.C., since 1993.

Johnson, Sargent (1888–1967)

Born in Boston, Johnson was primarily a sculptor. He studied at the California and Boston Schools of Fine Arts and the A.W. Best School of Art in San Francisco. He did several ceramic and enamel wall reliefs for the Federal Art Project of the WPA and for private businesses in San Francisco.

Jones, Calvin B. (b. 1934)

Born and raised in Chicago, Jones was awarded a full scholarship to study at the Art Institute of Chicago (BFA in drawing/painting and illustration, 1957). After college Jones worked in advertising for seventeen years. In 1970 he left advertising to become codirector of the avant-garde AFAM Gallery Studio and Cultural Center in Chicago. Since 1976 he has painted nine murals, seven in Chicago (often in collaboration with Mitchell Caton), one in Detroit, and one in Atlanta.

Jones, Frederick D. Jr. (b. 1914)

Born in Chicago, he studied at Clark College in Atlanta and at the Art Institute of Chicago. Study at the latter school was financed by the chairman of Coca-Cola, who was impressed by a sketchbook that the artist and part-time janitor accidentally left one night in the executive office after cleaning it.

Jones-Henderson, Napoleon (b. 1943)

He studied at the School of the Art Institute of Chicago (BFA, 1970) and Northern Illinois University, DeKalb (MFA in textile weaving, 1974). He also studied at the Student Continuum at The Sorbonne in Paris. Jones-Henderson works in different media, including sculpture, enamel, printmaking and tapestry. He is currently executive director of the Research Institute of African and African Diaspora Arts, Inc. in Roxbury, Boston, Massachusetts.

Jones-Hogu, Barbara (b. 1938)

Born in Chicago, she studied at Howard University (BA, 1959), the School of the Art Institute of Chicago (BFA), and Illinois Institute of Technology (MS). A participant in the original *Wall of Respect* in Chicago, she was a founding member of OBAC and AfriCobra. Jones-Hogu currently teaches at Malcolm X College in Chicago.

Jones, Lawrence A. (1910–1999)

Born in Lynchburg, Virginia, the eldest of twelve children, he studied at the School of the Art Institute of Chicago (BA in drama, 1939). In 1943 he won a Rosenwald Scholarship to study in Mexico, spending a year and a half at the Taller de Grafica Popular. During World War II he was a visual aids designer and a muralist in the U.S. Army. He headed the art departments at Dillard University in New Orleans and Fort Valley State College in Georgia before becoming head of the art department at Jackson State University in Mississippi in 1949. In 1971 he received an MFA in painting from the University of Mississippi.

Jones, Seitu

Seitu Jones studied at Morehouse College and the University of Minnesota (BA in art, 1985). He also attended Harvard University's Institute in Arts Administration under an NEA fellowship in 1974. Jones assisted Ta-Coumba Aiken on several murals beginning in 1973, receiving his first solo commission in 1979. He has created twenty-five to thirty public art works, ten of which are murals. He also does three-dimensional work, such as site-specific installations. He works in clay and wood, and is active in theater doing set designs. He is currently preparing to do graduate work in horticulture, as he often uses plants in his installations.

Jordan, Jack (b. 1927)

Born in Wichita Falls, Texas, he studied at Langston University in Oklahoma (BA, 1948), Iowa University (MA, 1949), the State University of Iowa (MFA, 1953), and Indiana University (MS and PhD in art education, 1975). His work has been exhibited in solo shows throughout the United States and Europe. From 1961 to 1990 he was the chair of the art department at Southern University. He continues to teach there.

Kambon, Akinsanya

A Vietnam veteran, he has been teaching since 1984 at California State University, Long Beach, in the Black Studies Department. In 1993 he painted a mural on the side of a public library in Long Beach to promote reading.

Kase 2 (Jeff Brown) (b. 1958)

Born in Harlem, Brown lost an arm and a leg at the age of ten after being electrocuted while playing on nearby freight tracks. He painted his first handball court in 1973 under the guidance of his street mentor, Butch 2. By 1976 he had painted fifty to seventy-five major pieces on the subway trains of New York City. His unique camouflaged letter style, where letters became cut, sliced and shifted, was referred to as "computer style." After taking a year off, Brown came back to the yards in 1977, painting in a more relaxed manner until 1984.

Kendrick, John A. (1952–1982)

Born in Virginia, he received a full scholarship from the Studio Museum to study at Skowhegan School of Painting and Sculpture in Maine. He also studied with Nelson Stevens at the University of Massachusetts, Amherst, receiving his Ph.D. in 1978. While at Amherst he painted murals on campus in New Africa House and in Springfield at a community center.

Khufu, Shyaam (b. 1947)

A self-taught artist, Khufu has painted twenty murals in the Los Angeles area over the past twenty-five years.

Lane, Doyle (b. 1925)

Born in New Orleans, he studied at Los Angeles City College (AA, 1953), East Los Angeles College, and the University of Southern California. A ceramist, he worked as a glaze technician for the L. H. Butcher Company. He designed a mosaic floor for Equitable Savings and Loan in Canoga Park (southern California), as well as ceramic floors for Mutual Savings and Loan in Pasadena, the Lutheran Nursing Home and Health Center in Alhambra, and a school in West Los Angeles.

Lawrence, Jacob (b. 1917)

Born in Atlantic City, New Jersey, Lawrence was formally trained under the auspices of two New York–based New Deal programs: the Harlem Art Workshop (1934–39) and the American Artists School (1938). Charles Alston was one of his teachers. One of this country's most celebrated artists, Lawrence has received numerous awards and solo exhibitions, and his work is in the collections of many major museums and corporations. His work has also appeared on the cover of *Time,* and he has been featured on several television documentaries.

Lewis, Charlotte (1934–1999)

Born Charlotte La Verne Graves in Prescott, Arizona, she and her family moved to Portland, Oregon, in 1937. She graduated from the Portland Art Museum School in 1955, then worked as a graphic designer for Meier & Frank for several years. In the late 1970s, Lewis began designing and making art for local community groups such as the Urban League, the Black United Fund, the American Friends Service Committee, the Red Cross, the American Cancer Society, and the Rainbow Coalition.

Lewis, Samella (b. 1924)

A major figure in African American art history, Lewis cofounded *Black Art: An International Quarterly* in 1975 (it became the *International Review of African American Art* in 1984). She was the founding director of the Museum of African American Art in Los Angeles, and she has written several books on African American artists. A painter, sculptor, graphic artist, and educator, she painted murals with William Walker at Columbus Gallery School of Art in Ohio in 1947–48. Born in New Orleans, she studied at Hampton Institute (BS, 1945), Ohio State University (MA and Ph.D. in fine arts and art history), New York University, and Tung-Hai University in Taiwan.

Lockard, Jon Onye (b. 1932)

A native of Detroit, he studied at Wayne State University and Meinzingers School of Art, both in Detroit. He also studied at the Fields School of Art, the Art Institute of Chicago, the University of Washington (Seattle), and the University of Toronto. Since 1969 he has taught in the Department of Humanities at Washtenaw Community College (Ann Arbor). Since 1970, he has been an adjunct lecturer at the University of Michigan's Center for AfroAmerican and African Studies. Lockard has exhibited at two World's Fairs and at galleries in Senegal, Nigeria, France, Canada, and Japan. He has received many awards and is currently working on a new series of murals for gaming casinos.

Lutz, John C.

While a day laborer on a WPA construction project in the 1930s, he showed a supervisor a drawing he'd done of a fellow worker. He was immediately transferred to the Federal Art Project's mural division. He painted farm scenes at Garfield School in Cleveland for the FAP.

McCray, Alvin M. (b. 1955)

He has lived in Brooklyn since age six. A film major in high school, McCray studied art at Brooklyn College and the School of Visual Art. He did his first two murals in 1981, one for a local nonprofit and the other with college students. He has also done a number of murals for churches in Brooklyn. In 1990 he completed a mural depicting neighborhood street life, located inside the post office where he was working as a mail handler.

McGee, Charles W. (b. 1924)

Born in Clemson, South Carolina, he moved to Detroit at age ten. He studied art at the Society of Arts and Crafts (now the Center for Creative

Studies) in Detroit (1947–59) and in Barcelona, Spain, for a year (1967–68) at the Escuela Massana and the Barcelona School of Graphics. He had his own art school and gallery during the 1970s, and was an associate professor of art at Eastern Michigan University from 1969 to 1987. In 1978 McGee helped found the Urban Wall Mural Program in Detroit, a community beautification effort funded by the Michigan Council of the Arts. Under its auspices about fifteen murals were created during the late '70s and early '80s. McGee also painted murals for the Martin Luther King Community Center and for Northern High School. In 1989 he created a metal relief for the East Lansing City Hall. He has received many awards and has exhibited widely throughout the United States.

McGhee, Allie (b. 1941)
Born in Charleston, West Virginia, he and his family moved to Detroit in 1951. He studied art at Ferris State College in Big Rapids (AA, 1961) and Eastern Michigan University (BA). He has taught art to senior shut-ins, children, college students, and prisoners. In 1982 he and Charles McGee painted murals for the Martin Luther King Community Center in Detroit; two years later they each created a mural while sharing an artist-in-residency at Northern High School. Other McGhee murals are located at the Michigan-Cass People Mover Station in downtown Detroit, Detroit Receiving Hospital, and Eastern Michigan University.

McIlvaine, Don (b. 1930)
While growing up in Washington, D.C., he attended Saturday-morning art classes taught by Lois Mailou Jones. Later, when she became dean of art at Howard University, she made it possible for McIlvaine to get a scholarship to study art at Howard. He also studied at the Corcoran Art School and Newark Academy of Art. In 1957 he moved to Chicago. Between 1969 and 1970, he painted six street murals in Chicago.

Middlebrook, Willie
Born and raised in Compton, Middlebrook studied at Art Center in Pasadena and Compton College (AA, 1979). During the mid-1970s he was active at the Compton Communicative Arts Academy, a large warehouse space that attracted many local black artists and musicians. His "photo-painted portraits" have been shown in 170 exhibitions throughout the United States, and he has received twenty-eight fellowships, including several from the NEA. Since 1978 Middlebrook has taught photography at the Watts Towers Arts Center and the Junior Arts Center at Barnsdall Art Park, and he is an adjunct professor in computer graphics at Compton College.

Miller, Aaron (b. c.1928)
Born in Oklahoma, Miller hitchhiked to San Francisco at age fourteen after the death of his parents. A self-taught artist, he believed he was divinely inspired to paint a mural depicting the crucifixion of Christ at Emanuel Church of God in Christ in San Francisco. It took him fourteen months, often working twelve-hour days, to complete the project.

Miller, Don (1923–1993)
Born in Jamaica and raised in Montclair, New Jersey, Miller was a graduate of Cooper Union in New York. He also attended the New School and the Art Students League. His work has been exhibited in museums, galleries, and private collections in the United States, Africa, and the West Indies.

Montgomery, Bernice
Montgomery received her BFA from North Texas State University. She has completed murals for Dallas Area Rapid Transit. In 1996 she was awarded a painting fellowship by the National Endowment for the Arts and the Mid-America Arts Alliance.

Motley, Archibald John Jr. (1891–1981)
Born in New Orleans, Motley grew up in Chicago. He graduated from the Art Institute of Chicago (1914–18). He won a Guggenheim Fellowship, spending a year (1929–30) in Paris. He worked in the New Deal art projects (FAP and Section), doing both easel paintings and murals. In 1928 his work was shown in a solo exhibition at the New Gallery in New York, the first for a black artist at a commercial gallery. That same year he won a Harmon Foundation gold medal in fine arts.

Noc (Melvyn Henry Samuels Jr.) (b. 1961)
Born in New York City, Noc started tagging at age eleven. Among the crews he painted with were The Death Squad and OTB (Out To Bomb). He stopped doing trains in 1980. During the early 1980s his work was regularly exhibited in group shows. He lives in Brooklyn.

Nsoroma, Ras Ammar (formerly Ammar Kevin Tate) (b. 1967)
Born and raised in Milwaukee, he studied at the Milwaukee Institute of Art and Design and the Art Institute of Chicago. While studying in Chicago, he collaborated on a mural *(The Circle Journey)* with artists from the Chicago Public Art Group. He has painted twenty-five to thirty murals in the Milwaukee area.

Odighizuwa, Paul
A Nigerian sculptor and painter, he collaborated on two murals with Isaka Shamsud-Din in Portland, Oregon, in 1989.

Ogburn, Steve (*see* Blade)

Owens, Maude Irwin (b. 1900)
A painter and an illustrator, Owens studied at Philadelphia Graphic Sketch Club. She did a fresco for the Polish Catholic Church in Philadelphia.

Padgett, James Arthur (b. 1948)

Born and raised in Washington, D.C., Padgett studied at Corcoran School of Art (1967–68), Skowhegan School of Painting and Sculpture (1971), and Howard University, College of Fine Arts (BFA, 1971, and MFA, 1973). In 1968 he was asked to join a mural painting project coordinated by visiting artist Hughie Lee-Smith and Jeff Donaldson, art department chair. Padgett painted four murals in Washington, D.C., between 1968 and 1973 as part of that project—two at Howard, one at Shaw Community Health Center, and the fourth at Anacostia Museum. He has been a professor of art at Wilberforce University in Ohio since 1973, and his work has been shown in more than fifteen one-man exhibitions and over forty group shows throughout the United States.

Parker, K. Jameel (b. 1963)

Originally from Elizabeth, New Jersey, Parker studied at Prairie View A & M College in Texas and the Boston Museum School (BFA). He teaches art in the Boston area. In 1992 he painted *We're All in the Same Gang* as a statement against black-on-black violence. In 1999 he completed a historical mural at Harriet Tubman House in downtown Boston.

Pate, James

Born in Birmingham, Alabama, Pate grew up in Cincinnati. After graduating from the Cincinnati High School for the Creative and Performing Arts, he began doing freelance illustration and graphic design. He currently lives in Dayton, where he has painted three murals.

Patrick, Alice (b. 1948)

Born and raised in Los Angeles, she studied at Art Center College of Design in Pasadena, California, at Otis Art Institute in Los Angeles, and privately with Anton Sabas. In the mid-1970s Patrick completed a mural on important African American women in history with the Citywide Mural Project in L.A., but it was soon destroyed when the site changed ownership. For about ten years she ran a local community gallery called Aliceland. Sculpture has been her passion for several years. She has recently done additional studies in ceramics and technique. Her most recent body of work is a collection of ceramic objects infused with the ancestral spirit, and narrative compositions in totems telling the story of jazz, life, and birth.

Phillips, (Charles) James (b. 1945)

Born in Brooklyn, he studied at Philadelphia College of Art from 1964 to 1965. A member of AfriCobra, Phillips was artist-in-residence at the Studio Museum in Harlem (1971–72), Howard University (1973–77), and San Francisco County Jail (1988–89). In the early 1980s he painted a mural based on Egyptian symbols in the Hunters Point neighborhood of San Francisco. He has also received mural commissions from the city of Baltimore and Howard University.

Pindell, Howardena (b. 1943)

Born in Philadelphia, she studied at Boston University (BFA in 1965) and Yale University (MFA in 1967), and she worked at the Museum of Modern Art in New York from 1967–1979. In 1971 she cofounded A.I.R. Gallery with other women artists. She joined the faculty of the State University of New York, Stony Brook in 1979, becoming a full professor of art in 1984. Pindell has received many awards, including a Guggenheim Fellowship in 1987, the College Art Association's Most Distinguished Body of Work Award in 1990, and the Studio Museum in Harlem's Artist Award in 1994.

Pinkney, Elliott (b. 1934)

A native of Georgia, Pinkney moved to southern California after serving in the U.S. Air Force. He earned a BA at Woodbury College in Burbank. A poet and sculptor as well as a painter, he has lived in Compton since the early 1970s. He was active at the Compton Communicative Arts Academy. During 1977 and 1978, funded by a special grant from the California Arts Council, he completed eight murals in Compton. Pinkney has completed many murals in the Los Angeles area (including Long Beach)—their underlying themes are most often African American pride and the importance of understanding among different cultures.

Polite, Arleen

Raised in a small town in Florida, Polite studied at Florida School of the Arts in Palatka (AS, 1982) and the Atlanta School of Art in Georgia (BFA in printmaking, 1984). She has created murals for St. James Episcopal Church, Holly Street Power Plant, and Wheatsville Food Co-op, all in Austin, Texas, where she lives. She has her own freelance illustration and design business.

Quik (b. 1958)

Born in Queens, he studied illustration at Pratt Institute in Brooklyn. He started painting subway trains as a spraycan artist when he was twelve years old. He did his first canvas in 1975. By the late eighties he had settled in Holland where his career blossomed, and he began giving solo and group showings.

Refa (Senay Dennis)

A spraycan artist based in Sacramento, Refa has painted extensively in the San Francisco Bay Area. Much of his work has political messages and themes. He has received a number of commissions and also works in gallery format.

Richards, Toby

Originally from southern Georgia, Richards has been Community Outreach Coordinator for the mural program sponsored by the Birmingham Museum of Art since 1995. Under her direction about forty-five murals have been created at schools, parks, community centers, and other neighborhood sites throughout Birmingham. She has received several local awards and honors for her work in exposing children to arts and culture.

Richardson, Earle (1913–1936)

Born in New York City, he studied at the National Academy of Design. He created cartoons for WPA-sponsored murals about African American sharecroppers and the fall of Crispus Attucks on Boston Commons, but his untimely death prevented their completion.

Richardson, Warrior (b. c. 1958)

He studied economics and played jazz saxophone at Howard University, and worked as an economist for the Agency for International Development for four years. He also taught mathematics at Ujamaa Shule, a private Washington, D.C., school. He lives in Omaha, Nebraska, where he teaches art and economics ("economystics") and gives music lessons to young people.

Richey, Ricardo (*see* Apex)

Rickson, Gary (b. 1942)

Born in Boston, Rickson studied at Boston University, the Moorish Science Temple in Baltimore (Ministry degree, 1964), and Roxbury Community College. In 1962 he cofounded the Boston Negro Artists' Association (now the Boston African American Artists' Association). A major force in the Boston area mural movement from 1968 to 1974, he created about fifty murals himself, mostly interior, and was a consultant on more than one hundred others. He produced a radio program, Artistically Revealing Truth, for Harvard University Radio Station WHRB from 1974 to 1984. For the past twenty years Rickson has been a landscaper involved in residential beautification. He also does live poetry readings and plays piano in Boston-area jazz clubs.

Riddle, John (b. 1933)

Born in Los Angeles, he studied at Los Angeles City College (AA, 1960) and California State University, Los Angeles (BA, 1966 and MA, 1973). He taught in Los Angeles area schools from 1966–1973. Riddle moved to Atlanta in 1974. He was executive director of the Neighborhood Art Center for six years, then assistant director of the Atlanta Civic Center from 1984 to 1997. He is currently Program Director of Visual Arts at the California African American Museum in Los Angeles.

Robinson, John A. (1912–1994)

Primarily self-taught, he studied briefly at Howard University with James A. Porter. He painted church murals in the Washington, D.C., area.

Sallée, Charles (b. 1913)

He studied at Western Reserve University, John Huntington Polytechnic Institute, and the Cleveland Museum of Art School. While employed by Cleveland's Federal Art Project in the late 1930s and early 1940s, he painted murals and was also active in printmaking. After serving in the army during World War II, Sallée did some commercial murals for bars and restaurants through the 1950s. He spent thirty-five years in the interior design business.

Sano1 (Ayumi Chisolm)

Sano1 is a spraycan artist from Cleveland, Ohio, active since the early 1980s.

Scott, John T. (b. 1940)

Scott is a multifaceted artist, probably best known for his kinetic sculpture. Born in New Orleans, he studied at Xavier University (BA, 1962) and Michigan State University (MFA, 1965). In 1984 he was the lead artist and concept designer on *I've Known Rivers,* the African American Pavilion at the World's Fair in New Orleans. In 1992 he received a "genius award" from the John D. and Catherine T. MacArthur Foundation. Scott has executed public art projects in Boston, Philadelphia, Nashville, Houston, Atlanta, New Orleans, and Kansas City. He has been a professor of fine arts at Xavier University since 1965.

Scott, William Edouard (1884–1964)

Born in Indianapolis, he studied at the Art Institute of Chicago (1904–1908) and at the Julian and Colarossi Academies in Paris under Henry O. Tanner. He is credited with having painted about seventy-five murals in hotels, banks, schools, and other public buildings, primarily in the Midwest.

Seabrooke Powell, Georgette (b. 1916)

A native of Charleston, South Carolina, she spent most of her youth in the Yorkville section of New York City. Seabrooke studied at Cooper Union Art School in New York (certificate, 1937). She created murals for Harlem Hospital and Queens General Hospital with the WPA's Federal Art Project, 1936–39. After her involvement in the FAP, she studied stage design at Fordham University. In 1959, Seabrooke and her family moved to Washington, D.C. In 1966 she started Arts in the Park, an annual event in Washington, D.C. In 1970 she founded Operation Heritage Art Center, which has been called Tomorrow's World Art Center since 1975. She has been a registered art therapist since 1972. Seabrooke received a BFA from Howard University in 1973. She has shown her mixed-media collages in exhibitions in Washington, D.C., New York, Dallas, and Florida, and her paintings can be found in the Johnson Publishing Company collection.

Searles, Charles (b. 1937)

Born in Philadelphia, he studied at the University of Pennsylvania and the Pennsylvania Academy of Fine Arts (BA, 1972). He has taught art at several colleges, arts centers, and museums since the early 1970s, most recently at Pratt Institute in New York (since 1995). His work has been shown in numerous solo and group exhibitions in the United States and abroad. Over the years his work has become more sculptural. He lives in New York City.

Shamsud-Din, Isaka (Isack Allen Jr.) (b. 1941)

Originally from rural east Texas, he and his family moved to Portland, Oregon, in 1947. He studied art with Robert Colescott at Portland State University (where he did his first mural in 1965), dropping out in 1965 to become a SNCC organizer in Arkansas. Shamsud-Din taught at San Francisco State College in 1966 as one of six original instructors in its Black Studies Program. He has initiated several collaborative mural projects in the African American community of Portland. He is currently a graduate student at Portland State University and a 1999 recipient of a Harold and Arlene Schnitzer Care Foundation fellowship.

Simmons, Mel

A native of Philadelphia, Simmons moved to San Francisco in 1971. It wasn't until 1980, when he was injured doing construction work, that he became involved in art. Simmons studied graphic printing at the Mission Cultural Center, and in 1983, he founded Culture on the Corner with money received from his injury. Culture on the Corner is a group of artists in the Western Addition neighborhood of San Francisco that does community art projects with local children.

Sims, John

A native of Birmingham, Alabama, Sims studied at Tuskegee University (BS, architecture). While a student he assisted on Nelson Stevens's *Centennial Vision,* a project that inspired him to learn more about African American history and culture. His paintings, often focusing on jazz themes, have been exhibited in many solo and group shows around the United States.

Smith, Kiela Songhay

A native of Chicago, she has created murals and mosaics in collaboration with artists, community and school groups, businesses, and city agencies. She studied at the School of the Art Institute of Chicago (BFA in photography, 1991), joining the Chicago Public Art Group while still a student. Shortly after graduating, she traveled to the Ivory Coast. In 1992, she was named Young Artist of the Year by the South Side Community Arts Center.

Smith, Vincent (b. 1929)

Born in Brooklyn, he has been a full-time artist since quitting a post office job at age twenty-three. He studied art with Reginald Marsh at the Art Students League and with Joseph Kongal at the Brooklyn Museum of Art School. In 1955 he received a scholarship to the Skowhegan School in Maine, where he studied with Ben Shahn and Sidney Simon. His work has been exhibited in numerous solo and group shows throughout the United States, as well as in Nigeria, Kenya, Tanzania, and Taiwan. He lives on the Lower East Side of New York City.

Smoot-Cain, Nina

She studied at the University of Illinois, Chicago, earning a BA in plastic and graphic arts in 1979 and an MFA in painting in 1981. She worked at Urban Gateways: The Center for Arts in Education from 1983 to 1998, serving as Director of Special Projects from 1992 to 1996 and as Director of Project Development and Training from 1996 to 1998. She has been a painting instructor at Roosevelt University in Chicago since 1989. Smoot-Cain has completed sixteen public art projects—paintings, mosaics, and sculptures—often in collaboration with other artists from the Chicago Public Art Group (CPAG). She is currently Vice President of the Board of Directors and a member of the Senior Artist Circle of CPAG.

Spon

Based in New York City, he is one of the newer, younger practitioners of spraycan art. Spon collaborated with Vulcan on *Roughneck Reality,* a visual story of the local street culture painted for the Graffiti Hall of Fame.

Stallings, Charles W. (c. 1916–1982)

Born in Gary, Indiana, Stallings was a printmaker, sculptor, and educator as well as a painter. He studied at Lincoln University (BA), University of Iowa (MA), Pennsylvania State University (Ph.D.), and the University of Baltimore School of Law (Ll.D.) He was professor of art at Morgan State College in Baltimore from 1946 to 1978. He also served as dean of faculty at Bowie State University from 1968 to 1978. He completed murals at Morgan State University and the Speech and Hearing Clinic at Pennsylvania State University.

Stephenson, A. G. Joe

Born and raised in Jamaica, Stephenson is of mixed Scottish, Danish, and Jamaican ancestry. Between 1979 and 1983 he worked as a muralist for CityArts Workshop in New York City. In 1984 he, Eva Cockcroft, Willie Birch, and Leslie Bender formed Artmakers, doing murals together in the New York City area until Stephenson moved to Albuquerque, New Mexico, in 1987. He has done many murals, often with youth, in Albuquerque.

Stevens, Nelson (b. 1938)

Born and raised in Brooklyn, New York, Stevens received his BFA from Ohio University (1962) and his MFA from Kent State University (1969). He taught in Cleveland and Illinois before joining the faculty of the University of Massachusetts, Amherst, in 1972. He was a founding member of AfriCobra, and is the founder and president of Spirit Wood Productions, Inc. The form and content of his paintings reflect his strong interest in jazz.

Sykes, Roderick

He has been involved in Los Angeles community arts since 1970. He and his uncle, Rozzell, cofounded St. Elmo Village, a neighborhood-based arts center. He often works with children to create murals in the schools. Sykes also teaches painting, drawing, and photography to children and adults.

Sylvain, Dorian

Dorian Sylvain studied fine arts at the American Academy of Art. She has had a longstanding interest in the theater, working as a scenic designer for fifteen years, beginning when she was a teen. In order to combine her interest in fine arts and theater, Sylvain returned to college, studying interdisciplinary arts at San Francisco State University. Mural painting evolved naturally for her. She is a member of the Chicago Public Art Group, and has done approximately twenty murals, many inside schools and community centers, often under the sponsorship of major Chicago-area arts organizations.

Tate, Ammar Kevin (*see* Nsoroma, Ras Ammar)

Taylor, Spencer (c. 1939–1998)

After growing up in New Orleans, Taylor studied at Louisiana State University and Southern University (BA in 1960), both in Baton Rouge, Louisiana. He later taught at LSU's New Orleans campus (now the University of New Orleans). He worked as an illustrator at Boeing Company's McDonnell Aircraft and Missile Systems Division in St. Louis from 1968 until his recent death. His sketches and paintings of aircraft are found in more than two hundred museum and corporate collections in the United States and Europe.

Thomas, Richard C. (b. 1953)

Born and raised in New Orleans, Thomas studied at Xavier University (BFA, 1978). He painted a mural in 1979 at the community center in Armstrong Park honoring Satchmo, and created a mural on music greats for the local airport. He has been active for many years working with local youth doing public art, and started his own organization called Pieces of Power. Thomas also owns and operates the Visual Jazz Art Gallery. His colorful silk-screen posters have been selected to officially represent several Mardi Gras and jazz festivals.

Toons (Tony Martin)

Part of the hip-hop generation, he often commuted from his home in Sacramento to San Francisco and Los Angeles where the culture was much more active. He was invited to Occidental College in Los Angeles where he spray painted a portrait of Martin Luther King Jr. for a conference on street art. Like many other young artists, he found his art more appreciated in Europe. He now lives in Berlin.

Vulcan

One of the early masters of "wildstyle" spraycan art, he was one of ten artists invited to Detroit to spray paint the "Art Train" the year the show concentrated on Pop Art. Living in an apartment at 106th Street and Madison Avenue in New York City, Vulcan had a total view of the Graffiti Hall of Fame. The large far wall was "reserved" for his art and he could be down on the street in a flash if he saw anyone messing with the numerous murals that graced the walls.

Wade, Eugene (*see* Eda, Eugene)

Walker, William (b. 1927)

Walker was born in Birmingham, Alabama. After serving in the Air Force, he attended Columbus Gallery School of Arts in Ohio (1947–54), where he worked on murals with Samella Lewis (1947–48). After travels through the South, he returned to Chicago in 1955 and spent several years working as a decorative painter for interior design companies. He played an important role in the creation of the *Wall of Respect* and a leading role in a series of murals in Detroit (1968–69). His first monumental mural, *The Wall of Peace and Understanding* (1970), led to the *Murals for the People* exhibit at Chicago's Museum of Contemporary Art. The Artists' Statement published with that exhibit, which Walker co-wrote, became the manifesto of the mural movement. Following the exhibit, Walker cofounded the Chicago Mural Group (now the Chicago Public Art Group) with John Pitman Weber. Walker left the group in late 1975, but continued to paint murals for several years. Only a few of his major outdoor murals survive.

Wane

A product of the Upper Bronx, he is one of the major "writers" in the C.O.D. crew. His large, colorful, broad-sweeping letters are easily recognizable. In an era of mobility, he has been all over Europe, and his name is as likely to show up on a wall in San Francisco as it is to appear on the side of a store in the Bronx.

Washington, Horace (b. 1945)

He grew up in New Jersey, working on his first mural—the state's tri-centennial mural—while in high school. He attended Columbus College of Art and Design in Ohio, the San Francisco Art Institute (BFA in 1970), and California State University, Sacramento (MA in 1973).

Watson, Richard J.

Born in Badin, North Carolina, Watson is a poet, actor, and singer-song-writer in addition to a painter. Since 1990 he has been the exhibits director at the African American Historical and Cultural Museum in Philadelphia. Sites of his murals in the Philadelphia area include the Church of the Advocate, branches of the Free Library, the Children's Hospital Adolescent Care Facility, and various neighborhood centers.

Webber, C. Siddha Sila (b. 1943)

A native of Chicago, Siddha is a poet and a holistic health doctor as well as a muralist. He studied at the Art Institute of Chicago. In the late 1960s and early 1970s, Siddha assisted Mitchell Caton on seven or eight murals. He has done more than forty murals in the Chicago area.

White, Charles (1918–1979)

Born and raised in Chicago, White became a professional sign painter at age fourteen. During his last year in high school he won three art scholarships. However, two commercial art schools refused him admission when they discovered that he was African American. The third, a national competition, provided him with a full scholarship to the Art Institute of Chicago. In 1941 he taught at Dillard University in New Orleans for a year and married his first wife, artist Elizabeth Catlett. In 1942 he won his first of two consecutive Rosenwald Fellowships, spending three months studying at the Art Students' League in New York and then doing a mural at Hampton Institute. In 1946 Elizabeth Catlett received a fellowship to study in Mexico, and the couple lived there for the next two years, for a time residing in the home of muralist David Alfaro Siqueiros. White studied at the government art school and at the Taller Graphica. In 1957 he and his second wife moved to Los Angeles to escape the New York rat race and to try to improve his health. As a teacher at Otis Art Institute in Los Angeles, White had a significant influence on younger artists, including muralist Richard Wyatt.

White, C. Ian

The son of Charles White, Ian shares his father's sense of responsibility to raise consciousness with his art. His initial interest in murals developed from an early exposure to the political billboardlike murals popular in Nicaragua during the rule of the Sandinistas. He visited Nicaragua several times while growing up. He studied at the San Francisco Art Institute (BFA in 1988) and Otis School of Art and Design (MFA in 1995). White has worked on several murals with young people in Los Angeles area schools. His works on canvas, which often use collage, have been exhibited in southern California, Washington, D.C., and New York.

Williams, Bernard (b. 1964)

A native of Chicago, Williams studied at the University of Illinois, Champaign-Urbana (BFA, 1988), and Northwestern University (MFA, 1990), as well as in Paris, Rome, and Germany. He first got involved with murals in 1991, when he became assistant director of mural projects at the nonprofit Marwen Foundation. He began working with the Chicago Public Art Group (CPAG) the following year when the two organizations collaborated on a mural project. In addition to painting his own murals, Williams has restored important older murals by William Walker and Calvin Jones. Since 1990 he has been a drawing instructor at the School of the Art Institute of Chicago. His work has been exhibited in numerous solo and group shows in Illinois, Indiana, Colorado, and Mexico City.

Williams, Caleb (b. 1946)

Born in Greenville, Mississippi, he was exposed to art at an early age by his mother, who worked with artists from the Greenville Art Association. He studied at the Art Institute of Chicago, the Art Institute of San Francisco (BFA), and Lone Mountain College (MFA). He is a teacher, muralist, and commission portrait painter.

Williams, Keith

After growing up in South Los Angeles, Williams majored in art at California State University, Long Beach. He had drawn as a child, but it wasn't until his senior year in college that he developed an affinity for painting. He has also done backdrops for bands and illustration work for Motown Records. In 1993 he moved from southern California to Oakland in northern California, where he continues to do murals, often with the help of youth.

Williams, William Thomas (b. 1942)

Born in North Carolina, he studied at the City University of New York (CUNY) (AAS, 1962), Pratt Institute (BFA, 1966), Skowhegan School of Painting and Sculpture (1965), and Yale University (MFA, 1968). Since 1971 he has been an art professor at CUNY, Brooklyn College. Williams has always worked in abstract modes. His paintings have been exhibited throughout the United States and Europe.

Wood, Clarence

In 1971 he was one of two artists hired by the Philadelphia Museum of Art's Department of Urban Outreach to coordinate neighborhood mural projects. He designed the first local *Walls of Respect* in 1972 at schools and recreation centers.

Woodruff, Hale (1900–1980)

Born in Cairo, Illinois, Woodruff was a painter, printmaker, and educator as well as a muralist. After a public-school education in Tennessee, he studied at Herron Art Institute in Indianapolis and at Fogg Art Museum at Harvard University. In 1926 Woodruff won a Harmon Foundation award that, with additional financial backing from a patron, enabled him to study art in Paris for four years. He taught at Atlanta University (now Clark-Atlanta University) from 1931 to 1945, and in 1941 began an annual art show at the university for black artists that became an important nationally known showcase. In 1934 Woodruff spent six weeks studying fresco painting in Mexico with Diego Rivera. From 1946 to 1967 he was professor of art education at New York University.

Wyatt, Richard (b. 1956)

Wyatt made his professional debut at age twelve, winning first place at a sidewalk art contest sponsored by the Watts Studio Workshop. He studied with Charles White at Otis Art Institute, then received a BFA in painting, sculpture, and graphic arts from UCLA in 1978. He did his first mural, a portrait of local artist Roland Welton, in 1976 under the auspices of Alonzo Davis's Brockman Gallery Productions. He has painted numerous murals in Los Angeles as well as in the southern California communities of Lompoc, Twentynine Palms, and Palm Desert.

Yancey, John (b. 1956)

Yancey studied at the School of the Art Institute of Chicago (BFA 1980) and Georgia Southern University (MFA 1993). He has been teaching at the University of Texas, Austin, since 1993. Before that he taught at Roosevelt University in Chicago and at the School of the Art Institute of Chicago. Yancey was active in the Public Art Workshop on Chicago's West Side, directing his first mural project in 1976. In 1982 and 1984 he did murals in Springfield, Illinois. Between 1985 and 1991 he worked on murals with children through a Chicago program called Urban Gateways. During the summers of 1991 through 1994 he painted murals at Boulevard Arts Center on the South Side.

Young, Bernard (b. 1952)

He studied at Temple University (BA) and Cornell University, and painted the *Wall of Consciousness* in Philadelphia in 1972.

Bibliography

BOOKS

Barnett, Alan W. *Community Murals: The People's Art*. Philadelphia: The Art Alliance Press, 1984.

Bearden, Romare, and Harry Henderson. *A History of African-American Artists From 1792 to the Present*. New York: Pantheon Books, 1993.

Biggers, John, and Carroll Simms. *Black Art in Houston: The Texas Southern University Experience*. College Station: Texas A&M University Press, 1978.

Cederholm, Theresa Dickason. *Afro-American Artists: A Bio-bibliographical Directory*. Boston: Trustees of the Boston Public Library, 1973.

Chalfant, Henry, and James Prigoff. *Spraycan Art*. New York: Thames and Hudson, Inc., 1987.

Changuion, Paul. *The African Mural*. London: New Holland Ltd., 1989.

Church of the Advocate. *Art and Architecture of the Church of the Advocate*. Philadelphia: Farmer Press, Inc., 1999.

Cockcroft, Eva, John Pitman Weber, and James Cockcroft. *Toward a People's Art: The Contemporary Mural Movement*. Albuquerque: University of New Mexico Press, 1998.

Cooper, Martha, and Henry Chalfant. *Subway Art*. New York: Henry Holt Company, 1984.

Dover, Cedric. *American Negro Art*. Greenwich, Connecticut: New York Graphic Society, 1969.

Dunitz, Robin J. *Street Gallery: Guide to 1,000 Los Angeles Murals*. Revised second edition. Los Angeles: RJD Enterprises, 1998.

Dunitz, Robin J., and James Prigoff. *Painting the Towns: Murals of California*. Los Angeles: RJD Enterprises, 1997.

Dunitz, Robin J., *Los Angeles Murals by African-American Artists: A Book of Postcards*. Los Angeles: RTD Enterprises, 1995.

Fax, Elton. *Seventeen Black Artists*. New York: Dodd, Mead & Company, 1971.

Franklin, John Hope. *Racial Equality in America*. Columbia: University of Missouri Press, 1993.

Harris, Moira F. *Museum of the Streets: Minnesota's Contemporary Outdoor Murals*. Minneapolis: Pogo Press, 1987.

Huggins, Nathan Irvin. *Harlem Renaissance*. London: Oxford University Press, 1986.

Igoe, Lynn Moody, and James Igoe. *Two Hundred Fifty Years of Afro-American Art: An Annotated Bibliography*. New York: R. R. Bowker, 1981.

Ketner, Joseph D. *The Emergence of the African-American Artist: Robert S. Duncanson, 1821–1872*. Columbia: University of Missouri Press, 1993.

Kirschke, Amy Helene. *Aaron Douglas: Art. Race, & the Harlem Renaissance*. Jackson: University Press of Mississippi, 1995.

Lewis, Samella. *Art: African American*. Los Angeles: Hancraft Studios, 1990.

Lewis, Samella, and Ruth Waddy. *Black Artists on Art*. Vol. 1, revised. Los Angeles: Contemporary Crafts, Inc., 1969.

———. *Black Artists on Art*. Vol 2. Los Angeles: Contemporary Crafts, Inc., 1971.

Lott, Tommy L. *The Invention of Race: Black Culture and the Politics of Representation*. Malden, Massachusetts: Blackwell Publishers, Inc., 1999.

Patton, Sharon F. *African-American Art*. New York: Oxford University Press, 1998.

Porter, James A. *Modern Negro Art*. Washington, D.C.: Howard University Press, 1992.

Powell, Richard J. *Black Art and Culture in the 20th Century*. New York: Thames and Hudson, 1997.

Powers, Stephen. *The Art of Getting Over: Graffiti at the Millennium*. New York: St. Martin's Press, 1999.

Schwartzman, Myron. *Romare Bearden: His Life and Work*. New York: Harry N. Abrams, 1990.

Sommer, Robert. *Street Art*. New York: Link Books, 1975.

Sorell, Victor A., ed. *Guide to Chicago Murals: Yesterday and Today*. Chicago: Council on Fine Arts, 1979.

Stewart, Ruth Ann. *WPA and the Black Artist: Chicago and New York*. Chicago: Council on Fine Arts and Chicago Public Library, 1978.

Taylor, Arnold. *Travail and Triumph: Black Life and Culture in the South Since the Civil War*. Westport, Connecticut: Greenwood Press, 1977.

Theisen, Olive Jensen. *The Murals of John Thomas Biggers: American Muralist, African American Artist*. Hampton, Virginia: Hampton University Museum, 1996.

Wheat, Ellen Harkins. *Jacob Lawrence: American Painter*. Seattle: University of Washington Press, 1986.

White, Frances Barrett. *Reaches of the Heart: A Loving Look at the Artist Charles White*. New York: Barricade Books, 1994.

Wright, John A. *Discovering African-American St. Louis: A Guide to Historic Sites*. St. Louis: Missouri Historical Society Press, 1994.

Younge, Gavin. *Art of the South African Townships*. New York: Rizzoli, 1988.

EXHIBITION CATALOGS

Beautiful Walls of Baltimore. Baltimore Museum of Art, April 30–June 18, 1978.

Charles Alston: Artist and Teacher. Kenkeleba Gallery, New York, May 13–July 1, 1990.

Claye, Charlene. *John Biggers: Bridges.* California Museum of Afro-American History and Culture, Los Angeles, March 11–May 13, 1983.

Dana Chandler: Retrospective 1967–1987. Massachusetts College of Art North Hall Gallery, March 1987.

Driskell, David C. *Two Centuries of Black American Art.* Los Angeles: Los Angeles County Museum of Art, 1976.

Eda, Eugene, William Walker, John Pitman Weber, and Mark Rovovin. "The Artist's Statement." In *Murals for the People.* Museum of Contemporary Art, Chicago, February 15–March 15, 1971. Reprinted by the Public Art Workshop in Chicago.

Hale Woodruff: 50 Years of His Art. Studio Museum in Harlem, April 29–June 24, 1979.

If the Shoe Fits, Hear It! Paintings and Drawings by Dana Chandler, 1967–1976. Northeastern University Art Gallery, March 8–April 2, 1976.

LeFalle-Collins, Lizzetta, and Shifra Goldman. *In the Spirit of Resistance: African-American Modernists and the Mexican Muralist School.* New York: The American Federation of Arts, 1996.

Lhote, Henri. *The Search for the Tassili Frescoes: The Story of the Prehistoric Rock-Paintings of the Sahara.* Trans. Alan Houghton Brodrick. New York: E. P. Dutton & Co., 1959.

Meyer, Ruth K. "Robert Scott Duncanson." In *Nicholas Longworth: Art Patron of Cincinnati.* Taft Museum, Cincinnati, February 4–March 20, 1988.

A New Deal for Public Art: Murals from Federal Work Programs. The Bronx Museum of the Arts, New York, October 1, 1993–January 23, 1994.

Patton, Sharon F., Ph.D. *Riding on a Blue Note: Vincent D. Smith.* Louis Abrons Arts Center Henry Street Settlement, New York, January 19–February 28, 1990.

The People's Art: Black Murals, 1967–1978. Philadelphia: The African American Historical and Cultural Museum, 1986.

Perry, Regenia A. *Free Within Ourselves: African-American Artists in the Collection of the National Museum of American Art.* San Francisco: Pomegranate Artbooks, 1992.

Powell, Richard J., et al. *Rhapsodies in Black: Art of the Harlem Renaissance.* Berkeley: University of California Press, 1997.

Reynolds, Gary A., and Beryl J. Wright. *Against the Odds: African-American Artists and the Harmon Foundation.* New Jersey: Newark Museum, 1989.

Ritter, Rebecca E. *Five Decades; John Biggers and the Hampton Art Tradition.* Hampton University Museum, Virginia, April 13–June 11, 1990.

Robinson, Jontyle Theresa, and Wendy Greenhouse. *The Art of Archibald J. Motley Jr.* Chicago Historical Society, Chicago, October 23, 1991–March 17, 1992.

Sorell, Victor. *Images of Conscience: The Art of Bill Walker.* University Gallery of Chicago State University, Autumn 1984.

Taylor, William E., and Harriet G. Warkel. *A Shared Heritage: Art by Four African Americans.* Indianapolis: Indianapolis Museum of Art, 1996.

To Conserve a Legacy: American Art from Historically Black Colleges and Universities. Addison Gallery of American Art and the Studio Museum in Harlem, Andover, Massachusetts, August 31–October 31, 1999.

Vincent Smith: An Overview. New Jersey: The Art Galleries of Ramapo College, 1988.

Vincent D. Smith: An Appreciation. Robeson Center Art Gallery, Rutgers University, Newark, New Jersey, January 25–February 24, 1994.

Wardlaw, Alvia J. *The Art of John Biggers: View from the Upper Room.* New York: Harry N. Abrams, Inc., in association with the Museum of Fine Arts, Houston, 1995.

ARTICLES

Ahola, Nola. "Two Major Murals Dedicated Feb. 27 at Kingdome." *The Arts: Newsletter of the King County Arts Commission* 9, no. 1 (January–February 1980): 1–5.

Andrews, Benny. "Dewey Crumpler Doesn't Crimp on His Murals." *Encore American and Worldwide News* (July 19, 1976): 28.

———. "Keeping Up with This Jones." *Encore American and Worldwide News,* 18 July 1977, 35. (About Lawrence Jones)

———. "On Understanding Black Art." *New York Times,* 21 June 1970, 22.

———. "The Street Artistry of Dana Chandler." *Encore American and Worldwide News,* 20 September 1976, 32–33.

"Arts and the Black Revolution." *Arts in Society* (summer/fall 1968).

Baigell, Matthew, and Julia Wilson, eds. "The Negro in American Culture." In *War and Fascism: Papers of the First American Artists' Congress.* New Brunswick, New Jersey, 1986.

Bambara, Toni Cade. "Centennial Vision." *Drum* 14, nos. 1 and 2: 60–62. Fall, 1983. (About Nelson Stevens)

Berman, Greta. "The Walls of Harlem." *Arts Magazine* (October 1977): 122–126.

Billops, Camille. "Georgette Seabrooke Powell." *Artist and Influence* XII (1993): 85–93.

Bontemps, Alex. "Black Painter's 1929 Mural Still Provocative." *Nashville Tennessean,* 14 February 1971. (About Aaron Douglas)

Brenson, Michael. "Public Art at New Federal Building in Queens." *New York Times,* 24 March 1989, C32.

Brunazzi, Ceci. "Portrait of a Muralist." *Common Sense* (June 1975): 12–13. (About Dewey Crumpler)

Butler, Anita M. "Richard Wyatt Jr., Young Artist." *Equalizer* (August 1970): 7ff.

Carber, Kristine M. "Muralist Horace Washington." *San Francisco Sunday Examiner & Chronicle,* 27 January 1991, F–4.

Catlett, Elizabeth. "The Role of the Black Artist." *Black Scholar* (June 1975): 10–14.

Cavinder, Fred D. "The Murals of Wishard." *Indianapolis Star Magazine,* 29 April 1984, 6–12. (Wishard Memorial Hospital murals by William Edouard Scott)

"Church Muralist." *Ebony,* 7 June 1952, 66–70. (Aaron Miller, San Francisco)

Churchwell, Robert. "Aaron Douglas Restoring Fisk Murals from 1930." *Nashville Banner,* 28 July 1965, 12.

Coker, Gilbert. "Mural restoration in Harlem is 'cultural victor.'" *New York Amsterdam News,* 31 March 1979, 45.

Coleman, Sandy. "The Prime-Time Painter." *Boston Globe,* 27 August 1996, Living Arts section. (About Paul Goodnight)

Dixon, Cheryl McKay. "Alonzo Davis." *International Review of African American Art* 6, no. 3 (1986): 16–32.

Donaldson, Jeff. "John A. Kendrick: A Salute." *Drum* 14, nos. 1 and 2: 44–45. (Fall 1983)

———. "Trans-African Art." *Black Collegian* (October–November 1980): 90–102.

Du Bois, W. E. B. "Of Our Spiritual Strivings." In *The Souls of Black Folk.* 1903; reprint, New York: New American Library, 1969.

Dunitz, Robin J. "Putting Art Where People Live: The African-American Murals of Los Angeles." *American Visions* (December–January 1995): 14–18.

Fancher, Brooke. "Tuzuri Watu." *Community Murals Magazine,* Summer 1987, 15.

Favre, Jeff. "Restored Glory." *Chicago Tribune,* 8 June 1995, Tempo section, 1. (About the restoration of a mural painted in 1909 by William Edouard Scott for Lane Technical High School.)

Fax, Elton. "John W. Outterbridge." In *Black Artists of the New Generation.* New York: Dodd, Mead & Company, 1977.

Felten, Eric. "Art Sold!–With Strings Attached." *Insight on the News,* 3 December 1990, 21. (About the destruction of Paul Goodnight's jazz mural and the legal ramifications)

Forwalter, John. "Dedication of Zeno's 55th Street South Wall Mural." *Hyde Park Herald,* 18 October 1972, 20. (About Albert Zeno of Chicago)

Fuetsch, Michele. "Painter Captures Spirit of Struggle." *Los Angeles Times,* 19 March 1989, 9–12. (About Elliott Pinkney)

Gragg, Randy. "Death of an Arts Angel." *Oregonian,* 20 August 1999, sec. F, p. 1ff. (About Portland artist Charlotte La Verne Lewis)

———. "Great Flood of Memory: A Portland muralist's hidden masterwork evokes the meaning of Vanport's sudden demise." *Oregonian,* 28 May 1998, sec. B, p. 1ff. (about Isaka Shamsud-Din)

Grier-Deen, Martha. "I Am Because We Are: Nelson Stevens." *Drum* 18, nos. 1 and 2 (May 1988): 67ff.

Hackett, Regina. "Borough of Queens (NY) is a new outpost of contemporary public art." *Seattle Post-Intelligencer,* 18 July 1989, C5.

Stuart Hall. "What is This 'Black' in Black Popular Culture?" In *Black Popular Culture.* Seattle: Bay Press.

Henderson, Rose. "Aaron Douglas, Negro Painter." *Southern Workman* 60, no. 9 (September 1931): 384–89.

Holbrook, Francis C. "William Edouard Scott, Painter." *Southern Workman* 53, no. 2 (February 1924): 72–76.

Howard, Carol. "Allie Ways." *Detroit Monthly* (April 1989): 64ff. (About Allie McGhee)

Hoyt, Roger Eric. "The Explosion of a Dormant Art Form: Chicago's Murals." *Chicago History* (spring/summer 1974): 28–35.

Jackson, David. "Black Artists and the WPA." *Encore American and Worldwide News,* 19 November 1979, 22–23.

Jones, Seitu. "Public Art That Inspires, Public Art That Informs." In *Critical Issues in Public Art.* New York: HarperCollins, 1992.

Kirschke, Amy Helene. "The Depression Murals of Aaron Douglas: Radical Politics and African American Art." *International Review of African American Art* 12, no. 4 (1995): 19–29.

LeFalle-Collins, Lizzetta. "Contributions of the American Negro to Democracy: a History Painting by Charles White." *International Review of African American Art* 12, no. 4 (1995): 51.

———. "Re-Defining the African-American Self." *In In the Spirit of Resistance: African American Modernists and the Mexican Muralist School.* New York: The American Federation of Arts, 1996.

Levy, Alan. "Interview: Jon Onye Lockard." *News-Link* (The University of Michigan Housing Division), 18 January 1993, 4–5.

Lewis Samella. "The Street Art of Black America." *Exxon USA* 12, no. 3 (Third Quarter 1973): 2–9.

Lewis, Samella, ed. "Institutional Murals." *International Review of African American Art* 12, no. 4 (special issue 1995).

Martin, Thad. "John Biggers: Artist Who Influenced a Generation." *Ebony,* March 1984, 87–90.

McDaniel, M. Akua. "Reexamining Hale Woodruff's Talladega College and Atlanta University Murals." *International Review of African American Art* 12, no. 4 (1995): 4–17.

Miller, Nory. "'Old Realist White,' Painting for People." *Chicago Daily News,* 20–21 March 1976, 13. (Interview with Charles White)

Morehouse, Lucille E. "New Interest Develops in Work of William Edouard Scott." *Indianapolis Star,* 2 May 1943, part 1, p. 19.

Muchnic, Suzanne. "A Children's Story Based in Paint." *Los Angeles Times,* 10 August 1982, part V, p. 1ff. (About Richard Wyatt mural *Inner City Relief*)

Neal, Larry. "The Social Background of the Black Arts Movement." *Black Scholar* 18, no. 1 (1987): 14.

Oren, Michel. "The Smokehouse Painters, 1968–70." *Black American Literature Forum* 24, no. 3 (fall 1990): 509–31.

Parish, Norman III. "'Wall of Respect': How Chicago Artists Gave Birth to the Ethnic Mural." *Chicago Tribune,* 23 August 1992, 1, 22.

Pool, Bob. "Muralist Enlightening School's Walls, Minds." *Los Angeles Times,* 26 August 1999, sec. B, p.10.

Roby, Thomas W. "The Humanizing Art of Eugene (EDAW) Wade." *City: A Journal of the City Colleges of Chicago* (spring 1987): 7–15.

"Race Bias Charged by Negro Artists." *New York Times,* 22 February 1936, 13. (About Harlem Hospital murals)

Rodrigues-Taylor, K. S. "Artist sues over ruined mural." *Boston Herald,* 6 September 1986, 29. (About Paul Goodnight)

Shaw, Brenda Thornton. "Artists design murals for Albina." *Downtowner,* August 1989. (About Isaac Shamsud-Din of Portland, Oregon)

Smith, Vincent. "The Painter Looks Back." *National Scene* supplement II, no. 10 (1980): 12.

Steele, Claude M. "Race and Schooling of Black Americans." *Atlantic Monthly* (April 1992): 69.

Taylor, William E. "William Edouard Scott: Indianapolis Painter." *Black History News & Notes,* no. 33 (August 1988): 4–7.

Treloar, James A. "Mural recounts meeting of Douglass, John Brown." *Detroit News,* 3 May 1972. (About mural by Leroy Foster)

Volland, Victor. "Aviation Artist Spencer Taylor Dies: Painted Mural African-Americans at Lambert Field." *St. Louis Post-Dispatch,* 8 October 1998, Metro section.

Von Blum, Paul. "The Black Panther Mural in L.A." *Z Magazine* (July–August 1995): 83–87.

Waldman, George. "Urban Mural." *Detroit Free Press,* 21 April 1989, 12F.

"The Wall of Black Heroes." *CityArts Quarterly* 2, no. 4 (fall/winter 1987): 21. (About a Detroit mural)

"The *Wall of Respect.*" *Ebony,* December 1967, 49.

"Walls of Fire: An Interview with Dewey Crumpler." *Arts Biweekly: The Bay Area Newsletter of Art & Politics,* no. 50 (June 15, 1977): 2–6.

White, Michelle-Lee. "Common Directions, Epic Dimensions: Jacob Lawrence's Murals at Howard University." *International Review of African American Art* 12, no. 4 (1995): 30–37.

Wilkins, Lloyd H. "Little-Known Murals in City Among Finest Art Works in State." *Indianapolis Sunday Star,* 7 January 1940, part 5, p. 1ff. (About William Edouard Scott)

ORAL HISTORIES/INTERVIEWS

Alston, Charles. Interview by Harlan Phillips. Smithsonian Archives of American Art, 1965.

———. Interview by Al Murray. Smithsonian Archives of American Art, 1968.

Douglas, Aaron. Interview by Charles L. James. Yale University Library, 1972.

———. Interview by L. M. Collins. 16 July 1971. Black Oral Histories, Fisk University Special Collections, Nashville, Tennessee.

———. Interview by David Levering Lewis. Voices of the Harlem Renaissance, July 1974. Schomburg Center for Research in Black Culture, New York.

———. Interview by Ann Allen Shockley. 19 November 1975. Black Oral Histories, Fisk University Special Collections, Nashville, Tennessee.

Lawrence, Jacob. Interview by Carroll Greene Jr. Smithsonian Archives of American Art, 26 October 1968.

Motley, Archibald John Jr. Smithsonian Archives of American Art, 1978–79.

Walker, William. Interview by Victor Sorell. Smithsonian Archives of American Art, 1991.

White, Charles. Interview by Betty Hoag. Smithsonian Archives of American Art, 1965.

Woodruff, Hale. Interview by Al Murray. Smithsonian Archives of American Art, 1968.

———. Interview by Winifred Stoelting. Smithsonian Archives of American Art, 1978. (Only available for reading in Washington, D.C.)

COLLECTED ARTISTS' PAPERS IN ARCHIVES

Alston, Charles. Smithsonian Archives of American Art.

Chandler, Dana. Smithsonian Archives of American Art.

Douglas, Aaron. Smithsonian Archives of American Art.

White, Charles. Smithsonian Archives of American Art.

Woodruff, Hale. Amistad Research Center, Tulane University, New Orleans, Louisiana.

PH.D. DISSERTATIONS/OTHER RESEARCH PAPERS

Report by group of concerned Harlem citizens to the NYC Art Commission on the condition of 40 WPA murals at 6 Harlem sites, all done by African-American artists

Berman, Greta. "The Lost Years: Mural Painting in New York City under the Federal Art Project, 1935–1943." Ph.D. diss., Columbia University, 1978.

Biggers, John. "The Negro Woman in American Life and Education: A Mural Presentation." Ed.D. diss., Pennsylvania State University, 1954.

Brown, Jacqueline R. "WPA/FAP and its Impact on African-American Artists." Ph.D. diss., Howard University College of Fine Arts, 1973.

Cureau, Harold. "Black Participation in the FAP." Research paper, Southern University, Art Department, Baton Rouge, 1975.

Ransaw, Lee Andrew. "Black Mural Art and its Representation of the Black Community." Ph.D. diss., Illinois State University, 1973.

Roberts, Peter J. "William Edouard Scott: Some Aspects of His Life and Work." Research paper, Emory University Department of the History of Art, 1981.

Stallings, Charles W. "Some Aspects of the Evolution of Negro Colleges in America as Depicted by the Execution of a Mural." Ed.D. diss., Pennsylvania State University, 1954.

WEB SITES

Adonis Dietrich and the Philadelphia Mural Art Program:
http://astro.ocis.temple.edu/~adonis1a/mural.html

Anderson, Darrell, Denver muralist:
www.artscomm.org/daartislife/

Amistad Research Center:
www.tulane.edu/~amistad/
Independent manuscript library at Tulane University in New Orleans dedicated to preserving African American history and culture. Holdings include the papers of Hale Woodruff.

B. Davis Schwartz Memorial Library:
www.liunet.edu/cwis/cwp/library/aavaahp.htm
African Americans in the Visual Arts: a Historical Perspective includes information on the Harlem Renaissance, WPA, and artists Charles Alston, Romare Bearden, John Biggers, Robert S. Duncanson, Aaron Douglas, and Jacob Lawrence.

Biggers, John; *Issues of Public Art and the Murals of John Biggers.*
http://www.artsednet.getty.edu/ArtsEdNet/Resources/Biggers/Public/

Blade, New York–based spraycan artist:
www.bladekingofgraf.com

Chicago Public Art Group:
www.cpag.net
This artist-run public art organization is one of the most active and exciting in the world.

Clark Atlanta University, Trevor Arnet Art Gallery:
www.cau.edu/artGallery/Images
Features murals by Hale Woodruff in detail.

Davis, Alonzo, Memphis–based artist:
http://globeart.com/alonzo/statement.html

Goodnight, Paul, Boston–based artist:
www.paulgoodnight.com/state.htm

Jones, Lawrence A.:
http://cedar.olemiss.edu/depts/art/MVAI/J/JonesL_info.html

Percent for Art program, New York City:
www.ci.nyc.ny.us/html/dcla/html/pahome.html
Features images of murals and other public art by a number of artists, including Melvin Clark, Vincent Smith, Houston Conwill, Michael Kelly Williams, and Willie Birch.

RJD Enterprises:
www.muralart.com
Features information and publications about murals.

Thomas, Richard C., New Orleans–based artist who owns a gallery:
www.visualjazz.com

VIDEOCASSETTES

Griots of Imagery: A Comment on the Art of Romare Bearden And Charles White. Praisesong on a Shoestring Inc., New York, 1993. 27 min.

Jacob Lawrence: The Glory of Expression. 28 min. L & S Video. Chappaque, NY, 1993.

John Biggers's Journeys (A Romance). Produced by Chloe Productions, Newport News, Virginia, 1995. 76 min.

John Biggers: The History of Negro Education in Morris County, Texas, An Interview with Alton Dacus. Produced by Northeast Texas Community College Learning Resource Center, Mt. Pleasant, Texas, 1985.

Kindred Spirits: Contemporary African American Artists Produced by KERA-TV, Dallas, 1990. 30 min.

Romare Bearden: Visual Jazz. 28 min. L & S Video.

Stories of Illumination and Growth: John Biggers's Hampton Murals. Script by Juliette Harris Bowles. Produced for Hampton University Museum by Cinebar Productions, Newport News, Virginia, 1992. 28 min.

OTHER MEDIA

Slide collection of works by black artists, Art Department, University of Southern Alabama, Mobile, (205) 344-3400.

Index